Department of International Economic and Social Affairs

ST/ESA/SER.A/102/Add.1

Population Studies   No. 102/Add.1

World Population Policies

Volume II

Gabon to Norway

 United Nations   New York, 1989

NOTE

The designations employed and the presentation of the material in this publication do not imply the expression of any opinion whatsoever on the part of the Secretariat of the United Nations concerning the legal status of any country, territory, city or area or of its authorities, or concerning the delimitation of its frontiers or boundaries.

The term "country" as used in the text of this report also refers, as appropriate, to territories or areas.

The designations "developed" and "developing" economies are intended for statistical convenience and do not necessarily express a judgement about the stage reached by a particular country or area in the development process.

Symbols of United Nations documents are composed of capital letters combined with figures. Mention of such a symbol indicates a reference to a United Nations document.

The printing of this volume was made possible by a publications grant from the United Nations Population Fund.

ST/ESA/SER.A/102/Add.1

UNITED NATIONS PUBLICATION

Sales No. E.89.XIII.3

02800

ISBN 92-1-151175-5

PREFACE

The information contained in the present report is based on the continuous monitoring of population policies by the Population Division of the Department of International Economic and Social Affairs of the United Nations Secretariat as part of its programme of work. World Population Policies presents, in three volumes, comparable and up-to-date information on the population policies of the 170 Member States of the United Nations and Non-Member States. The countries are arranged in alphabetical order, volume I (Sales No. E.87.XIII.4) covering countries from A to F, volume II from G to N, and volume III from O to Z. The present publication replaces Population Policy Briefs: Current Situation in Developing Countries (ST/ESA/SER.R/62), Population Policy Briefs: Current Situation in Developed Countries (ST/ESA/SER.R/63) and Population Policy Compendium.

Responsibility for this report rests with the United Nations Secretariat; however, the assessment was facilitated to a great extent by the close co-operation among the United Nations bodies. In particular, the contribution of the United Nations Population Fund in support of this publication is gratefully acknowledged.

Except where otherwise noted, the demographic estimates and projections cited in this report are based on the tenth round of global demographic assessments undertaken by the Population Division.

For additional information and data relating to demographic estimates and projections, reference should be made to World Population Prospects: Estimates and Projections as Assessed in 1984 (United Nations publication, Sales No. E.86.XIII.3).

CONTENTS

EXPLANATORY NOTES

Reference to "dollars" ($) indicates United States dollars, unless otherwise stated.

Reference to "tons" indicates metric tons, unless otherwise stated.

The term "billion" signifies a thousand million.

A hyphen between years (e.g., 1984-1985) indicates the full period involved, including the beginning and end years; a slash (e.g., 1984/1985) indicates a financial year, school year or crop year.

A point (.) is used to indicate decimals.

The following symbols have been used in the tables:

Three dots (...) indicate that data are not available or are not separately reported.

A dash (--) indicates that the amount is nil or negligible.

A hyphen (-) indicates that the item is not applicable.

A minus sign (-) before a number indicates a deficit or decrease, except as indicated.

Details and percentages in tables do not necessarily add to totals because of rounding.

INTRODUCTION

The realization that population is a vital component of the development process has led an increasing number of countries to formulate and implement policies to influence either directly or indirectly the demographic character of their population. To meet the growing demand for information on national population policies, this publication presents in a systematic and comparable manner, for developed and developing countries, an overview of the Governments' perceptions and policies in relation to such factors as population growth and age structure, mortality and morbidity, fertility and the family, international migration, urbanization and spatial distribution and the status of women.

In order to place Government perceptions and policies within the proper context, the relevant demographic indicators are also provided. The definitions of the various indicators may be found in annex I. In addition, the institutional arrangements for the formulation and implementation of such policies are also described.

The major sources of information for this report were the Population Policy Data Bank maintained by the Population Division of the Department of International Economic and Social Affairs, Population Policy Compendium (now discontinued) and the five United Nations inquiries on population policy. The Population Policy Data Bank contains, among other things, government documents and publications, such as development plans and position papers, speeches and publications of other international organizations. The status of the responses to the five inquiries are contained in annex II.

GABON

DEMOGRAPHIC INDICATORS	CURRENT PERCEPTION
SIZE/AGE STRUCTURE/GROWTH	The Government considers the rate of population growth to be <u>unsatisfactory</u>, because it is <u>too low</u>.
Population: 1985 2025 (thousands) 1 151 2 607 0-14 years (%) 34.6 33.5 60+ years (%) 9.4 8.1 Rate of: 1980-85 2020-25 growth 1.6 1.7 natural increase 15.7 17.0	
MORTALITY/MORBIDITY	Current conditions of health and levels of mortality are perceived as <u>unacceptable</u>.
1980-85 2020-25 Life expectancy 49.0 65.0 Crude death rate 18.1 8.5 Infant mortality 111.9 46.7	
FERTILITY/NUPTIALITY/FAMILY	Present levels and trends are considered to be <u>unsatisfactory</u> because they are <u>too low</u>.
1980-85 2020-25 Fertility rate 4.5 3.0 Crude birth rate 33.8 25.4 Contraceptive prevalence rate ... ... Female mean age at first marriage 17.7 (1960)	
INTERNATIONAL MIGRATION	Immigration is viewed as <u>significant</u> and <u>too high</u>, although the Government feels it has been favourable to economic development. Emigration is considered to be <u>significant</u> and <u>too high</u>.
1980-85 2020-25 Net migration rate 0.0 0.0 Foreign-born population (%)	
SPATIAL DISTRIBUTION/URBANIZATION	Spatial distribution is viewed as <u>inappropriate</u>. Both urban and rural growth are seen as <u>unsatisfactory</u> since they are, respectively, <u>too high</u> and <u>too low</u>.
Urban 1985 2025 population (%) 40.9 69.6 Growth rate: 1980-85 2020-25 urban 4.2 2.5 rural -0.1 0.0	

GENERAL POLICY FRAMEWORK

Overall approach to population problems: The main goal of Gabon's population policy is to increase the rate of growth in order to enlarge the labour pool. Measures are directed towards improving conditions of family welfare and population distribution. The Government has not developed a broad network of demography-oriented measures.

Importance of population policy in achieving development objectives: The Government feels that population growth occupies an important position in the process of socio-economic development. Unlike many African countries which must limit growth in order to attain development objectives, Gabon believes it must increase its native population in order to achieve its goals. The policy to increase population size aims at counteracting acute labour shortages. Rural labour deficits have disrupted needed agricultural production. The current development plan stresses the need to mobilize all human resources to participate actively in achieving development goals.

INSTITUTIONAL FRAMEWORK

Population data systems and development planning: Censuses were held in 1960, 1970 and 1981. None are considered completely accurate. Improving the collection and analysis of data is a governmental priority. The most recent development plan is the fifth, covering 1984-1988.

Integration of population within development planning: No single government agency formulates and co-ordinates population policies. La Direction de la planification des ressources humaines and Le Commissariat général au plan et au développement have been responsible for integrating demographic variables into planning, particularly in regard to employment planning. Since 1960 Le Commissariat général has prepared population projections. La Direction des enquêtes statistiques et de la démographie under the supervision of La Direction général de la statistique et des études économiques conducts demographic inquiries.

POLICIES AND MEASURES

Changes in population size and age structure: Government policy is to increase the growth rate by raising fertility rates. The main goal of population policy is to create an environment conducive to couples having larger families. In its effort to increase population size, the Government has set targets for the growth rate. It plans to achieve a 2.3 per cent growth rate by the year 1990 and a 3.0 per cent rate by 2000. The National Social Guarantee Fund is responsible for creating a social insurance system. Measures to protect the aged figure prominently in the system. The social security scheme extends coverage to employed persons, while a special system exists for public employees.

<u>Mortality and morbidity</u>: Government policy to improve health care is supported by the adoption of the strategy "Health for all by the year 2000". Policy objectives stress the reduction of disparities between urban and rural areas in health services, expansion of health care facilities to the village level, the quantitative and qualitative improvement of health personnel, and the improvement of environmental conditions. The Government's programmes consist of a maternal and child health project, immunization for adults and children, and the improvement of the food supply in order to combat malnutrition.

<u>Fertility and the family</u>: The Government has instituted a wide range of measures to increase fertility rates, improve the health of mothers and children, and promote family well-being. A 1975 law guarantees family benefits. Maternity benefits include leave for women in insured employment of at least four months and free maternity care. The 1978 Labour Code added the following maternity benefits: women are entitled to full salary while on maternity leave and nursing breaks for 15 months after the resumption of work. Mothers with large families also receive medals. Family and child welfare benefits include lump-sum birth grants, allowances for children under the age of 16 with working mothers, and yearly school allowances dispensed at the beginning of the school year. The Government has expressed deep concern over infertility as a reason for the insufficient growth rate. It is reported that up to 30 per cent of Gabonese women are infertile. With the assistance of a private company, the Government established a research centre to investigate the causes of infertility. The Government has recently changed its position in regard to family planning and contraception, and now permits access to modern methods of contraception, but without government support. Abortion is available only for narrow medical reasons. A mother and child health care project includes activities to promote child-spacing.

<u>International migration</u>: The Government has an active policy to reduce future immigration. Gabon maintains a sizable foreign-born population, due to the lack of qualified Gabonese. The Government has concluded arrangements with neighbouring countries to supply labour to Gabon, but expelled foreign nationals in 1978 and in 1981. The Government has expressed concern over the growing number of refugees within its borders. In an attempt to control illegal immigration, it requires all workers to obtain a permit. Government policy is to reduce the level of emigration in the future.

<u>Spatial distribution/urbanization</u>: Official policy is to decelerate internal migration, decrease urban growth, and increase rural growth. The current development plan emphasizes the objectives of reducing intra- and interprovincial disparities and modifying the urban and rural distribution of population. One priority is improving the development of the interior and rural areas. The Government maintains strategies for rural development and the improvement of lagging regions. Measures include public infrastructure subsidies, the improvement of housing and social services, human resource investment, and job training. The Government has instituted a long-term programme to improve infrastructure and increase investment in water utilities and electricity.

Status of women and population: The Government has expressed the desire to improve the status of women, particularly in relation to fertility. Measures include improving the health of women and planning a "House of Women" in the capital, Libreville. The Gabonese Democratic Party's Women's Union is active in educating women in family economics, introducing them to political life, and encouraging them to devote time to the arts. It supports the establishment of country-wide women's centres but lacks qualified cadres to carry out its work. The minimum legal age at marriage for women is 15 years.

Other issues: Gabon considers itself to be an underpopulated country in respect to its endowment of natural resources. Because of its relatively small population and high revenues from oil production, Gabon has a high per capita income, thus disqualifying it for some international aid which the Government feels is needed. The Government has disputed the population estimates used by donor agencies to calculate per capita income.

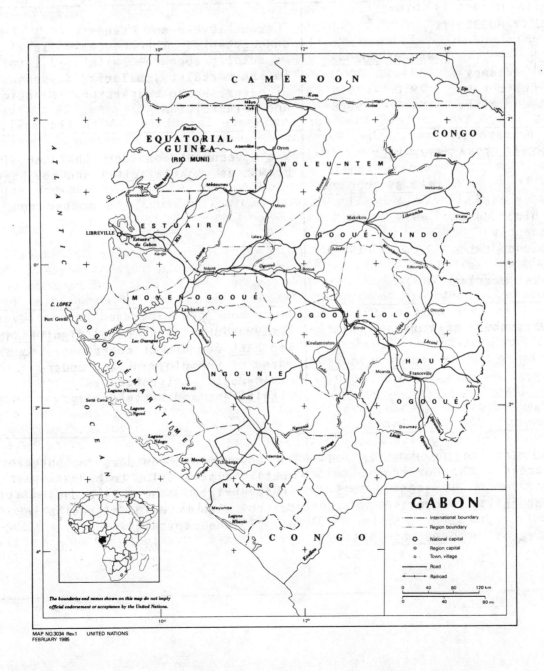

MAP NO.3034 Rev.1   UNITED NATIONS
FEBRUARY 1985

GAMBIA

DEMOGRAPHIC INDICATORS	CURRENT PERCEPTION
SIZE/AGE STRUCTURE/GROWTH Population: 1985 2025 (thousands) 643 1 494 0-14 years (%) 42.5 36.4 60+ years (%) 5.0 5.9 Rate of: 1980-85 2020-25 growth 1.9 1.6 natural increase 19.4 15.6	The Government considers the rate of population growth <u>unsatisfactory</u> and <u>too high</u> due to a general deterioration of the environment and the difficulties of providing the population with goods and services.
MORTALITY/MORBIDITY 1980-85 2020-25 Life expectancy 35.0 51.0 Crude death rate 29.0 13.8 Infant mortality 174.1 93.8	Current levels and trends are <u>unacceptable</u>. The Government is especially concerned with high levels of infant mortality, malaria, diarrhoeal diseases, acute respiratory infections and malnutrition.
FERTILITY/NUPTIALITY/FAMILY 1980-85 2020-25 Fertility rate 6.4 3.6 Crude birth rate 48.4 29.3 Contraceptive prevalence rate 1.0 (1977) Female mean age at first marriage	The Government considers the rate of growth as <u>unsatisfactory</u> and <u>too high</u>.
INTERNATIONAL MIGRATION 1980-85 2020-25 Net migration rate 0.0 0.0 Foreign-born population (%) 11.1 (1973)	Immigration is considered <u>significant</u> and <u>too high</u> because it contributes to high rates of unemployment and under-employment. Emigration is <u>not significant</u> and <u>satisfactory</u>.
SPATIAL DISTRIBUTION/URBANIZATION Urban 1985 2025 population (%) 20.1 48.4 Growth rate: 1980-85 2020-25 urban 4.0 3.3 rural 1.5 0.1	The Government considers the pattern of spatial distribution to be <u>inappropriate</u>. There is a desire to control high rates of migration into Banjul, the capital.

GENERAL POLICY FRAMEWORK

<u>Overall approach to population problems</u>: The Government's objectives are to reduce substantially population growth by lowering fertility and mortality rates and the level of immigration and rural-to-urban migration, through direct intervention. Mortality and fertility are to be reduced through an integrated approach combining family planning with maternal and child health services. Although there is no explicit policy regarding spatial distribution, the Government plans to reduce massive rural-to-urban migration by rural development and employment programmes.

<u>Importance of population policy in achieving development objectives</u>: The Government recognizes the role of population factors in national development. The second five-year plan, 1982-1986, observed, "While population growth affects economic growth, the latter influences mortality, fertility and migration and thereby affects the growth and distribution of population....The aim of national development is to improve the quality of life of the nation through a combination of economic and population policies. This implies that population policy is not to be pursued in isolation but as part of an overall development policy."

INSTITUTIONAL FRAMEWORK

<u>Population data systems and development planning</u>: The Government has made significant progress in the past two decades collecting and analysing demographic data. Modern censuses were conducted in 1963, 1973 and 1983. In addition there are vital registration data, covering only Banjul, and data from demographic surveys. The Socio-economic Survey and Evaluation Unit of the National Rural Development Programme has also collected demographic data on a sample basis, for documenting annual and seasonal fluctuations in population growth. The first (1976/77-80/81) and second (1981/82-85/86) five-year plans specified objectives of rural development, balanced human and material resources development, and an equitable income distribution. As of early 1987 no new plan was envisaged, since planning had been incorporated in the Economic Recovery Plan, launched in August 1985.

<u>Integration of population within development planning</u>: The Ministry of Economic Planning and Industrial Development, created in 1974, is the sole agency responsible for formulating and co-ordinating population policies. There is no unit charged with taking into account population variables in planning. The Government has considered establishing at least one post for that purpose within the Population and Employment Section of the Ministry of Economic Planning and Industrial Development. The First National Conference of Parliamentarians on Family Planning, Population and Development, held in 1983, recommended that the Government establish an official Population Commission to review and analyse population matters in relation to development, but the recommendation has yet to be implemented. The Department of Information and Broadcasting and various organizations play supporting roles in the population field.

GAMBIA

POLICIES AND MEASURES

Changes in population size and age structure: The long-term objective is to reduce population growth by lowering mortality, fertility and immigration. The Government's policy of socio-economic restructuring is aimed at diversifying the economy and achieving self-reliance through the development of manpower and natural resources, and the promotion of equality and welfare. Programmes such as primary health care, primary education and non-formal education, rural water supply, and low-cost housing are designed to influence indirectly fertility, mortality and rural-to-urban migration. A pension scheme covers all employed workers.

Mortality and morbidity: The Government reports that the integrated maternal and child health programme has contributed to reducing infant mortality. Policies aim at expanding curative and preventive services and increasing rural health-care coverage. The second five-year plan indicated that social services would be directed at satisfying basic needs, reducing rural/urban disparities and increasing the accessibility of the rural population to basic health facilities. One of the targets of the primary health-care programme is to reach every village of 200 or more inhabitants by the year 2000. The Government reported that every village would be encouraged to form a development committee to select candidates for training as village health workers and to encourage traditional birth attendants to accept training. A health education curriculum, emphasizing practical applications, will be introduced in schools, and wells will continue to be constructed for supplying safe water to villages. The immunization programme will be expanded, vector and mosquito control extended, and environmental health services strengthened.

Fertility and the family: Official policy is to reduce fertility, in order to lower population growth and improve maternal/child health and family well-being. The Government has no quantitative target for reducing fertility but hopes to provide all married women with family planning information and education through health service units and maternal and child health clinics. The second five-year plan emphasized the extension of family planning to rural areas and the training of additional birth attendants to provide family planning education in villages. The proposed women's centres, which would be established under the community development programme, will include family planning. The Government has urged all organizations involved in information, education and communication to encourage the limiting of family size by making parents aware of the need to have only the number of children for whom they can provide adequate care. The Government provides direct support for contraceptive methods. Abortion is permitted only for broad medical reasons. Information concerning the status of sterilization is not readily available.

International migration: Reducing immigration has become a primary objective, because the Government is concerned with providing a sufficient number of jobs for its nationals. In the second five-year plan, the Government reported that the continued, uncontrolled influx of labour from neighbouring countries would aggravate problems of unemployment and under-employment. It noted, in addition, that sharp annual fluctuations in immigration levels distorted the population estimates used for planning purposes and therefore interfered with the development planning process. The Government plans to strengthen its machinery for controlling immigration by introducing a system of identity cards for all adult Gambians.

Spatial distribution/urbanization: There are as yet no explicitly formulated policies to influence spatial distribution and internal migration, but the desire to reduce rural-to-urban migration is implicit in several government policy statements. In order to reduce rapid migration into the Banjul area, the Government has focused attention on developing two small cities, Basse and Farafenni. When the objectives of the first plan for Basse and Farafenni were not realized, the Government revised its spatial policy, placing more emphasis on the complementary aspects of urban and rural development and on planning for and managing the growth of urban areas. A strategy to institute country-wide physical planning, improve the institutional framework, provide basic infrastructure and facilities, raise rural living standards, and reduce disparities between urban and rural areas and among regions has been implemented. The Government has also incorporated a rural employment policy into the second plan.

Status of women and population: The Government has created a Bureau for Women's Affairs and a National Women's Advisory Council within the President's Office. The main objective of the Bureau is to promote the interests and welfare of women and to enhance their full participation in national development. There is no minimum age at marriage for women.

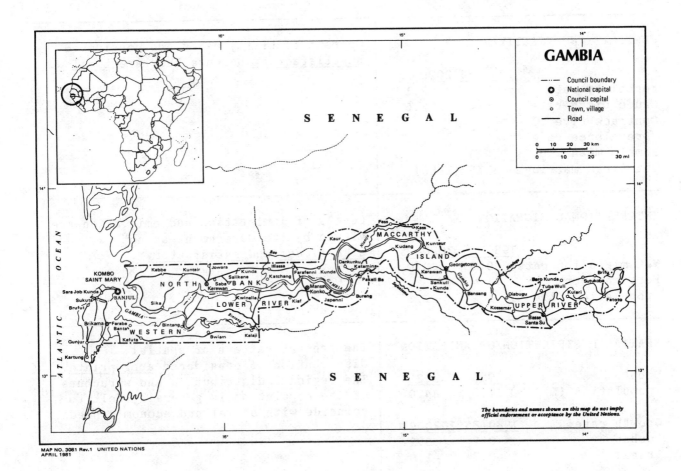

MAP NO. 3061 Rev.1 UNITED NATIONS
APRIL 1981

GERMAN DEMOCRATIC REPUBLIC

DEMOGRAPHIC INDICATORS	CURRENT PERCEPTION

SIZE/AGE STRUCTURE/GROWTH
 	
Population: 1985   2025
 (thousands)   16 766   17 570
  0-14 years (%)   19.4   19.0
  60+ years (%)   18.1   25.2
 	
Rate of: 1980-85   2020-25
 growth   0.0   0.0
 natural increase   0.3   0.1
	Population growth rates are <u>unsatisfactory</u> because they are <u>too low</u>. The Government attaches great importance to securing population replacement to ensure continued economic growth.

MORTALITY/MORBIDITY 1980-85 2020-25 Life expectancy 72.1 77.0 Crude death rate 14.1 12.5 Infant mortality 11.1 5.4	The present conditions of health and levels of mortality are considered <u>acceptable</u>.
FERTILITY/NUPTIALITY/FAMILY 1980-85 2020-25 Fertility rate 1.9 2.1 Crude birth rate 14.4 12.6 Contraceptive prevalence rate ... ... Female mean age at first marriage 21.5 (1980)	Current fertility rates are considered <u>unsatisfactory</u> because they are <u>too low</u>.
INTERNATIONAL MIGRATION 1980-85 2020-25 Net migration rate 0.0 0.0 Foreign-born population (%)	Levels of immigration and emigration are viewed by the Government as <u>not</u> <u>significant</u> and <u>satisfactory</u>.
SPATIAL DISTRIBUTION/URBANIZATION Urban 1985 2025 population (%) 77.0 84.0 Growth rate: 1980-85 2020-25 urban 0.2 0.2 rural -0.7 -1.0	The present pattern of spatial distribution is considered <u>appropriate</u>. The regional distribution and structure of the population is generally felt to coincide with social and economic needs.

GENERAL POLICY FRAMEWORK

<u>Overall approach to population problems</u>: The utmost importance is attached to all questions of population and development proceeding from the premise that social and economic relations are the decisive bases for demographic processes. The Government encourages families to have at least two or three children, in order to secure population replacement. Importance is given to the promotion of the family and the care of mothers and children, support for large families and newly-wed couples, lowering mortality and reducing differentials in living and working conditions.

<u>Importance of population policy in achieving development objectives</u>: It is the Government's view that problems of population development can only be dealt with in a constructive and purposeful manner if population development and related questions are treated in terms of their social and economic interrelationships. Population policy is considered a very important factor in the continued systematic construction of the country.

INSTITUTIONAL FRAMEWORK

<u>Population data systems and development planning</u>: Demographic estimates, which are prepared by the Central Statistical Office, are an important tool for the formulation of population policies and economic planning. Censuses were conducted in 1950, 1964, 1971 and 1981. Economic planning is based on general five-year plans which are disaggregated into detailed one-year plans. The plans are produced by the State Planning Commission. The 1986-1990 plan was presented to the Eleventh Party Congress in April 1986.

<u>Integration of population within development planning</u>: Demographic processes and their implications are taken into account in social and economic policy. Research on demographic and social problems and their relationships is carried out on a planned basis. A Scientific Council for Social Policy and Demography works on the basis of a central research plan. The Institute for Sociology and Social Policy, established within the Academy of Sciences in 1978, and demography departments in nearly all the universities assist in the task of data collection and research.

POLICIES AND MEASURES

<u>Changes in population size and age structure</u>: The Government has a policy of intervention to raise the growth rate by pursuing the goal of two- or three-child families. The Government believes that its policy has demonstrated that a socialist society is able to exert a positive influence on birth rates with a policy sensitive to the interests and needs of young couples. The current two-child norm is considered a great improvement over the one-child families of the mid 1970s. Also noted with satisfaction is the reversal since the early 1970s of the trend towards a steadily diminishing working-age population

and an increasing number of old-age pensioners. Efforts are concentrated on ensuring solid vocational training and a place in the workforce for youth. To ensure that the elderly live in dignity, pensions and other benefits were improved in 1984. The policy is aimed at balancing distortions in the age structure, which were a consequence of the two World Wars, the economic crisis and post-War developments. Growing attention is being devoted to the economic and social consequences of aging.

Mortality and morbidity: The largest possible reduction in morbidity and mortality remains a government priority, with the greatest emphasis being given to primary health care. The Government has noted that, in future, further efforts will be taken to improve public health and social welfare service, including extended use of scientific findings, further improvement of training programmes and adult education of the staff of public health and social welfare services, and better doctor/patient contact. Greater importance is also being attached to medical treatment and rehabilitation, prophylaxis, and care for the physically and mentally disabled.

Fertility and the family: Intervention to raise the rates is a cornerstone of the Government's fertility policy. The Government encourages families to have at least two children. Measures are taken to improve material conditions, thereby encouraging parents to have children, and to assist women in combining labour-force activities with child-bearing and child-rearing. A series of such measures were introduced in the Eighth Congress of the Socialist Unity Party and reaffirmed in the Ninth, Tenth and Eleventh Party Congresses. In May 1987 child allowances were substantially increased to 100 marks (M 2.6 = $US 1) monthly for the first and second child and to 150 marks for the third and subsequent child. At the same time interest-free loans for young married couples under age 30 were raised to 7,000 marks. As of May 1986, working women have been entitled to 12 months paid maternity leave while those with two or more children can take paid leave to care for their sick children. Access to modern methods of fertility regulation is not limited, and direct Government support is provided. Family planning services include the statutory right to terminate a pregnancy. Abortions are permitted until the twelfth week of pregnancy; after 12 weeks, termination is permissible if there is a risk to the mother's life. The cost of contraceptives are defrayed by the Social Insurance Scheme, and the Government declines restrictive measures in the field of family planning. Sterilization is permitted if no other method is suitable.

International migration: Immigration is not a major policy concern. Some movement exists - mainly the temporary exchange of specialists, vocational or professional teaching or training assignments, and family reunification. The Government has recruited foreign workers from other countries of the Council for Mutual Economic Assistance and Algeria, while limiting emigration by imposing travel restrictions and building a strong sense of national identity. In September 1986 the Government announced that it had agreed to halt the flood of third-world refugees seeking passage through the country. Henceforth, only refugees in possession of a visa from a Western country would be permitted transit. In a previous agreement, signed in December 1985, the Government would not provide transit visas to refugees headed to Denmark.

<u>Spatial distribution/urbanization</u>: The policy concerning internal migration is to decelerate the basic trend by promoting small towns and intermediate cities, rural development and regional development for lagging regions. Measures include public infrastructure subsidies, direct restrictions and controls on industrial sites, direct State investment, transport rate adjustments, housing and social services, human resource and job training, and residential controls. The modification and reorganization of working places in industrial, building and transport enterprises which have been implemented in the past few years are important measures. Also, every effort is being made to create more favourable living and working conditions in rural areas.

<u>Status of women and population</u>: The Government indicates that the priority given to women in population and family policies does not result only from their roles as mothers and educators of their children. Great efforts are taken to enable women to benefit more from their equal status in society. Both sexes enjoy equal rights in all fields of social, public and personal life. Equal pay for equal work is guaranteed by the Constitution and is observed in practice. Female labour-force participation is fostered through State-subsidized improvements in infrastructure such as crèches and kindergartens. Despite the considerable equality gained in the socio-economic and political realms, an uneven division of household duties is reported to still prevail. Although fathers are eligible to request the "baby year" leave in lieu of the mother, few do so. The minimum legal age at marriage for women is 18 years.

MAP NO. 2771.1   UNITED NATIONS
DECEMBER 1988

GERMANY, FEDERAL REPUBLIC OF

DEMOGRAPHIC INDICATORS	CURRENT PERCEPTION
SIZE/AGE STRUCTURE/GROWTH	The rate of growth is considered <u>too low</u>. The Government is concerned about aging and declines in total population.

Population:	1985	2025
(thousands)	60 877	53 490
0-14 years (%)	15.4	16.0
60+ years (%)	20.0	31.1

Rate of:	1980-85	2020-25
growth	-0.2	-0.4
natural increase	-2.3	-4.3

DEMOGRAPHIC INDICATORS	CURRENT PERCEPTION
MORTALITY/MORBIDITY	The present conditions of health and levels of mortality are considered <u>acceptable</u>.

	1980-85	2020-25
Life expectancy	73.7	77.3
Crude death rate	12.3	15.4
Infant mortality	10.6	5.5

DEMOGRAPHIC INDICATORS	CURRENT PERCEPTION
FERTILITY/NUPTIALITY/FAMILY	The Government regards the present level of fertility as <u>too low</u>, because it is inadequate to ensure population replacement.

	1980-85	2020-25
Fertility rate	1.4	2.0
Crude birth rate	10.1	11.1
Contraceptive prevalence rate	77.9 (1985)	
Female mean age at first marriage	23.6 (1980)	

DEMOGRAPHIC INDICATORS	CURRENT PERCEPTION
INTERNATIONAL MIGRATION	The level of immigration is considered <u>significant</u> and <u>too high</u>, while the level of emigration is considered <u>not significant</u> and <u>satisfactory</u>.

	1980-85	2020-25
Net migration rate	0.0	0.0
Foreign-born population (%)	7.4 (1983)	

DEMOGRAPHIC INDICATORS	CURRENT PERCEPTION
SPATIAL DISTRIBUTION/URBANIZATION	The spatial distribution of the population is considered <u>partially appropriate</u>.

Urban	1985	2025
population (%)	85.5	88.6

Growth rate:	1980-85	2020-25
urban	0.1	-0.4
rural	-1.8	-0.5

GENERAL POLICY FRAMEWORK

Overall approach to population problems: The Government aims at achieving
a steady population growth rate, improving the situation of families,
providing for the health of individuals, and improving the pattern of
spatial distribution.

Importance of population policy in achieving development objectives:
There is no explicit population policy. Population policy measures have
been elements of social and family policy and of legislative, regional
planning and labour market policies. The Government considers population
policy to be an important component of its development aid strategy.

INSTITUTIONAL FRAMEWORK

Population data systems and development planning: Census-taking is the
responsibility of the Federal Statistical Office. The last two population
censuses were undertaken in 1961 and 1970. It was not possible to hold
the census planned for April 1983, owing to disputes concerning the
confidentiality of the information. Despite challenges, a census was held
in May 1987. Vital registration is complete and is the responsibility of
the Ministry of Interior, Population Statistics Office.

Integration of population within development planning: The Government has
charged the Interministerial Working Group on Population Questions,
chaired by the Federal Minister of Interior, with drawing up a
comprehensive report on population developments in the country. Since
1950, the Federal Statistical Office has been responsible for preparing
population projections. The Federal Institute for Population Research
(BIB) was established in 1973, and it has been chiefly responsible for
providing information on population-development interrelationships and for
conducting special demographic surveys to meet specific planning needs.

POLICIES AND MEASURES

Changes in population size and age structure: Although the Government does
not have an explicit population policy to increase population growth, in March
1984 a pro-natalist programme, estimated to cost $3 billion a year, was
launched with the goal of encouraging an additional 200,000 births annually.
It is hoped that this will help to reduce the declines in total population
that the country is currently experiencing. The Government is very concerned
about the fall in fertility rates, estimated to be the lowest in Western
Europe, and the consequent aging of the population.

Mortality and morbidity: Maternal and infant mortality are of special policy
concern. Carcinogenic diseases, heart and circulatory diseases (particularly
coronary diseases), dental caries, and mental illness are identified as being
of special policy concern. The programme for the promotion of health-related

research and development includes preventing heart and circulatory diseases, further improving cancer care through early diagnosis, improving care for the mentally ill and preventing a large proportion of disabilities in early childhood through early treatment.

Fertility and the family: Concerned by a total fertility rate that fell to 1.4 in 1985, the Government has emphasized that efforts must be made in every sphere of society to make the country a better place for children. In 1984, the Government launched a pro-natalist programme. Twenty million dollars has been set aside for a Mother and Child Foundation, to steer unwed expectant mothers away from abortion clinics. The goal is to increase the number of births by 200,000 annually, so as to maintain the current population level. Major new tax incentives form part of the programme, along with a programme that would supply all women with "motherhood vacation money" of $ 200 a month for a full year after giving birth. In January 1986 the post-natal maternity allowance was replaced by a parental leave of 10 months, which is to be extended to one year in 1988. The leave is payable at the rate of 600 deutsche mark a month (DM 2.5 = $US 1). Diffusion of information on, and access to, all modern methods of contraception is permitted by law. The promotion of family planning is aimed at enabling young couples to decide for themselves when they want to have a child. Those insured under the statutory health insurance scheme are entitled to a physician's counselling on questions of birth control, a medical examination, the prescription of contraceptives, and financial assistance in connection with legal sterilization. The Government has promoted a model programme to develop counselling services in the field of family planning, psychological and social conflicts during pregnancy, sexual counselling and counselling on partner-related problems. Abortion is legal during the first 12 weeks for social or psychological reasons; within 22 weeks for eugenic reasons; and within any period for medical reasons. Sterilization is legal.

International migration: While current policy aims at reducing the level of immigration in the future, government officials in 1987 indicated that the persistence of population declines may have to be compensated for by increasing the number of immigrants entering the country. Statistics indicate that the numbers of foreigners living in the country rose in 1987 to approximately 4.6 million. The integration of foreigners living in the country is an important goal of the Government's policy. Foreigners who want to return to their home countries are provided with financial assistance. In January 1986, a new law came into force concerning a housing construction subsidy for foreigners returning to their country of origin, which aims at facilitating the reintegration of foreign workers who return to their own countries. In February 1986, the Federal Government set up an interministerial commission to look into the whole complex of questions relating to the granting of asylum. In September 1986, the Government announced measures designed to discourage immigration. Airline companies will risk fines of $ 1,000 if they fail to check the papers of passengers flying to the Federal Republic. Refugees from developing countries will have to apply for visas even if they plan to spend only a few days in the country, and those awaiting a decision on their asylum requests may seek employment only after five years. To stem the flow of asylum seekers, the German Democratic

Republic agreed, as of October 1986, to grant transit passage only to those in possession of a third country visa. Since 1979, the Federal Agency for the Recognition of Foreign Refugees has dealt with over 400,000 asylum requests.

Spatial distribution/urbanization: Minor changes are desirable, such as changes in the urban/rural balance. The main goal is to decrease out-migration from rural areas and in-migration into the largest metropolitan area and to maintain internal migration at current levels in other urban areas. Through its area planning policy, the Government is working towards a balanced distribution of the population. Its aim is to create and maintain equally favourable living conditions in all regions.

Status of women and population: A Department for Women's Affairs was set up at the Federal Ministry for Youth, Family Affairs and Health in July 1979 with a view to promoting equal rights for women. A guide to vocational advancement for women, recommending measures to be taken in private industry, has been issued by the Government. Guidelines with the same objective became effective on 1 March 1986 in the federal administration. The Government places major emphasis on the situation of particularly disadvantaged women. The minimum legal age at marriage for women is 16 years.

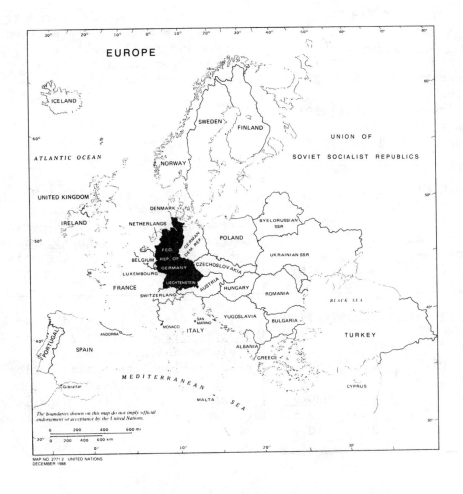

GHANA

DEMOGRAPHIC INDICATORS	CURRENT PERCEPTION

SIZE/AGE STRUCTURE/GROWTH
 	
Population: 1985   2025
 (thousands)   13 588   47 020
  0–14 years (%)   46.7   38.7
  60+ years (%)   4.5   5.2
 	
Rate of: 1980–85   2020–25
 growth   3.2   2.3
 natural increase   32.2   23.0
	The rate of growth is considered <u>unsatisfactory</u> because it is <u>too high</u>. The current high rate is perceived as detrimental to individual and family welfare.

MORTALITY/MORBIDITY 1980–85 2020–25 Life expectancy 52.0 67.5 Crude death rate 14.6 5.8 Infant mortality 98.3 37.1	Levels and trends are <u>unacceptable</u>. Major concerns are maternal, infant, and child mortality, and the poor health status of the rural population, due to inadequate sanitation, housing, water supply, nutrition, and health services.
FERTILITY/NUPTIALITY/FAMILY 1980–85 2020–25 Fertility rate 6.5 3.6 Crude birth rate 46.9 28.9 Contraceptive prevalence rate 10.0 (1979) Female mean age at first marriage 19.4 (1971)	Current rates are considered <u>too high</u> in relation to both the rate of population growth and family well-being. There is concern over the high frequency of induced abortions.
INTERNATIONAL MIGRATION 1980–85 2020–25 Net migration rate 0.0 0.0 Foreign-born population (%) 6.6 (1970)	Immigration is <u>significant</u> and <u>too high</u>, due to the depressed economy and the returning migrants from Nigeria. Emigration is <u>not significant</u> and <u>satisfactory</u>. However, there is concern over the brain drain.
SPATIAL DISTRIBUTION/URBANIZATION Urban 1985 2025 population (%) 31.5 56.6 Growth rate: 1980–85 2020–25 urban 3.8 3.6 rural 3.0 0.7	The pattern of spatial distribution is <u>inappropriate</u>. Primary concerns are rapid urbanization and rural depopulation, unbalanced regional development, and fear that many returning migrants expelled from Nigeria would concentrate in already overcrowded Accra.

- 19 -

GHANA

GENERAL POLICY FRAMEWORK

Overall approach to population problems: There is direct intervention in order to reduce the rate of population growth, morbidity and mortality, fertility, immigration and emigration and urbanization, accompanied by social and economic restructuring. Modifying fertility is the primary official means of decreasing population growth.

Importance of population policy in achieving development objectives: National development plans since 1962 have underscored the importance of linking population policies with development efforts if development objectives are to be reached.

INSTITUTIONAL FRAMEWORK

Population data systems and development planning: Decennial censuses have been conducted relatively regularly since 1891, and post-Independence censuses since 1960. The latest census was taken in 1984. Registration of births and deaths is incomplete. A formal system of development planning has existed since 1951, with the most recent plan being the five-year development plan, 1981-1985. An Economic Recovery Programme was launched for the period 1986-1988.

Integration of population within development planning: The Ghana Manpower Board, responsible for overall population policies, is located in the Ministry of Finance and Economic Planning. Within that Ministry is also located the National Family Planning Programme Secretariat. The Government has received international assistance in order to strengthen the integration of population variables in development planning.

POLICIES AND MEASURES

Changes in population size and age structure: High growth rates are felt to hinder the attainment of development objectives by aggravating pressure on scarce public services, worsening the employment situation, and straining shrinking food supplies. Policy since 1969 has aimed at decreasing the rates of population growth and natural increase. Measures have been implemented to reduce fertility, adjust spatial distribution, and reduce immigration. The National Family Planning Programme and the Aliens Compliance Order, both of which date from 1969, are designed to decrease fertility and immigration levels. Integrated socio-economic development efforts, particularly rural development, are intended to affect the population growth rate indirectly. Since a decrease in the growth rate is acknowledged to be unlikely in the immediate future, the Government hopes that effective economic growth can offset the rise in population. In 1984, the Government reaffirmed its target of a 1.75 per cent population growth rate by the year 2000, although there are indications that this ambitious goal has now been raised to 2.0 per cent. The social security scheme covers employees of firms with at least five workers, while voluntary affiliation is available to those in smaller firms and the self-employed.

Mortality and morbidity: The official policy is to reduce morbidity and mortality levels. This is to be accomplished by emphasizing both preventive and curative health measures, with a new focus on the former. A major shortcoming of Ghana's health system has been that virtually all of its resources are located in urban hospitals and clinics, and not in rural areas. To overcome this, the primary health care system has aimed at decentralization, intersectoral collaboration, and extending community orientation and participation. Specific measures promoted - but not always fully implemented - include rural projects in maternal and child health, water supply, sanitation, and basic education, and programmes that stress child-spacing. There has also been an expansion in the immunization programme and the training of health personnel.

Fertility and the family: The Government sees the goal of fertility reduction as intimately related to standards of family health, nutrition, hygiene, and the overall standards of living, and believes these latter conditions must be improved to make fertility modification more feasible. The policy to reduce fertility is oriented towards the voluntary reduction of fertility by couples, through the services of Ghana's extensive National Family Planning Programme, which provides family planning services at every hospital and health centre. There are efforts under way to strengthen the Programme. Besides family planning, disincentives include limiting maternity benefits, and restricting child labour. A major indirect measure lowering fertility has been an emphasis on increasing the participation of women in development by broadening their educational base and creating job opportunities for them. Access to contraception is not limited and receives direct government support. In 1985 the law on abortion was liberalized to permit abortion on broad health, eugenic and juridical indicators. Sterilization is legal, with conditions. Since 1969, the Government has maintained the target of a total fertility rate of four children per woman by the year 2000.

International migration: The official policy is to curb future immigration. Several measures have been adopted in the past to control immigration levels, the most notable being the far-reaching Aliens Compliance Act of 1969. The Government is currently considering a variety of new methods to curb immigration. It reluctantly accepted the forced return of Ghanaians from Nigeria in 1983. In late 1985 the Interior Ministry announced that under the 1985 Investment Code, it was an offense for aliens in Ghana to engage in retail trade. Some restrictive measures have been imposed to halt the emigration of skilled personnel, but no explicit policy regarding emigration has been declared. The Economic Recovery Programme for 1984-1986 was designed to encourage skilled workers and professionals to remain in Ghana.

Spatial distribution/urbanization: The official policy is to adjust spatial distribution by curbing internal migration. Among the comprehensive measures that have been adopted are rural development strategies and slowing the growth of Accra. Partial strategies have included regional development policies for lagging regions. Ghana is highly urbanized, and policies have been addressed to the resultant problems (e.g., rural depopulation, increasing pressures on urban services). Returnees from Nigeria have been frequently dispersed to regions distant from Accra, so as to avoid further overcrowding the capital. Within Accra and other major towns, the Government has increased outlays on public services, to accommodate a growing urban population.

Status of women and population: Improving women's status is seen as essential to the achievement of Ghana's demographic objectives. In particular, it is hoped that a lower total fertility rate and reduced maternal morbidity and mortality will result from improvements made in women's education and employment. The Government has stressed the importance of broadening women's activities and integrating them into the larger frame of population development.

Other issues: The Government acknowledges that greater participation by men in contraceptive practices must be encouraged in the future. The Government fears the strain that is being placed on the country by the almost 2 million nationals who have had to return to Ghana from Nigeria since 1983.

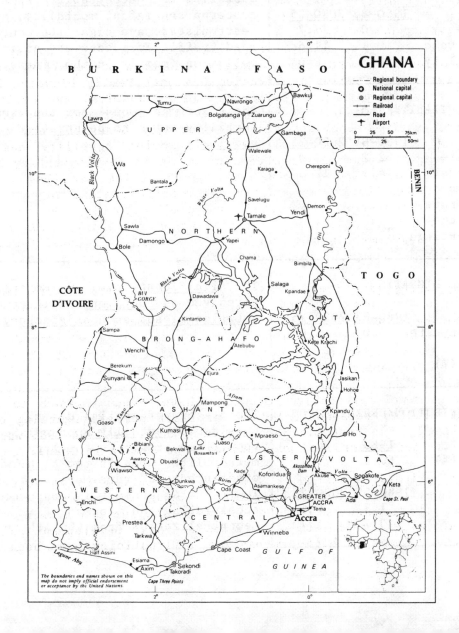

GREECE

DEMOGRAPHIC INDICATORS	CURRENT PERCEPTION

SIZE/AGE STRUCTURE/GROWTH

Population:	1985	2025
(thousands)	9 878	10 789
0-14 years (%)	21.5	18.6
60+ years (%)	17.8	23.8

Rate of:	1980-85	2020-25
growth	0.5	0.1
natural increase	4.8	0.9

The view of population growth rates has changed within the past few years, from satisfactory to too low. It is feared that the continuation of demographic trends, including population aging, will have unfavourable economic and social consequences. Preserving the country's demographic vigour is seen as being closely related to the safeguarding of the country's fundamental identity.

MORTALITY/MORBIDITY

	1980-85	2020-25
Life expectancy	74.0	77.7
Crude death rate	10.1	11.6
Infant mortality	16.3	8.0

The Government regards morbidity and mortality as unacceptable. Particular concerns are infant mortality, cancer, heart disease and cigarette consumption, road traffic accidents and environmental pollution (mainly in the Athens area).

FERTILITY/NUPTIALITY/FAMILY

	1980-85	2020-25
Fertility rate	2.2	2.0
Crude birth rate	14.9	12.5
Contraceptive prevalence rate	...	...
Female mean age at first marriage	...	...

The Government considers the current fertility rates to be unsatisfactory and too low.

INTERNATIONAL MIGRATION

	1980-85	2020-25
Net migration rate	0.0	0.0
Foreign-born population (%)	...	...

The significant level of immigration is perceived as too high. Emigration is not significant and satisfactory.

SPATIAL DISTRIBUTION/URBANIZATION

Urban	1985	2025
population (%)	60.1	79.1

Growth rate:	1980-85	2020-25
urban	1.3	0.6
rural	-0.7	-1.7

The pattern of spatial distribution is considered partially appropriate. Population growth in the largest metropolitan area is too high, while in other urban and rural areas, it is too low. The Government is concerned with accelerating the process of decentralization from the Athens area.

GENERAL POLICY FRAMEWORK

Overall approach to population problems: Demographic issues and population policy formation are considered of primary importance, and the Government has taken several concrete measures against the problems of low population growth, an unacceptable health care system, declining fertility, and an unfavourable urban/rural balance. The solution of these problems is seen as a national concern.

Importance of population policy in achieving development objectives: The Government considers international co-operation in the field of population to be an integral part of the development process. It stresses the need for training on population distribution and for special programmes on the status of women, children, youth and the aged.

INSTITUTIONAL FRAMEWORK

Population data systems and development planning: The most recent census was conducted in 1981. The Five-Year Economic and Social Development Plan 1983-1987 embodies the Government's basic strategy and was prepared by the Centre for Planning and Economic Research. The Centre, established in 1961, is responsible for the technical preparation of medium-term plans and is the main economic research and planning institute. There is a recognized need for training and advisory services for population policies and programmes, and, specifically, population communication and education.

Integration of population within development planning: There is no single government agency responsible for the formulation or co-ordination of population policies. The National Statistical Service of Greece has been responsible since 1960 for preparing population projections and demographic surveys.

POLICIES AND MEASURES

Changes in population size and age structure: The policy of non-intervention of 1980 has been changed to one of boosting growth rates, although the Government has specified no quantitative targets. It feels that the determinants of population change, intricately connected with life-styles and the prevailing social and economic conditions, can be affected by removing the disincentives created as a result of modern conditions of life and by regional development. Towards this goal, improvements are aimed at social services and the quality of life as well as the protection of purchasing power of wage earners, especially those with lower incomes.

Mortality and morbidity: Of primary importance to the Government has been the reform of the health care system by increasing resource allocation to the health sector, particularly to provision of pharmaceuticals and health care, and by placing emphasis on preventive medicine, particularly for lower-income

GREECE

groups in rural areas. To improve a system considered fragmented and inadequate, a new health law was passed in 1983, establishing a national health system. The goal is to provide high-quality health services to the entire population within five years. Among the specific objectives are unifying health services throughout the country; increasing the quantity and quality of auxiliary medical and hospital staff; and increasing funding to establish a technical infrastructure, including the construction of health centres and the creation of new hospitals throughout the country. To provide integrated care to the entire population, 400 health centres are being created, so that no one is more than 30 minutes away from a centre. Tobacco advertisements on television are banned and a Government bill proposed health warnings in all cigarette advertisements and packages.

Fertility and the family: The maintenance of the fertility rate above replacement level is to be brought about chiefly by improving maternal and child health and family well-being. The Ministry of Social Services sees the main purpose of family planning programmes as enabling couples to control the number and spacing of the children they desire rather than curbing population growth. To maintain the level, a number of measures have been implemented, such as family planning programmes, measures to improve the status of women, child welfare allowances, a 14-week maternity leave, more centres for the care of the newborn and nurseries, and improved housing schemes for families with more than three children. Act No. 1483 of 1984 granted parental leave of up to three months for each parent and forbade dismissal of women during pregnancy and for one year after childbirth. Concerning the effective use of modern methods of fertility regulation, access is not limited, and indirect government support is provided. In June 1986, the Parliament passed a law permitting abortion on demand at State expense. Sterilization is allowed only for medical purposes.

International migration: Policy aims at curbing future immigration but maintaining the already established immigrant population. The Greek Ministry of Public Order has been deporting growing numbers of unauthorized migrants chiefly from Africa and West Asia, on the grounds that they increase unemployment and various social problems. As of 1986, those working illegally in Greece were estimated to number about 20,000. Currently, an active policy concern is immigration for permanent resettlement and the refugee/asylum-seeker situation. Policy is also aimed at curbing emigration in the future. Of special concern is the harmonious social and economic integration of returning emigrants into the country's population. To facilitate the reintegration of returning migrants, a number of measures have been implemented, such as granting housing facilities to the returnees and allowing them to import goods free of exchange formalities. Other measures are favourable loan terms for migrant workers; special incentives for labour-force mobility, from which Greek migrants can also profit; vocational training and guidance; and investment incentives. The Government also assists Greeks working abroad by contributing to the costs of vocational training for Greek expatriates and their children and by giving training benefits to children of Greeks working abroad.

Spatial distribution/urbanization: Policies concerning internal migration aim to decrease migration to the largest metropolitan area and decrease out-migration from other urban and rural areas. Strategies aim at slowing metropolitan growth and encouraging the development of lagging regions. Enterprise-oriented measures include public infrastructure subsidies, grants, loans, and tax incentives to new industries and relocatees, and growth-centre strategies. Individual-oriented incentives include migration subsidies and worker relocation assistance, housing and social services, human resource investments and job training. To control excessive population concentration in Athens and Salonika, the Government provides incentives to encourage labour-force mobility. Industrial zones have been established throughout the country by the National Council of Regional and Physical Planning.

Status of women and population: The Government has repeatedly expressed its goal of creating equality between the sexes in social, economic and political activities. To end discrimination and change discriminatory attitudes, the Civil Code has been revised according to the constitutional principle of equality of the sexes. In addition, the Family Law has been reformed, and family guidance centres and day-care centres established. Specific measures concerning recruitment and retraining have been taken in all occupations, and education programmes for females in traditionally male-dominated occupations have been established. Of special concern is the right of women to head agricultural concerns. Act. No. 1414/84 of the Ministry of Labour provides for the elimination of sex discrimination, while the General Equality Secretariat, created in 1985, is competent to receive complaints concerning the application of the principle of sexual equality in employment. The minimum legal age at marriage for women was raised to 18 years in 1983.

GRENADA

DEMOGRAPHIC INDICATORS	CURRENT PERCEPTION
SIZE/AGE STRUCTURE/GROWTH	The Government perceives current growth rates to be <u>unsatisfactory</u> and <u>too high</u>.

Population: <u>1985</u>   <u>2025</u>
(thousands)   112   185
  0-14 years (%)   ...   ...
  60+ years (%)   10.0   ...

Rate of: <u>1980-85</u> <u>2020-25</u>
  growth   1.0   ...
  natural increase   21.0   ...

| **MORTALITY/MORBIDITY** | The Government considers mortality levels to be <u>unacceptable</u>. |

     <u>1980-85</u> <u>2020-25</u>
Life expectancy   ...   ...
Crude death rate   8.0   ...
Infant mortality   13.0   ...

| **FERTILITY/NUPTIALITY/FAMILY** | Current fertility rates are <u>unsatisfactory</u> and <u>too high</u>. |

     <u>1980-85</u> <u>2020-25</u>
Fertility rate   ...   ...
Crude birth rate   29.0   ...
Contraceptive
  prevalence rate   ...   ...
Female mean age
  at first marriage   ...   ...

| **INTERNATIONAL MIGRATION** | The <u>insignificant</u> immigration levels are considered <u>satisfactory</u>. Emigration is <u>significant</u> and <u>satisfactory</u>. |

     <u>1980-85</u> <u>2020-25</u>
Net migration rate -11.0   ...
Foreign-born
  population (%)   2.3 (1981)

| **SPATIAL DISTRIBUTION/URBANIZATION** | The spatial distribution is considered <u>inappropriate</u>. |

Urban   <u>1985</u>   <u>2025</u>
  population (%)   ...   ...

Growth rate: <u>1980-85</u> <u>2020-25</u>
  urban   ...   ...
  rural   ...   ...

GENERAL POLICY FRAMEWORK

<u>Overall approach to population problems</u>: Although the Government has no explicit population policy, it is concerned with the quality of life, health and general welfare of its population. Due to its young population, Government priorities are concerned with the demands for basic services in the areas of health, housing, education, water, food and employment.

<u>Importance of population policy in achieving development objectives</u>: In order to alleviate severe economic problems, Government development objectives include improving the management of the country's population resources in relation to its natural resources. Government policy aims at broadening the productive base of the economy while having well-trained people assisting and managing those efforts. Since tourism is a major development area, a safe, healthy, and attractive environment is another Government priority.

INSTITUTIONAL FRAMEWORK

<u>Population data systems and development planning</u>: The most recent population census was taken in 1981. Vital registration of births and deaths is considered virtually complete.

<u>Integration of population within development planning</u>: The Government has set up a multidisciplinary Task Force on Population in order to improve plans for social and economic growth. The Task Force serves to monitor the basic indicators of population such as fertility, nutritional intake, infant mortality and migration, in order to reach its planning objectives.

POLICIES AND MEASURES

<u>Changes in population size and age structure</u>: Due to high fertility rates and substantial emigration, the Government is faced with an increasingly young population, with over half the population under 21 years of age. Government priorities include improving basic services and giving special attention to the elderly, who have been left without support, due to the emigration of young adults. Community health workers pay special visits to the aged, and district health teams handle geriatric care and treatment. A pension plan, implemented in 1983, was incorporated into the National Insurance Scheme, offering a general pension to employed persons.

<u>Mortality and morbidity</u>: The main priority of the Government is providing primary health services to the total population and upgrading those already in operation. The Three-Year Health Sector Plan, initiated in 1983, deals specifically with maternal and child health care. The Plan's priorities are directed towards care of mothers, including education for high-risk mothers, the care of children, the fertile female age group, the rural and urban poor,

the elderly and the disabled. General health care strategies involve raising levels of health awareness in the general population, expanding educational projects, preventing communicable and vector-borne diseases, providing safe water and waste disposal, developing a health information system, and providing essential drugs. Additional goals include expanding the production and consumption of local crops, providing food supplements to families in need, encouraging breast-feeding, and expanding nutrition programmes. Because of a recurring deficit in the budget, the Government indicated in 1986 that it would be necessary to make cutbacks in various areas, including health projects.

Fertility and the family: The Government has not cited any direct measures taken to lower fertility. The Government considers fertility to be an individual matter and believes that women should have access to information on family planning as well as on nutrition and child care. Family planning and health education programmes operate in co-ordination with maternal and child health care programmes. The Grenada Planned Parenthood Association provides family planning services through government health centres and the community-based distribution programme, with support from the Ministry of Health. Since 1974 the Government has considered family planning programmes an important component in the country's development. In 1985, a three-year family planning and family life education project was implemented to increase contraceptive coverage throughout the country and to reduce the incidence of teen-age pregnancy. Maternity benefits fall under the National Insurance Scheme and entitle a woman to 60 per cent of her previous earnings for 12 weeks or until six weeks after the date of confinement. Abortion is legal if the life of the mother is at risk. There is no information readily available on the status of sterilization.

International migration: Immigration is not an active policy concern, given its insignificant level. The levels of emigration are perceived by the Government as significant. The high levels of emigration, which have helped to limit population growth, have been due mainly to limited employment possibilities, political unrest and the proximity of more developed islands.

Spatial distribution/urbanization: Policies concerning internal migration consist of decelerating the movement of migrants to urban areas. A Model Farms Programme is expected to help in stemming the exodus of young people from the agricultural sector.

Status of women and population: Two projects concerning the advancement of women were implemented in 1987. One project is designed to train women to operate, service and maintain both light and heavy equipment under the Women's Apprentice Motor Mechanic Scheme. The other project, operating through the Women's Resource Centre, will establish a documentation centre within the Ministry of Health, Housing and Women's Affairs and conduct research on the situation of women. Information on the minimum legal age at marriage for women is not readily available.

Other issues: The Government's development strategies include a reduction in the level of unemployment, an improvement in income distribution and living standards, control of inflation and a real growth rate of 4 per cent per annum in the period 1986-1990. Because the promotion of tourism plays an important role in development activities, the Government is very concerned about preserving a healthy and attractive environment. Consequently, development projects are monitored, in order to minimize the negative environmental consequences.

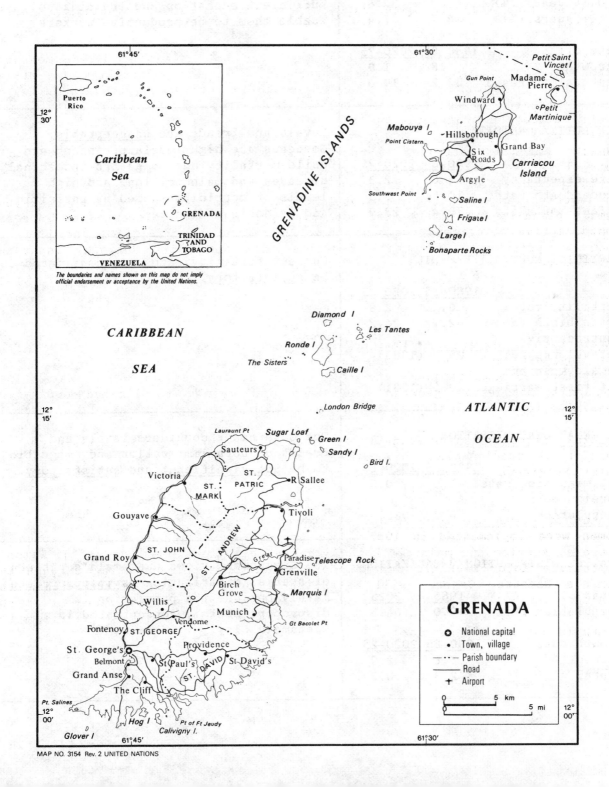

GUATEMALA

DEMOGRAPHIC INDICATORS	CURRENT PERCEPTION

SIZE/AGE STRUCTURE/GROWTH
 	
Population: 1985   2025
 (thousands) 7 963 21 668
  0-14 years (%) 45.9   32.6
  60+ years (%)   4.7   7.4
 	
Rate of: 1980-85 2020-25
 growth   2.8   1.9
 natural increase 32.2   19.0
	The Government views the country's rate of population growth as <u>unsatisfactory</u> because it is <u>too high</u>. The primary concern is providing the population with sufficient education and training to enable them to be productive workers.

MORTALITY/MORBIDITY 1980-85 2020-25 Life expectancy 59.0 72.3 Crude death rate 10.5 5.3 Infant mortality 70.4 23.9	Levels and trends are <u>unacceptable</u>. Concerns are high levels of infant and child mortality due to gastro-intestinal diseases and malnutrition, and high levels of morbidity caused by parasitic and infectious disease.
FERTILITY/NUPTIALITY/FAMILY 1980-85 2020-25 Fertility rate 6.1 2.9 Crude birth rate 42.7 24.2 Contraceptive prevalence rate 25.0 (1983) Female mean age at first marriage 20.5 (1981)	Current fertility rates are considered to be <u>satisfactory</u>.
INTERNATIONAL MIGRATION 1980-85 2020-25 Net migration rate -4.0 0.0 Foreign-born population (%) 0.7 (1981)	The Government considers levels and trends of both immigration and emigration to be <u>not significant</u> and <u>satisfactory</u>.
SPATIAL DISTRIBUTION/URBANIZATION Urban 1985 2025 population (%) 40.0 64.5 Growth rate: 1980-85 2020-25 urban 3.6 2.9 rural 2.3 0.2	The Government views Guatamala's pattern of spatial distribution as <u>inappropriate</u>, mainly because the population is disproportionately concentrated in Guatamala City.

GENERAL POLICY FRAMEWORK

Overall approach to population problems: There is no explicit population policy. The Government's major population concern is the interaction between internal migration and patterns of employment. Increasing importance has been given to spatial distribution, largely as a means of achieving economic integration and promoting national security.

Importance of population policy in achieving development objectives: The Government has not formulated an explicit population policy, although studies have been conducted as to the feasibility of incorporating a population policy into future development plans. In development plans to date, discussion has centred mainly on the relationship between population growth, migration and employment.

INSTITUTIONAL FRAMEWORK

Population data systems and development planning: Census-taking is the responsibility of the Department of Demographic and Social Statistics of the Directorate of Statistics. Eleven censuses have been conducted - the latest in 1981. Registration of births and deaths is classified as complete. Development planning is carried out through the National Council for Economic Planning. The eighth national development plan for the period 1987-1991 is currently in effect.

Integration of population within development planning: The Government began integrating population factors into development planning in 1978. The Population and Employment Department of the National Planning Secretariat is charged with formulating population policies, developing population programmes and integrating population variables into macro, sectoral and regional planning. The Department is the technical secretariat for the National Population Commission.

POLICIES AND MEASURES

Changes in population size and age structure: There is no specific policy designed to modify the rate of population growth, and no quantitative targets have been set with respect to growth. Under the social security scheme, employed persons, including agricultural workers, are covered, while public employees are included in a special scheme.

Mortality and morbidity: Policy objectives include a reduction in maternal/child mortality and morbidity and mortality from preventable diseases; a decrease in malnutrition; improvement in sanitary conditions, and increased efficiency in the health care sector. Measures to achieve these goals include the expansion of health care services in rural areas, improvements in the management and administration of health programmes, extension and improvement of the Guatemalan Social Security Institute, strengthening the immunization programme and increasing environmental sanitation activities. The Government is increasingly committed to a policy of preventive primary care. It has established programmes for diarrhoea control and sanitary food preparation and the provision of clean water. The army has conducted mass immunization campaigns. Non-governmental organizations have had a striking impact on infant mortality reduction through their promotion and distribution of oral rehydrator salts. The National Commission for the Promotion of Breast-Feeding has undertaken national campaigns to encourage breast-feeding and has established 18 human milk banks in hospitals to serve high-risk children.

Fertility and the family: The Government does not have an explicit policy to modify fertility, although recent planning documents have mentioned the desirability of reducing fertility in the context of providing employment, increasing human resource potential and satisfying basic needs. The right to family planning is enshrined in the 1985 Constitution, and direct and indirect support to family planning programmes is provided through the Department of Maternal/Child and Family Health. In co-operation with the Ministry of Education, the Guatemala affiliate of the International Planned Parenthood Federation has developed population education projects and communication programmes. Since approximately three out of four births are attended by one of the country's 13,000 traditional birth attendants, only 40 per cent of whom have received any formal training, the Department of Mother/Child Health of the Ministry of Public Health intends to draw up a participatory training methodology to train the midwives. Abortion is illegal except to save the life of the mother. Voluntary sterilization is performed in both government and private institutions.

International migration: No official policy has been established concerning immigration or emigration beyond normal visa and passport controls. However, it is estimated that as many as 100,000 nationals have left Guatemala without official sanction in recent years. As of mid 1986, roughly 45,000 Guatemalans had sought refuge in neighbouring Mexico. With the change of Government in January 1986, the new President of Guatemala extended an invitation to all Guatemalan refugees abroad to return to their native villages or to any other area of their choice in Guatemala. This represents a change in policy from the previous administration which had grouped returnees together in "development centres" (payos de desarrollo), model villages that were under army supervision. Given the limited resources available, however, the Government has encountered difficulties in reabsorbing the returning refugees.

Spatial distribution/urbanization: The Government wishes to increase migration to areas other than Guatemala City and to promote rural-to-rural migration. Recently, the Government has promoted resettlement policies to aid in controlling internal security. Government-sponsored programmes aim at eventually developing growth poles. Successive Governments have encouraged settlement of virgin lands, but for the most part these efforts have not been completely successful, since the indigenous population is reluctant to leave its ancestral lands. A project has been undertaken to activate small and medium-sized cities in order to consolidate the economic base and create a basic infrastructure within the framework of territorial management.

Status of women and population: The minimum legal age at marriage for women
is 14 years.

Other issues: The situation of extensive illiteracy, poor health, low income,
high unemployment and malnutrition in which many families had been living has
been exacerbated by family and community disintegration as a result of civil
strife.   Many communities have been destroyed, substantial numbers of people
displaced and countless women and children widowed and orphaned.   Unofficial
estimates place the number of orphans at approximately 200,000.

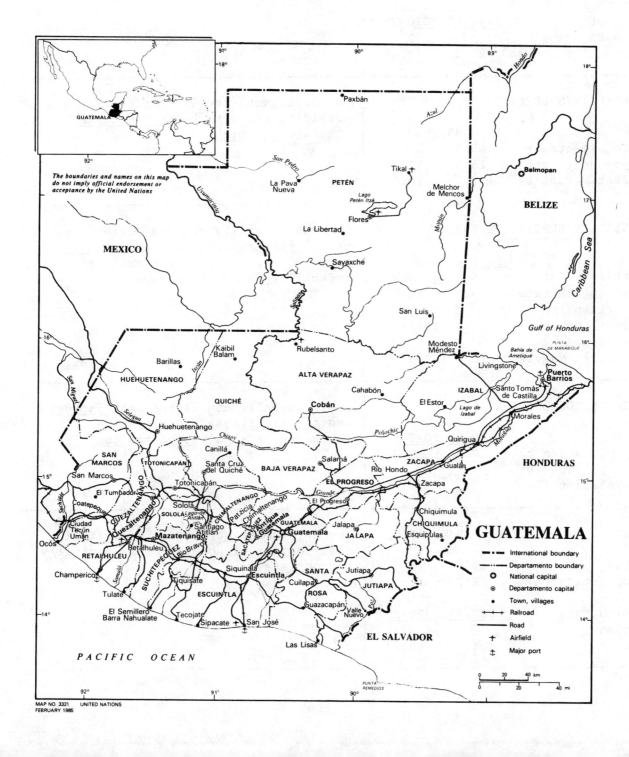

GUINEA

DEMOGRAPHIC INDICATORS	CURRENT PERCEPTION

SIZE/AGE STRUCTURE/GROWTH
 	
Population: 1985   2025
 (thousands) 6 075 15 561
  0-14 years (%) 43.1   36.5
  60+ years (%)   4.9   5.9
 	
Rate of: 1980-85 2020-25
 growth   2.3   1.7
 natural increase 23.3   17.4
	The Government considers the level of population growth to be <u>satisfactory</u>.

MORTALITY/MORBIDITY 1980-85 2020-25 Life expectancy 40.2 56.2 Crude death rate 23.5 11.1 Infant mortality 159.1 80.2	The Government considers mortality and morbidity rates to be <u>unacceptable</u> because they are <u>too high</u>.
FERTILITY/NUPTIALITY/FAMILY 1980-85 2020-25 Fertility rate 6.2 3.4 Crude birth rate 46.8 28.5 Contraceptive prevalence rate 1.0 (1977) Female mean age at first marriage 16.0 (1955)	Current fertility rates are viewed as <u>unsatisfactory</u> because they are <u>too high</u>. Concerns are adolescent fertility, infertility and illegal abortions.
INTERNATIONAL MIGRATION 1980-85 2020-25 Net migration rate 0.0 0.0 Foreign-born population (%)	Immigration is considered <u>satisfactory</u> and <u>not significant</u>. Emigration is perceived as <u>significant</u> and <u>too high</u>.
SPATIAL DISTRIBUTION/URBANIZATION Urban 1985 2025 population (%) 22.2 52.8 Growth rate: 1980-85 2020-25 urban 5.4 3.2 rural 1.5 0.2	The Government perceives the spatial distribution of population as <u>partially appropriate</u>.

GENERAL POLICY FRAMEWORK

Overall approach to population problems: The Government has begun to
enact measures to combat high fertility and infant mortality,
malnutrition, and food supply problems. The main goals of Guinea's
population policy are reforming the health care system, reducing
emigration, and rehabilitating rural regions. The new Government has
sought aid from international agencies to assist it in restructuring the
economy and improving conditions for the population. International aid
for data collection and analysis is seen as necessary for defining an
adequate population policy. Education on population and general matters
is considered vital to improving the welfare of the population. The
eradication of causes of underdevelopment, rather than family planning, is
viewed as the path to solving population problems.

Importance of population policy in achieving development objectives: The
Government considers solving population problems to be a main priority in
the development process. Interactions are seen between demographic
phenomena and development. The strategy of economic development must
include the rational utilization of human resources. The Government has
reversed the pro-natalist policy of the previous Government because it
feels that population growth does not necessarily bring about economic
development.

INSTITUTIONAL FRAMEWORK

Population data systems and development planning: The 1955 demographic
survey served as the major source of demographic data until the 1983
census. The Government conducted a census in 1971 without international
aid and another in 1977; results from the latter were not processed.
Registration of births, deaths, marriages, and divorces was made
compulsory in 1962; however, information is not available regarding the
completeness of vital registration. The first Republic instituted a
system of five-year development plans. The current Government established
an Interim National Recovery Plan for 1985-1987 and a Medium-Term
Development Strategy, 1987-1991.

Integration of population within development planning: The Government
established the Population Planning Unit within the Ministry of Planning
in 1984 to formulate, co-ordinate, and evaluate population policies. The
Unit is also responsible for data analysis and utilization, and
integration of population variables into development planning. The
present interim plan provides for the establishment of government units to
plan for investments in development and to deal with the food-supply
situation.

GUINEA

POLICIES AND MEASURES

Changes in population size and age structure: The population growth rate has been depressed by net emigration and high infant and child mortality. Government policy to alleviate the shortage of skilled manpower aims to continue the repatriation of emigrants, especially of skilled workers and entrepreneurs, and to improve the health care system in order to lower morbidity and mortality rates. Old-age benefits are available to employed persons, including public employees.

Mortality and morbidity: Government policy gives a high priority to reducing high rates of morbidity and mortality. A primary concern is improving the health and nutrition of mothers and children. Measures have been in effect since 1975 to promote maternal and child health services and to reduce infant mortality and morbidity. One of the goals of the new Government is to reform the health care system so that it provides better services.

Fertility and the family: The change in Government in 1984 brought about a reversal of fertility policy. The Government would now like to reduce fertility rates but considers direct intervention inappropriate. Although family planning has been available in Guinea since 1972, the Government has only recently provided direct support for such services and for modern contraception. The Government would like to increase resources available for family planning. L'Association guineénne de bien-être familiale was sanctioned by the new Government to aid in family planning at maternal and child health centres and to distribute information. Family allowances are available for children under age 17 with a working parent enroled in the insurance system. In 1984 the allowances were raised to 150 sylis (22 sylis = $US 1) per child up to a maximum of 10 children. Birth grants and pre-natal allowances, which had been suspended since 1974, were reinstated in 1985. Abortion is available for broad medical reasons. Information on the status of sterilization is not readily available.

International migration: Immigration is not of active policy concern, but emigration is. Emigration policy aims at curbing out-migration in the future and attracting return migrants. It is estimated that there are up to 2 million Guineans living abroad, mainly in neighbouring West African countries. The new Government granted an amnesty in 1984 to all expatriates. Incentives were provided to encourage students, intellectuals, and entrepreneurs to return. The movement back, which is mainly informal and spontaneous, has placed an additional strain on scanty national resources and on basic health and community services. The United Nations High Commissioner for Refugees plans to provide basic medical support and some essential agricultural instruments to aid in the integration of the returnees.

Spatial distribution/urbanization: Government policy, explicitly stated in the interim plan, is to rehabilitate existing infrastructure and to embark upon a coherent rural development plan. Policy measures include utilizing peasant labour, efficiently using previous investments, and slowing the growth of the primate city, Conakry, where 15 per cent of the total population is located. The Government also aims at reducing urban/rural disparities. The interim plan calls for the establishment of a development office in each rural district to facilitate the process of improving conditions. Other Government measures include public infrastructure subsidies, housing and social services, and human resource and job training. International aid is helping to finance projects such as highway reconstruction and urban development planning.

Status of women and population: The Government emphasizes improving the status of women and of the general population. The 1983 census indicated that women comprised the majority of the population but were predominantly excluded from the work force or were under-employed. A national committee is responsible for training women in rural and urban areas in nutrition, home economics, and vocational skills. The committee has succeeded in establishing centres for the advancement of women but suffers from a lack of funds. The National Directorate for the Status of Women initiates studies on the legal, economic and social situation of women in Guinea. The new Government has stressed judicial reforms to guarantee rights to all citizens and educational reforms to aid in socio-economic development. The reason for the emphasis on education is highlighted by the estimate that only 33 per cent of primary-school-age children were enroled in school in 1981. The minimum legal age at marriage for women is 17 years.

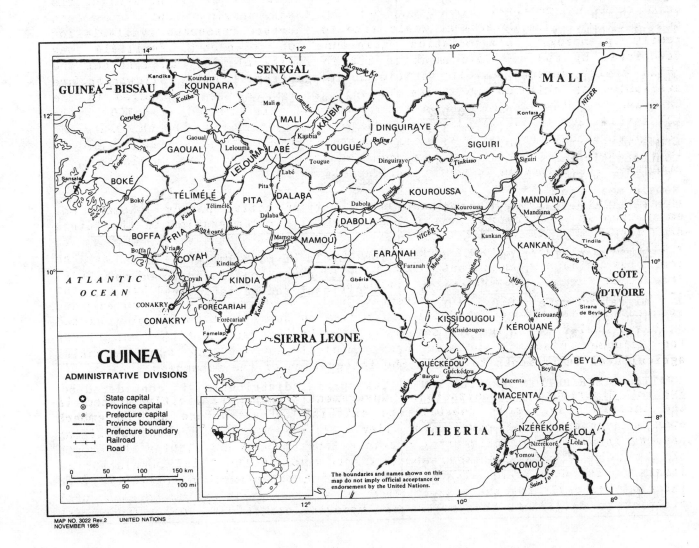

MAP NO. 3022 Rev.2   UNITED NATIONS
NOVEMBER 1985

GUINEA-BISSAU

DEMOGRAPHIC INDICATORS	CURRENT PERCEPTION
SIZE/AGE STRUCTURE/GROWTH	The current growth rate of the population is perceived as <u>satisfactory</u>.

Population:	1985	2025
(thousands)	889	2 014
0-14 years (%)	40.7	34.6
60+ years (%)	6.8	7.0

Rate of:	1980-85	2020-25
growth	1.9	1.7
natural increase	19.1	17.1

MORTALITY/MORBIDITY

Present conditions of health and levels of mortality are considered to be <u>unacceptable</u>.

	1980-85	2020-25
Life expectancy	43.0	59.0
Crude death rate	21.7	10.4
Infant mortality	142.8	68.9

FERTILITY/NUPTIALITY/FAMILY

Current fertility levels are considered to be <u>satisfactory</u>.

	1980-85	2020-25
Fertility rate	5.4	3.3
Crude birth rate	40.7	27.5
Contraceptive prevalence rate	...	...
Female mean age at first marriage	18.3 (1950)	

INTERNATIONAL MIGRATION

The levels of both <u>immigration</u> and <u>emigration</u> are considered to be <u>not significant</u> and <u>satisfactory</u>.

	1980-85	2020-25
Net migration rate	0.0	0.0
Foreign-born population (%)	1.7 (1979)	

SPATIAL DISTRIBUTION/URBANIZATION

The spatial distribution is considered to be <u>partially appropriate</u>.

Urban	1985	2025
population (%)	27.1	57.7

Growth rate:	1980-85	2020-25
urban	4.5	3.0
rural	1.0	0.1

GENERAL POLICY FRAMEWORK

<u>Overall approach to population problems</u>: The Government considers population problems to be closely related to those of development. It wishes to find a balance between population numbers and the effective launching of a development process capable of ensuring guaranteed food self-sufficiency. The main concerns are reducing the high levels of morbidity and mortality and achieving a pattern of spatial distribution appropriate to the country's development goals.

<u>Importance of population policy in achieving development objectives</u>: No official population policy has yet been formulated. However, the Government is aware of the importance of considering population variables for achieving development objectives. The Government has received international assistance to strengthen the statistical base for the eventual formulation of a population policy.

INSTITUTIONAL FRAMEWORK

<u>Population data systems and development planning</u>: Vital registration, which is incomplete, is the responsibility of the Directorate of Statistics. Planning is hampered by lack of reliable data. Several population censuses were conducted during the colonial era, but little record remains of them. The 1979 population census was the first and only data collection operation of any significance conducted since independence at the national level and provides the only statistical information now available to the Government for planning purposes. There are ongoing efforts to strengthen the capabilities of the Directorate of Statistics to collect, process and analyse demographic, social and economic data. The first national development plan covered the period 1983-1986. Implementation of a second development plan, due to start in 1986, has been postponed pending the conclusion of negotiations with international lending organizations. In early 1987 it was reported that the second four-year development plan, for 1988-1991, would give priority to agriculture and fishing, as the first plan had done.

<u>Integration of population within development planning</u>: Although there is no explicit national population policy, the Ministry of Planning has been charged with the responsibility of taking into account population variables in planning. Population projections are prepared by the Directorate of Statistics. It is also responsible for providing information on population/development interrelationships and for undertaking demographic surveys.

POLICIES AND MEASURES

<u>Changes in population size and age structure</u>: There has not been any policy of intervention on either the size or the age structure of the population. However, the Government wishes to maintain a balance between population size

GUINEA-BISSAU

and food self-sufficiency. There is no information readily available on the status of pension schemes.

Mortality and morbidity: The Government's objective in the health sector is to make health care available to all by the year 2000. It has embarked on a health policy which focuses on primary health care and shifts priority from curative to preventive care. The Government's primary objective is to reduce morbidity and maternal and infant mortality. The fight against malaria, diarrhoea and measles are of special policy concern. A target has been set to lower infant mortality to 50 per 1,000 by the year 2000. Maternal and child health and child-spacing have been integrated into the basic health services, mainly in the Bissau and Gabu areas. A national health strategy was integrated into the four-year national development plan for 1983-1986.

Fertility and the family: Although there is no policy of intervention to affect fertility directly, measures for the improvement of the status of women and for improving maternal and child health may have an indirect effect upon fertility. The Government has recognized family planning as one of several initiatives to improve the welfare of mothers and children. The number of maternal and child health centres with integrated family planning services has been increasing. The Government plans to implement nation-wide population education and training programmes in family health for rural women. Seminars and radio programmes on maternal and child health and family planning have increased awareness of those services. The Government has received international assistance for a project to encourage child-spacing, a higher age at marriage and the development of responsible attitudes towards sex and parenthood. The Government wants to achieve at least a two-year spacing of births as part of an overall programme to reduce mortality and morbidity. Abortion is legal to preserve a woman's health or in the case of rape or incest. Information on the status of sterilization is not available.

International migration: There is no policy of intervention concerning either immigration or emigration. However, the Government has expressed concern regarding illegal/undocumented immigration.

Spatial distribution/urbanization: The Government considers changes in the urban/rural balance to be desirable due to an unbalanced spatial distribution exacerbated by periodic drought and famine. Policies concerning internal migration consist of decreasing out-migration from the rural areas and increasing out-migration from the largest metropolitan area.

Status of women and population: The conviction that there can be no real progress without improving the status of women and ensuring their full participation in development is an integral part of Government policy. The Government has undertaken a number of initiatives focused on specific needs and concerns of women, such as income-generating activities and training in family health, family welfare and food conservation. International assistance has been proposed for an integrated rural development project for women, to be executed by the Women's Democratic Union. The Government intends to implement a family-life education programme at the national level as a contribution to improving the status of women. Information concerning the minimum legal age at marriage for women is not available.

<u>Other issues</u>: Since independence in 1974, the country has faced severe shortages of trained manpower, food and foreign exchange. Severe droughts struck the country in 1977, 1979, 1980 and 1983, resulting in a drastic fall in agricultural production and chronic food deficits.

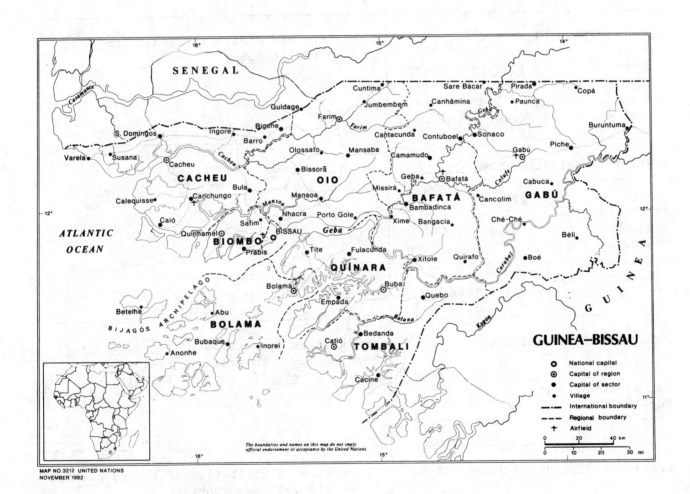

GUINEA–BISSAU

MAP NO.3212 UNITED NATIONS
NOVEMBER 1982

GUYANA

DEMOGRAPHIC INDICATORS	CURRENT PERCEPTION
SIZE/AGE STRUCTURE/GROWTH	The current growth rate is perceived as <u>satisfactory</u>.

Population:	1985	2025
(thousands)	953	1 562
0-14 years (%)	37.0	21.7
60+ years (%)	6.0	16.4

Rate of:	1980-85	2020-25
growth	2.0	0.8
natural increase	22.6	8.3

DEMOGRAPHIC INDICATORS	CURRENT PERCEPTION
MORTALITY/MORBIDITY	Mortality and morbidity levels are considered <u>acceptable</u>.

	1980-85	2020-25
Life expectancy	68.2	75.9
Crude death rate	5.9	6.6
Infant mortality	36.2	11.9

DEMOGRAPHIC INDICATORS	CURRENT PERCEPTION
FERTILITY/NUPTIALITY/FAMILY	Fertility rates are viewed as <u>satisfactory</u>.

	1980-85	2020-25
Fertility rate	3.3	2.1
Crude birth rate	28.5	14.8
Contraceptive prevalence rate	31.0 (1975)	
Female mean age at first marriage	20.7 (1980/81)	

DEMOGRAPHIC INDICATORS	CURRENT PERCEPTION
INTERNATIONAL MIGRATION	Immigration is considered <u>not significant</u> and <u>too low</u>. Emigration levels are viewed as <u>significant</u> and <u>too high</u>.

	1980-85	2020-25
Net migration rate	-3.1	0.0
Foreign-born population (%)	0.8 (1980/81)	

DEMOGRAPHIC INDICATORS	CURRENT PERCEPTION
SPATIAL DISTRIBUTION/URBANIZATION	The spatial distribution of the population is considered <u>inappropriate</u>.

Urban	1985	2025
population (%)	32.2	60.5

Growth rate:	1980-85	2020-25
urban	3.0	2.0
rural	1.5	-0.8

GENERAL POLICY FRAMEWORK

Overall approach to population problems: The Government has sought to reduce population outflow from rural regions by emphasizing agricultural development. The strategy has the additional goal of attaining food self-sufficiency. Official measures are also aimed at improving the population's health and welfare.

Importance of population policy in achieving development objectives: The Government includes measures in its development strategy which have direct and indirect influences on population. Development strategies announced in 1983 and 1985 state that improving health conditions, manpower training, education, food production, and agricultural development are government priorities.

INSTITUTIONAL FRAMEWORK

Population data systems and development planning: Censuses have been conducted since 1911 at fairly regular 10-year intervals, with the most recent census in 1980. The next census is planned for 1990. There has been civil registration of births and deaths since the nineteenth century, and it is now considered complete. Since independence from Great Britain in 1966, Guyana has formulated several development plans with different foci. The Guyana Development Plan for 1966-1970 and a second plan for 1972-1976 focused on urban development. A five-year agricultural development plan was issued in 1986.

Integration of population within development planning: No governmental agency is viewed as solely responsible for integrating population variables into planning. The State Planning Commission, the Ministry of Finance and Economic Planning, and the Bank of Guyana are responsible for the formulation and monitoring of development plans. The Statistical Bureau, along with other governmental agencies, is responsible for vital registration. The Government established a Health Policy Committee in 1981.

POLICIES AND MEASURES

Changes in population size and age structure: Although the current population growth rate is considered satisfactory, concern has been expressed that the population size may be too small. The Government desires increased immigration as one way of increasing resource utilization. Health care for the aged is included in the overall plan to improve medical services. In addition, the 1980 Constitution specifies that all citizens have the right to social care in their old age. Pension coverage is available to all employed persons as well as to the self-employed.

Mortality and morbidity: The Government's development strategy includes the improvement of health conditions by emphasizing nutrition and health education. The Government also emphasizes the regionalization of services as a continuation of the 1970 National Health Plan. The system focuses on primary health care and preventive services, which are provided free of charge. The Constitution guarantees free medical care. Mortality and morbidity concerns are respiratory infections, nutritional deficiencies, cardio-vascular diseases, malignant neoplasms, mental disorders, and accidents. Infants, children, mothers, and the elderly are among the target populations of health measures. Teen-age pregnancy is also a concern, as is the resurgence of malaria. The Government has instituted measures to improve maternal and child health care and dental care. A programme began in 1977 to train mid-level medical employees, in order to expand services. Additional measures address the low level of immunization, nutrition, and health education. The economic crisis and the lack of foreign exchange, however, have severely hampered the implementation of health projects. A national survey for the period 1979-1984 indicates that infant mortality has probably increased.

Fertility and the family: The Government has not announced an explicit fertility policy. However, family planning and maternal and child health services attracted increased attention during the early 1980s. Family planning services have been expanded. The Government has changed its position since 1982 and now gives direct support to information on and access to modern methods of contraception. Maternity benefits are available for employed women in the form of a partially paid 13-week maternity leave. A new benefit, the maternity allowance, introduced in March 1986, consists of a flat-rate cash benefit of $G 300 ($G 4.2 = $US 1). It is intended to partially cover the costs of pregnancy and confinement and is payable to women who are entitled to maternity benefits and whose spouse is covered by the social insurance scheme. Abortion is available only for health reasons.

International migration: Official policy is to achieve a higher rate of immigration. Although the level of emigration - particularly that of skilled workers   is considered to be high, there is no known policy statement concerning emigration.

Spatial distribution/urbanization: Government policy is to decelerate internal migration and slow the growth of Georgetown, the primate city. The strategy to control internal migration and adjust spatial distribution of the population focuses on rural and agricultural development. Agricultural development is a stated priority in the 1985 development strategy announcement. The Government has instituted programmes for irrigation and land colonization and maintains a strategy of border region development. Additional measures pertain to housing and social services, human resource development, and job training.

Status of women and population: The Government is committed to improving the status of women. The 1980 Constitution guarantees equal rights and special health protection for women. A 1983 legislative act removes discrimination against women in employment matters. The Women's Revolutionary Socialist Movement aims to develop political awareness among women and provide women

with opportunities in political, economic, and social life. The Movement has
a representative on the Council on the Affairs and Status of Women in Guyana.
The minimum legal age at marriage for women is 14 years.

<u>Other issues</u>: National development strategies are based on the realization
that the country must rely on its own efforts. As identified in the 1985
budget speech, the critical task confronting the country is the necessity of
reducing progressively the public deficit, while pursuing national development
priorities, which include the provision of welfare services at a politically
acceptable level. The country's deteriorating economy has resulted in budget
reductions in all social services, including health, education and
environmental sanitation.

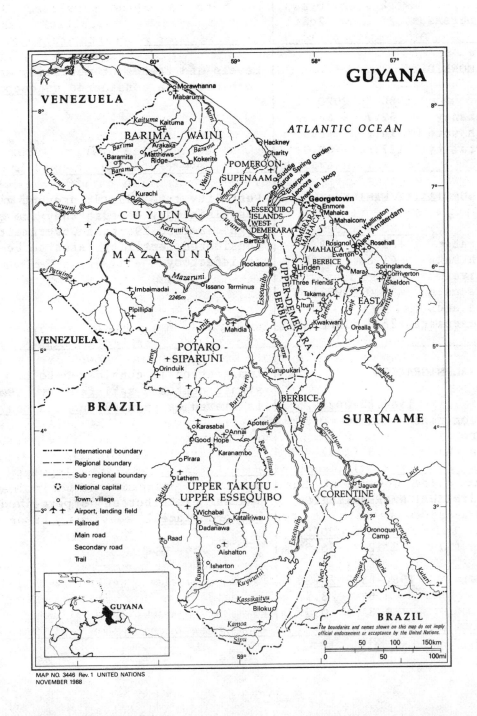

HAITI

DEMOGRAPHIC INDICATORS	CURRENT PERCEPTION

SIZE/AGE STRUCTURE/GROWTH
 	
Population: 1985   2025
 (thousands)   6 585   18 312
  0-14 years (%)   43.6   37.2
  60+ years (%)   5.4   5.6
 	
Rate of: 1980-85   2020-25
 growth   2.5   2.2
 natural increase   27.2   22.3
	Population growth is considered <u>unsatisfactory</u> because it is <u>too high</u>. This represents a change in perception since 1980, when growth was viewed as satisfactory.

MORTALITY/MORBIDITY 1980-85 2020-25 Life expectancy 52.7 66.0 Crude death rate 14.2 6.5 Infant mortality 127.8 49.3	Levels and trends of mortality and morbidity are considered <u>unacceptable</u>.
FERTILITY/NUPTIALITY/FAMILY 1980-85 2020-25 Fertility rate 5.7 3.5 Crude birth rate 41.3 28.8 Contraceptive prevalence rate 7.0 (1983) Female mean age at first marriage 23.8 (1982)	Fertility rates are at present viewed as <u>unsatisfactory</u> because they are <u>too high</u>. Before 1982 the Government considered fertility rates to be satisfactory.
INTERNATIONAL MIGRATION 1980-85 2020-25 Net migration rate -2.1 -0.7 Foreign-born population (%) 0.3 (1982)	Immigration is considered to be <u>not significant</u> and <u>satisfactory</u>. Emigration is viewed as <u>significant</u> and <u>too high</u>.
SPATIAL DISTRIBUTION/URBANIZATION Urban 1985 2025 population (%) 27.2 56.5 Growth rate: 1980-85 2020-25 urban 4.6 3.5 rural 1.8 0.6	Spatial distribution is perceived as <u>inappropriate</u>.

GENERAL POLICY FRAMEWORK

<u>Overall approach to population problems</u>: In the early 1980s, the Government recognized the need to deal with population problems in order to solve other societal problems. The Government stressed measures to reduce fertility and mortality, to improve health conditions and living standards, to narrow regional disparities and improve rural life to reduce internal migration. There is no indication whether the Government that assumed power in early 1986 holds the same views or policies regarding population as the previous Government. The report below is based on the perceptions and policies of the previous Government.

<u>Importance of population policy in achieving development objectives</u>: The Government sought to create conditions more suitable for socio-economic development, given the rate of demographic growth, available resources and ability to finance services. Government sectors were instructed to formulate policies aimed at bringing population growth into accord with economic possibilities. An understanding of demographic processes was deemed necessary for formulating a population policy and integrating population variables into socio-economic planning. The Government focused on lowering fertility and mortality in order to reduce constraints on social and economic development.

INSTITUTIONAL FRAMEWORK

<u>Population data systems and development planning</u>: Censuses were conducted during the nineteenth century; however, the first modern census was held in 1950. Subsequent censuses were taken in 1971 and 1982. Both governmental and non-governmental offices maintain vital registration systems. Registration is not well co-ordinated and is considered to be incomplete. Haiti has had three five-year development plans, the most recent of which covered the years 1981-1986. A biennial plan for 1984-1986 updated and reiterated the Third Five Year Plan. The Fourth Five-Year Plan, for 1986-1991, was in preparation in 1986. An interim development programme was prepared in October 1986 by the National Council which, among other things, intends to revive the national economy and tackle the problems of unemployment and underemployment.

<u>Integration of population within development planning</u>: Although no single governmental agency was responsible for formulating and implementing population policy, an administrative infrastructure had been created to deal with population problems. In September 1986 a National Population Commission was created. The Haitian Statistical Institute (IHSI), established in 1974, includes a Demographic Research and Analysis Unit which has been responsible since 1980 for projections, policy formation, and the integration of demographic variables into planning. The Division of the Census and National Research within IHSI plans, organizes, and conducts censuses. The United Nations provided support in 1984 to programmes aimed at increasing demographic research for development planning purposes.

HAITI

POLICIES AND MEASURES

<u>Changes in population size and age structure</u>: The policy is to reduce population growth in order to achieve a rate and age structure compatible with the country's economic capabilities. Rapid population growth and the young age structure are viewed as limiting national development. The Government's strategy is to reduce fertility and mortality gradually and simultaneously while maintaining the growth of the active population. Measures are being taken on contraceptive use and improving health and nutrition, population education, and the control of migration. Old-age pensions are available for employed persons at age 55 with 20 years of contribution.

<u>Mortality and morbidity</u>: In 1987 the Ministry of Health of the new Government received international assistance for developing a new national health policy to satisfy the health needs of the population. The previous Government had established a National Health Plan in 1982 to stress primary health care and to set quantitative targets for the reduction of mortality rates. The primary objectives were to improve health conditions, nutrition, and sanitary conditions, particularly in new urban areas. The mortality of mothers, children, and the working age population was of great concern. Measures were taken to reduce infant and particularly neo-natal mortality, birth defects, and mortality due to social and environmental factors. Infectious diseases and parasitic diseases were of special concern. Acquired Immune Deficiency Syndrome (AIDS) has recently become a concern. The Government's strategy is to regionalize and evenly distribute health services. Efforts are made to train personnel, increase community involvement, and provide health education. Special programmes include immunization against infectious diseases, oral rehydration for diarrhoeal diseases, and safe drinking water projects. Quantitative targets for the year 2000 include a crude death rate of 8 per 1,000, an infant mortality rate of 50 per 1,000, maternal mortality rate of 0.7 per 1,000, and life expectancy at birth of 65 years.

<u>Fertility and the family</u>: The policy is to lower fertility rates primarily by promoting family planning. Family planning objectives are to improve maternal and child health and to provide education on family matters. The Government focuses on increasing contraceptive usage. Contraceptive prevalence surveys indicated a low percentage of users among women at risk of pregnancy. Programmes administered by the Ministry of Health include establishing pre-natal clinics in rural and marginal urban areas, mass media campaigns to motivate contraceptive usage, and the placement of vending machines for condoms in urban areas. Goals for the year 2000 include a 60 per cent family planning coverage, a crude birth rate of 20 per 1,000, and two or three children per woman. Abortion is prohibited except for narrow medical reasons, but sterilization is allowed for contraceptive purposes.

<u>International migration</u>: Immigration is not an active policy concern. Emigration policy aims to reduce the outflow of population which has caused a serious manpower drain. Although the policy is to reduce emigration, the Government acknowledges that the outflow produces important revenue through the issuance of exit visas and remittances. Undocumented emigration has produced great concern in the receiving countries. In 1981, a United States/ Haitian agreement attempted to end such migration and to work towards repatriation. Concern has also arisen in the Dominican Republic over the

treatment of Haitian immigrants living in that country. It is believed that the number of Haitians living abroad exceeds 1 million, or approximately one-sixth of the country's population. Repatriation of Haitians from the Dominican Republic was begun in 1985. In 1986 the new Government reached an agreement with the Dominican Republic for the supply of almost 20,000 Haitians to help with the 1987 sugar harvest.

Spatial distribution/urbanization: The Government wants to effect major changes in the patterns of spatial distribution by decreasing in-migration to the primate city, Port-au-Prince, and redirecting migratory flows to small and intermediate-sized towns. The Government planned to develop growth poles outside of Port-au-Prince by decentralizing political administration and localizing industry. Means to reduce motivation for rural out-migration include expanding employment opportunities, improving rural living conditions and directing infrastructure subsidies and irrigation projects towards rural areas. A National Office of Housing, created in 1982, is responsible for attending to housing problems and needs.

Status of women and population: Improving the status of women is viewed mainly in regard to reducing fertility. The 1981-1986 Five-Year Plan stated the goal of increasing female labour-force participation. The educational status of the entire population is low, and the Government has stressed the need for education among its population. Information on the legal age at marriage for women is not readily available.

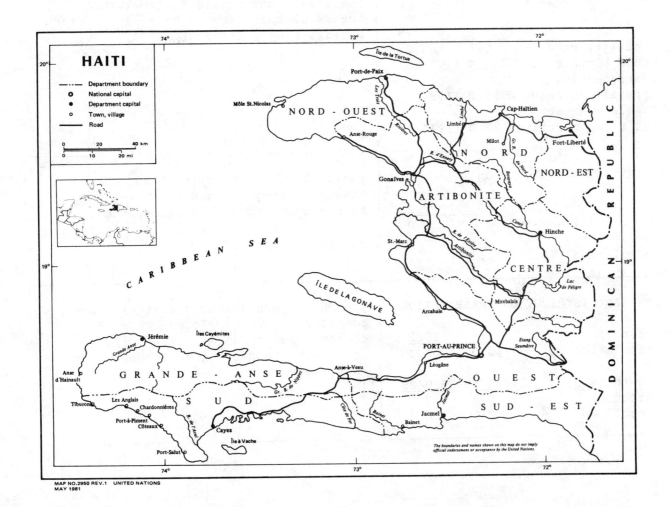

MAP NO.2950 REV.1   UNITED NATIONS
MAY 1981

HONDURAS

DEMOGRAPHIC INDICATORS	CURRENT PERCEPTION
SIZE/AGE STRUCTURE/GROWTH	The rate of growth is considered <u>unsatisfactory</u> because it is <u>too high</u>. Problems of particular concern include a young age structure and a high dependency ratio.

Population:

(thousands)	1985	2025
	4 372	13 293
0-14 years (%)	46.9	34.1
60+ years (%)	4.6	6.8

Rate of:	1980-85	2020-25
growth	3.4	2.1
natural increase	33.8	20.9

MORTALITY/MORBIDITY

Levels and trends are <u>unacceptable</u>. Concerns are the high level of infant mortality - one of the highest in Latin America - urban/rural differentials in mortality and health services, and the high incidence of diarrhoeal disease.

	1980-85	2020-25
Life expectancy	59.9	72.2
Crude death rate	10.1	4.9
Infant mortality	81.5	29.3

FERTILITY/NUPTIALITY/FAMILY

The Government considers levels and trends of fertility to be <u>unsatisfactory</u> because they are <u>too high</u>.

	1980-85	2020-25
Fertility rate	6.5	3.2
Crude birth rate	43.9	25.8
Contraceptive prevalence rate	35.0 (1984)	
Female mean age at first marriage	20.0 (1974)	

INTERNATIONAL MIGRATION

Immigration is <u>significant</u> and <u>unsatisfactory</u> because it is <u>too high</u>. Refugees are considered an economic and social burden. Emigration is <u>significant</u> and <u>too high</u>.

	1980-85	2020-25
Net migration rate	0.0	0.0
Foreign-born population (%)	...	...

SPATIAL DISTRIBUTION/URBANIZATION

Trends in population distribution are considered <u>inappropriate</u>. There is concern that urban migration will contribute to shortages in housing and basic services.

Urban	1985	2025
population (%)	40.0	68.3

Growth rate:	1980-85	2020-25
urban	5.4	2.9
rural	2.1	0.4

GENERAL POLICY FRAMEWORK

Overall approach to population problems: Direct intervention to modify demographic variables is combined with a policy of economic and social restructuring. Official policy is to decrease population growth, chiefly by means of modifying fertility, and to restrict large-scale immigration in the future. The Government also seeks to reduce mortality, adjust patterns of spatial distribution and reduce the emigration of qualified personnel.

Importance of population policy in achieving development objectives: Population policy is increasingly viewed as a means of attaining overall development objectives. The Government drafted a Population Strategy in 1982, and in 1983 a decree made family planning a priority area within the national primary health care programme.

INSTITUTIONAL FRAMEWORK

Population data systems and development planning: Twelve censuses have been conducted since 1844, the latest being in 1974. A census had been provisionally scheduled for 1988. Vital registration is incomplete. A National Demographic Survey was conducted in 1983. The National Economic Planning Council (CONSUPLANE) formulates the country's five-year development plans, the most recent being prepared for the 1986-1989 period.

Integration of population within development planning: The Government has established a population department within the National Economic Planning Council (CONSUPLANE). It is charged with assessing the impact of macro and sectoral policies on demographic trends and assisting in the formulation of population policies. It drew up guidelines for the National Development Strategy, 1986-1989, and has prepared methodologies for integrating demographic variables into national and regional development plans.

POLICIES AND MEASURES

Changes in population size and age structure: Official population policy is reflected in the National Population Plan for 1982-1986. The policy aims at decreasing fertility levels, decreasing large-scale immigration and adjusting economic and social factors. The Government's policy sought to reduce the annual population growth from 3.4 to 3.1 per cent between 1982 and 1986. It views guaranteed free access to family planning as the most direct means of population regulation. By reducing the current rate of natural increase, which the Government acknowledges to be one of the highest in Latin America, it hopes to raise slightly the median age from 16 to 16.5 years during 1982-1986 and to reduce the dependency ratio from 102 to 100 within the same period. The social security scheme covers employed persons in public and

private enterprises but excludes domestic casual and agricultural workers
(except those with more than 10 employees). Coverage is being gradually
extended to other areas.

Mortality and morbidity: The official policy for the health sector is to
cover the entire population with primary health care by the year 2000.
Measures include the regionalization of services and decentralization of
administrative functions. By expanding basic health services through the
formation of rural health centres, a link between the formal and informal
health care system is provided. At the community level, services include
rural health care, basic education in sanitation, vaccination programmes,
family planning and maternal and child health. The Government set a target of
reducing the crude death rate from 10.1 to 8.4 per thousand and increasing
life expectancy from 60 to 63 years during 1982-1986. The Government has a
long-term target of ensuring that by the year 2000 the infant mortality rate
does not exceed 30 per thousand live births.

Fertility and the family: Official policy states that all decisions regarding
limitation of family size should be freely made by the couples concerned and
not as a result of the imposition of governmental views. The Government has
stressed that family planning should be seen as a health measure with
important benefits for mothers, children, the family and community. The
Government has emphasized that all persons, particularly those in marginal
urban areas and rural areas, should have free access to services. To heighten
awareness of family planning and child-spacing, considerable emphasis has been
placed on information programmes and literacy. In addition, the importance of
basic education, particularly for women, and sex education and education on
family life for all those of reproductive age, and especially adolescents, is
recognized. Access to modern methods of contraception is not limited, and the
Government provides direct support. Abortion is legal to preserve the life or
health of the mother. While sterilization is not promoted as a method of
family planning, it is permitted with medical certification. The Government's
fertility target was to reduce the crude birth rate from 44 to 39 per thousand
and the total fertility rate from 6.5 to 5.6 births per women between 1982 and
1986.

International migration: The Government has maintained a strict policy with
respect to immigration for permanent settlement, although it has admitted
large numbers of refugees from neighbouring Central American countries in
recent years. The Government hopes that realistic programmes will be carried
out to avert new flows of refugees and to seek durable solutions to the
problem of refugees and displaced persons, including voluntary repatriation or
resettlement in third countries. As of June 1986 almost 50,000 refugees in
Honduras had received assistance from the United Nations High Commissioner for
Refugees. In October 1987 the President of Honduras reiterated his
Government's willingness to continue offering its co-operation as an asylum
country in providing the necessary facilities for the repatriation of
refugees. Although Honduras wishes to avoid large-scale immigration, it has
expressed a willingness to allow continuing immigration of qualified persons
with skills to contribute to the country's development. Because of its
concern with the brain drain, the Government's policy was to reduce the
emigration of qualified personnel by 80 per cent during the period 1982-1986.

Spatial distribution/urbanization: The Government would like to reduce migration to the larger cities and towns. Its policy supports intermediate cities located ouside the central corridor. A target to reduce out-migration from the country's major sending areas by 30 per cent during 1982-1986 was set. The Government has been attempting to develop new initiatives to address the growing housing and basic service deficits affecting the urban poor. In an extensive programme of agrarian reform, efforts have been made to resettle landless farmers in small groups which, although not as an explicit spatial measure, work on a co-operative basis. Comprehensive regional programmes for severely deteriorated territories and border zones have also been formulated.

Status of women and population: The National Population Plan for 1982-1986 specifically addresses the issue of women's status. It recommends programmes to increase female literacy and encourages greater female labour-force participation. The Department of Social Promotion within the National Planning Council is responsible for the inclusion of women's issues in national plans. The minimum legal age at marriage for women is 12 years.

Other issues: The Government's overall strategy is to promote industrial and agricultural growth through large-scale infrastructure investments and to accelerate the implementation of various social projects, particularly those related to rural development, health, education, water supply and sewerage, in order to improve the welfare of Honduran citizens directly.

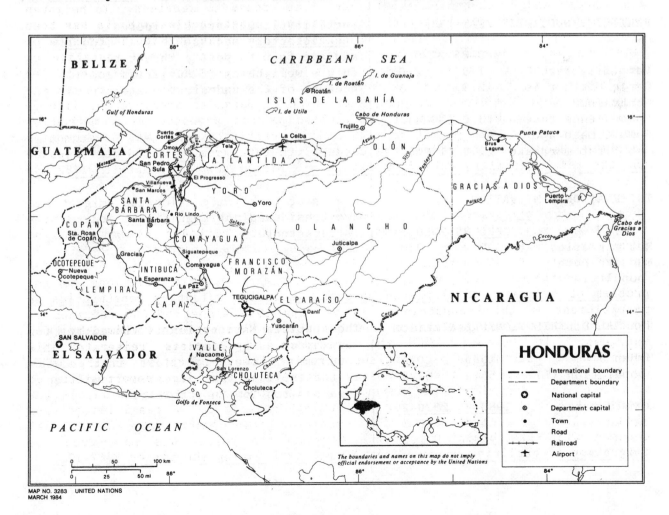

MAP NO. 3283   UNITED NATIONS
MARCH 1984

HUNGARY

DEMOGRAPHIC INDICATORS	CURRENT PERCEPTION
SIZE/AGE STRUCTURE/GROWTH Population: 1985 2025 (thousands) 10 697 10 598 0–14 years (%) 21.6 17.8 60+ years (%) 18.2 24.2 Rate of: 1980–85 2020–25 growth 0.0 −0.1 natural increase −0.3 −0.6	Growth is perceived as <u>unsatisfactory</u> because it is <u>too low</u>. Concerns are population aging and declining population size.
MORTALITY/MORBIDITY 1980–85 2020–25 Life expectancy 70.3 76.4 Crude death rate 13.1 12.9 Infant mortality 20.1 7.0	The Government has changed its perception since 1982, and now considers levels and trends to be <u>unacceptable</u>. Concerns are the high mortality levels of men aged 40–59 and suicide rates.
FERTILITY/NUPTIALITY/FAMILY 1980–85 2020–25 Fertility rate 1.9 2.0 Crude birth rate 12.9 12.3 Contraceptive prevalence rate 73.0 (1986) Female mean age at first marriage 21.0 (1980)	Fertility levels are considered <u>unsatisfactory</u> because they are <u>too low</u> and are felt to pose a threat to the future well-being of Hungarian society because of the undesirable age structure.
INTERNATIONAL MIGRATION 1980–85 2020–25 Net migration rate 0.0 0.0 Foreign-born population (%)	Levels of both immigration and emigration are considered <u>not significant</u> and <u>satisfactory</u>.
SPATIAL DISTRIBUTION/URBANIZATION Urban 1985 2025 population (%) 56.2 67.5 Growth rate: 1980–85 2020–25 urban 1.0 0.0 rural −1.2 −0.3	The spatial distribution is viewed by the Government as <u>appropriate</u>. The Government, however, believes that growth is too rapid in the largest metropolitan area and too low in rural areas.

GENERAL POLICY FRAMEWORK

Overall approach to population problems: The Government seeks to increase population growth by increasing fertility levels and improving living conditions. Population policies have as their goal a more equitable age composition of the population, decreasing the mortality rate and improving the general health of the population.

Importance of population policy in achieving development objectives: Population policy is considered an integral part of socialist socio-economic policies and is continually adjusted to reflect Hungary's demographic situation and social and economic possibilities.

INSTITUTIONAL FRAMEWORK

Population data systems and development planning: Censuses were published in 1960, 1970, and 1980. Vital registration is considered complete. A formal system of development planning has existed since 1956; the latest plan is the seventh five-year plan (1986-1990).

Integration of population within development planning: No single governmental agency is responsible for the formulation or co-ordination of population policies. The Unit for Long-Term Planning of the State Planning Board, established in the early 1960s, is responsible for integrating population projections into long-term development planning. The Demographic Research Institute of the Hungarian Central Statistical Office (HCSO) conducts demographic surveys and prepares population projections for planning purposes.

POLICIES AND MEASURES

Changes in population size and age structure: There is an official policy of intervention to increase the rate of population growth. The objective is to reduce the speed of population decline in the short run and stop it in the long run (early in the twenty-first century). By enlarging the size of generations born in the future, it is hoped that the age structure of the population will become more equitable, thus alleviating some of the undesirable consequences of population aging. The Government's policies aim at modifying the attitudes of couples and individuals concerning desired family size, since those are seen as the most crucial determinant of population growth. Most official policies regarding population growth relate to fertility. Population size and growth are also to be altered by decreasing the mortality rate of middle-aged men, which has risen since the mid 1960s. The quantitative target is to attain and maintain a level of population growth that ensures population replacement. To cope with the rapid and advanced aging process, various social policy measures have been undertaken, in such areas as pensions and health care, to improve the economic and social situation of the elderly.

HUNGARY

<u>Mortality and morbidity</u>: Policy measures include a programme for the study of mortality, administered by the Central Statistical Office in conjunction with various international organizations, monitoring the health conditions of the population, programmes for the prevention of the most frequent causes of death and disease, care and treatment of chronically sick people and development of maternal and child care. Under the Health Act of 1972 all citizens are entitled to medical care at State expense. Particular attention has been given to halting the declining male life expectancy at birth by decreasing the high mortality levels of men aged 40-59 which have resulted from diseases of the circulatory system. No quantitative overall mortality targets have been established. Public information campaigns that emphasize the negative consequences of excessive alcohol consumption, smoking, poor diet and lack of exercise are being created.

<u>Fertility and the family</u>: So as to raise population growth and improve maternal and child health and family well-being, a policy of intervention exists to boost fertility levels. Policies aim at raising fertility in order to ensure the replacement of population, adjusting distortions in the age structure, and realizing the socialist ideal of the family. Various maternity and family benefits are designed to encourage fertility. Mothers are entitled to maternity leave with full wages for the first five months after delivery. The maternity fee, introduced in 1985, pays 75 per cent of the mother's average income after the first five months until the child reaches one and a half years of age. After that, a maternity allowance is available until the child is three years old. In addition, there is a "birth aid", a lump-sum payment given at a child's birth, and sick pay for parents to stay at home and nurse a sick child. There are also family allowances. Nurseries for children under age three and kindergarten and day-homes for children aged 6-14 are also intended to encourage childbirth. Family planning services are provided by the Government through the national health system. Contraceptives are available at all pharmacies. However, a 1984 law forbids the provision of contraceptives to women under age 18 without a medical prescription. Abortion is legal on health, eugenic, juridical, social and medical grounds during the first 12 weeks of pregnancy for single women and for married women over 35 or with three or more living children. In 1987 a decree was issued permitting sterilization for contraceptive purposes for women over age 30 with at least four children, women over age 35 with at least three children, and to all women over the age of 40.

<u>International migration</u>: Levels of immigration and emigration are viewed as insignificant and are not active policy concerns of the Government.

<u>Spatial distribution/urbanization</u>: No explicit policies have been formulated concerning spatial distribution and internal migration. However, the National Settlement System concept has several indirect aims, including the narrowing of large differentials in living conditions and income between the urban and rural populations; meeting housing requirements; reducing the amount of internal migration; and establishing functional relations between settlements suitable for long-term spatial location of productive resources.

<u>Status of women and population</u>: Measures such as child-care allowances and maternity benefits are aimed at facilitating the combination of motherhood with work outside the home. The Government has affirmed its commitment to

improving the status of women by outlawing sex discrimination in hiring, unequal conditions for the sexes at the workplace, not hiring pregnant women, and dismissal of pregnant employees. In 1986 the minimum legal age at marriage for women was raised to 18 years in order to promote more stable marriages and lower the incidence of divorce.

Other issues: In 1984 a resolution of the Council of Ministers stated that for the period 1986-1990 special emphasis should be given to three aspects of a long-term population policy: a scientific foundation for population policy; the mutual relationship between population and socio-economic development; questions of the health, biological state and reproductive quality of the population. Based on these areas of emphasis, the Demographic Committee of the Hungarian Academy of Sciences issued a research plan in the area of population policy for 1986-1990.

ICELAND

DEMOGRAPHIC INDICATORS	CURRENT PERCEPTION

SIZE/AGE STRUCTURE/GROWTH
 	
Population: <u>1985</u>   <u>2025</u>
  (thousands)   243   304
  0-14 years (%) 26.6 18.0
  60+ years (%) 13.8 23.7
 	
Rate of: <u>1980-85</u> <u>2020-25</u>
 growth   1.2   0.2
 natural increase 12.3   2.3
	The Government perceives current growth rates as <u>satisfactory</u>.

MORTALITY/MORBIDITY <u>1980-85</u> <u>2020-25</u> Life expectancy 76.8 78.3 Crude death rate 7.2 9.6 Infant mortality 6.4 5.0	The Government considers current levels of mortality to be <u>acceptable</u>.
FERTILITY/NUPTIALITY/FAMILY <u>1980-85</u> <u>2020-25</u> Fertility rate 2.4 1.9 Crude birth rate 19.5 11.9 Contraceptive prevalence rate ... ... Female mean age at first marriage 23.8 (1980)	Current fertility rates are considered <u>satisfactory</u>.
INTERNATIONAL MIGRATION <u>1980-85</u> <u>2020-25</u> Net migration rate 0.0 0.0 Foreign-born population (%)	Immigration levels are <u>not significant</u> and <u>satisfactory</u>. Emigration, which is also <u>not significant</u>, is considered <u>satisfactory</u>.
SPATIAL DISTRIBUTION/URBANIZATION Urban <u>1985</u> <u>2025</u> population (%) 89.4 93.3 Growth rate: <u>1980-85</u> <u>2020-25</u> urban 1.5 0.3 rural -1.0 -0.3	The spatial distribution is considered <u>partially appropriate</u>. There is concern with the primacy of Reykjavik, the capital.

GENERAL POLICY FRAMEWORK

Overall approach to population problems: Government policy is to strengthen health services in rural areas. The Government does not intervene to influence either population growth or fertility.

Importance of population policy in achieving development objectives: The Government has not reported any explicit population policy intended to achieve development objectives.

INSTITUTIONAL FRAMEWORK

Population data systems and development planning: The most recent population census was taken in 1970. Vital registration of births, begun in 1785, is considered virtually complete and is the responsibility of the Statistical Bureau. A national population register, established in 1952, is responsible for the registration of every person having a domicile in Iceland and in recent years has been used to yield statistics concerning the number of Icelanders living abroad.

Integration of population within development planning: There is no reported governmental agency charged with integrating population variables into development planning. In 1985 new population projections up to the year 2020 were issued.

POLICIES AND MEASURES

Changes in population size and age structure: There is no official policy concerning population growth rates. Government policy concerning the aged includes recent acts passed concerning the health services that give special attention to the health and social problems of the elderly and the handicapped.

Mortality and morbidity: Iceland, with one of the highest life expectancies in the world, has as its main priority primary health care and greater emphasis on comprehensive care. The 1973 Act on Health Services, updated in 1983, outlines the activities of the health centres, which provide general health care as well as x-rays, rehabilitation, home nursing, preventive and specialist services. Government strategies include the strengthening of rural health centres, the promotion of healthy lifestyles through health education campaigns and greater access to primary health care for all socially and geographically disadvantaged and under-served groups. Recent acts concerning medical care include the policy that everyone has a right to adequate access to health services. The health system is supported mainly by comprehensive

ICELAND

community health centres, which receive their support from the State. Of particular concern are diseases of the circulatory system and cancer, the leading causes of death. To promote healthy lifestyles, health education campaigns have been undertaken in schools and support provided to various national societies. As of 1986, the Act on Health Services was being reviewed by a committee appointed by the Minister of Health and Social Security in order to focus on urban primary health care.

Fertility and the family: There is no explicit Government policy regarding fertility. Family planning services are available at hospitals, and physicians are legally required to give advice. In January 1981, new parental benefits were introduced, consisting of three months of maternity leave, with a daily allowance not exceeding 75 per cent of the average wage during the previous two months, and one month of paternity leave. In addition, employers are forbidden to dismiss a pregnant woman or a parent during parental leave unless there is a valid and urgent reason. Family benefits are paid by the Pensions Department of the State Social Security Institute. Abortion is legal on health, juridical and social grounds up to 12 weeks of pregnancy. Sterilization is available upon request for those over 25 years of age.

International migration: There is no specific government policy concerning immigration or emigration. Immigration to a large extent consists of return migration. As a consequence of a boom in consumer expenditures in 1987, serious labour shortages have cropped up in the country, with unemployment falling below 1 per cent. To alleviate the situation, the Federation of Icelandic Industries has proposed schemes to attract labour from abroad. Individual employers have undertaken recruitment drives in Norway, where demand for labour is already very high. Historically, emigration has been substantial, especially among the student population. There is a large share of emigration from, and immigration to, Iceland with countries such as Denmark, Sweden and Norway. This, again, is particularly true among students who make up the bulk of the heavy migration flows. Since 1969, the Nordic countries have had a joint agreement on the registration of persons moving from one country to another. This includes a procedure whereby students from Nordic countries remain registered in the country in which they are residing and not in the country of origin. As of 1982, citizens of other Nordic countries may work in Iceland without a permit. As a consequence of substantial emigration, it is estimated that as of 1985, 7 per cent of Icelandic citizens were living abroad.

Spatial distribution/urbanization: There exists in Iceland heavy out-migration from rural areas into urban areas, especially into the capital region. As a result, the population of all regions outside the capital has fallen. The Reykjavik area, which covers less than 1 per cent of the country, in 1986 contained 55 per cent of the population and has received 93 per cent of the population growth since 1981.

Status of women and population: In 1976 a law was passed to promote equality between women and men. The law declared it unlawful for employers to discriminate on grounds of sex and declared that schools must provide instruction on equal rights for women and men. On 24 October 1985 almost 50,000 women, including Iceland's woman President, staged a one-day strike by staying away from offices and refusing to perform homemaking tasks. The strike was called to emphasize the role of women in the economy and to highlight the significant wage disparities between men and women, and the exclusion of women from most managerial positions. The minimum legal age at marriage for women is 18 years.

INDIA

DEMOGRAPHIC INDICATORS	CURRENT PERCEPTION
SIZE/AGE STRUCTURE/GROWTH	The Government views the rate of growth as <u>too high</u> in relation to the poverty and unemployment in the country.
Population: 1985 2025 (thousands) 758 927 1 228 829 0-14 years (%) 36.8 21.3 60+ years (%) 6.8 14.4 Rate of: 1980-85 2020-25 growth 1.9 0.7 natural increase 19.4 7.0	
MORTALITY/MORBIDITY	Present levels and trends are <u>unacceptable</u>.
1980-85 2020-25 Life expectancy 55.4 71.6 Crude death rate 12.3 7.7 Infant mortality 110.3 34.5	
FERTILITY/NUPTIALITY/FAMILY	Current fertility rates are viewed as <u>unsatisfactory</u> because they are <u>too high</u>.
1980-85 2020-25 Fertility rate 4.3 1.9 Crude birth rate 31.7 14.8 Contraceptive prevalence rate 34.0 (1980) Female mean age at first marriage 18.7 (1981)	
INTERNATIONAL MIGRATION	Immigration and emigration are considered to be <u>not significant</u> and <u>satisfactory</u>. Concerns are the brain-drain, refugees and temporary emigration for employment.
1980-85 2020-25 Net migration rate 0.0 0.0 Foreign-born population (%) 1.2 (1981)	
SPATIAL DISTRIBUTION/URBANIZATION	The pattern of spatial distribution is considered to be <u>partially appropriate</u> with regard to the urban/rural imbalance, uneven development and economic disparities between and within regions.
Urban 1985 2025 population (%) 25.5 53.6 Growth rate: 1980-85 2020-25 urban 3.6 2.2 rural 1.4 -0.9	

GENERAL POLICY FRAMEWORK

Overall approach to population problems: The Government considers its
population problem to be extremely serious, particularly in relation to
alleviating poverty. The main goals of demographic policy are to control
population growth by reducing fertility, decrease morbidity and mortality
by integrated health care programmes, and enhance social and economic
advancement, mainly through industrial, agricultural and rural development
programmes.

Importance of population policy in achieving development objectives: The
Government has accorded very high priority to intervention in regard to
population growth. The family welfare programme, which includes family
planning and maternal and child care, seeks to reduce fertility, mortality
and - ultimately - the growth rate. The anti-natalist policy aims at
overall socio-economic development by limiting population size, in order
to provide adequate nutrition, housing, health care, education, employment
etc.

INSTITUTIONAL FRAMEWORK

Population data systems and development planning: India has the
distinction of having had an uninterrupted period of 100 years of
census-taking. Censuses have been conducted at regular 10-year intervals
since 1881. The most recent population census was conducted in 1981. The
vital registration system provides up-to-date statistics, but is
considered incomplete. The seventh five-year plan, for the period
1985/86-1989/90, is currently in effect.

Integration of population within development planning: The Government,
through the Planning Commission, integrates population concerns within
overall development planning. Although the Ministry of Health and Family
Welfare has overall responsibility for family welfare, including family
planning, there is close co-ordination with other ministries, such as
Information and Broadcasting, Human Resource Development, Labour and
Agriculture. Responsibility for implementing population programmes rests
with the individual States, and is often carried out in co-operation with
the organizational and administrative structures utilized for implementing
agriculture, rural development and other development projects. The
Central Health and Family Welfare Council and the Population Advisory
Council, are the units responsible for advising on broad policy issues.

POLICIES AND MEASURES

Changes in population size and age structure: The Government, which sees
population control as a primary development priority, is committed to reaching
zero population growth by the year 2050 with a population of 1.3 billion. The
Family Welfare Programme attempts to link population planning with broader

INDIA

economic and social reforms, especially those related to child survival and the status of women. Old-age benefits under the Provident Fund are given to employees of firms established for at least three years, with at least 50 employees and to firms (using power) established for five years with 20-49 employees. Under the Gratuity Fund, employees of firms, factories, and plantations with fewer than 10 employees earning above a certain limit, are excluded from coverage. States are being persuaded to give preference to parents of small families in providing pensions and admission to senior citizens homes.

Mortality and morbidity: The policy concentrates on reducing morbidity and mortality among children and mothers and on the equitable distribution of health services between urban and rural areas. By integrating health services into the overall programme of social services, an alternate model of health care service is being developed, which emphasizes the preventive, promotive and rehabilitative aspects along with the curative aspect and is directed primarily at rural areas and the poorer segments of the population. A "Health for All by the Year 2000" policy has been adopted, aimed at providing universal primary health care even in the remotest areas. In addition, it stresses the need to view health and human development as vital for integrated national socio-economic development. Specified targets for 1990 are a death rate of 10.4 and an infant mortality rate of 87 per 1000 live births.

Fertility and the family: The Government recognizes that with its large population, it cannot wait for development to change the attitudes of couples towards smaller families, since the development process itself is stifled by high population growth. In 1977 policy was modified to eliminate all forms of compulsion in the family planning programme and to make it a family welfare programme embracing all aspects of family welfare - particularly, maternal and child health, nutrition, women's education and women's rights. The seventh five-year plan aims at establishing the two-child family norm and attaining replacement-level fertility by the year 2000. All methods of family planning are widely available. Financial incentives are provided to acceptors of sterilization and the IUD, by compensating for lost wages. New incentive schemes include premium-free insurance to those who limit and space child-bearing and the provision of social security to aged couples with one child and no male offspring. The revamped family welfare campaign is based on five main principles: families should be limited to two children; the law that bars marriage for girls under age 18 should be enforced; families should not continually produce children until a son is born; all infants should be immunized in their first year; and births should be spaced at intervals of three years. A birth rate target of 29.1 by 1990 has been specified.

International migration: Since immigration and emigration levels are insignificant, there are no policies directed at international migration. The 1983 Emigration Act sought to protect the interests of emigrants, which had been prone to exploitation by recruiting agents. Indians can not take up work abroad without receiving a certificate of clearance from the Protector of Emigrants. The Government is providing assistance to Tamils, refugees from Sri Lanka, who have been arriving in southern India since 1983. It is estimated that approximately 130,000 arrived between 1983 and late 1986.

<u>Spatial distribution/urbanization</u>: The policy aims at slowing metropolitan growth, promoting small towns and intermediate cities, and adjusting the spatial distribution pattern by agricultural and rural development and industrial location policies. To develop industries in less developed areas, enterprise-oriented public infrastructure subsidies, grants, loans and tax incentives are provided. In the five-year plans, integrated technological advancement, rural development and employment generation have been emphasized. Although there is no national urbanization policy, the five-year plans have emphasized urbanization as an important aspect of economic and social development. Urban development schemes aim to provide adequate infrastructure and facilities in small, medium and intermediate-sized towns to strengthen those market centres and equip them to serve as growth and service centres for rural areas.

<u>Status of women and population</u>: The Government stresses the correlation between population policies and women's status in terms of their health and nutrition, age at marriage, literacy and employment. For the social and economic emancipation of women, a strategy was developed which emphasizes health, education and employment. The minimum age at marriage has been raised to 18 years for girls. To promote female employment a major step has been the expansion and diversification of education and training opportunities and legislative measures ensuring the protection of benefits for working women.

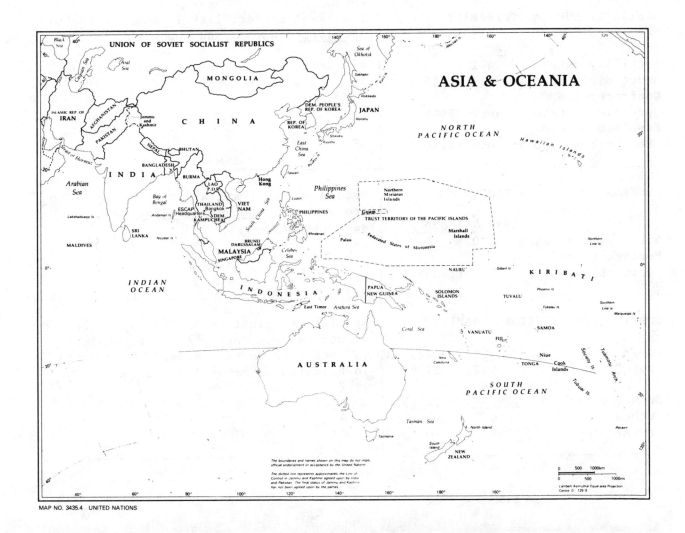

INDONESIA

DEMOGRAPHIC INDICATORS	CURRENT PERCEPTION
SIZE/AGE STRUCTURE/GROWTH	The present rate of population growth is perceived as <u>unsatisfactory</u> because it is <u>too high</u>.

Population: 1985   2025
  (thousands)   166 440   272 744
  0-14 years (%)   38.7   22.6
  60+ years (%)   5.6   13.1

Rate of: 1980-85   2020-25
  growth   2.0   0.8
  natural increase   19.5   8.0

MORTALITY/MORBIDITY

	1980-85	2020-25
Life expectancy	53.5	70.8
Crude death rate	12.6	7.9
Infant mortality	84.4	26.2

The present conditions of health and mortality are considered to be <u>unacceptable</u>. The Government has indicated that children under five years of age and pregnant mothers in rural areas are of special concern.

FERTILITY/NUPTIALITY/FAMILY

	1980-85	2020-25
Fertility rate	4.1	2.0
Crude birth rate	32.1	15.9
Contraceptive prevalence rate	38.0 (1985)	
Female mean age at first marriage	20.0 (1980)	

The level of fertility is considered to be <u>unsatisfactory</u> and <u>too high</u>.

INTERNATIONAL MIGRATION

	1980-85	2020-25
Net migration rate	0.0	0.0
Foreign-born population (%)	0.1 (1980)	

The levels of immigration and emigration are viewed as <u>not significant</u> and <u>satisfactory</u>.

SPATIAL DISTRIBUTION/URBANIZATION

	1985	2025
Urban population (%)	25.3	55.9

Growth rate:	1980-85	2020-25
urban	4.6	2.2
rural	1.1	-0.8

Spatial distribution of the population is viewed as <u>inappropriate</u>. The population is perceived to be unevenly distributed in relation to natural resources.

GENERAL POLICY FRAMEWORK

Overall approach to population problems: The objectives of population policy are to reduce population growth, chiefly by family planning programmes, achieve a more equitable pattern of population distribution, and enhance job prospects and living conditions. The Government believes that it is imperative to launch a two-pronged approach to development; a population-centred development policy and a development-oriented population policy. The Family Planning Programme and the Transmigration Programme have been the Government's major initiatives in the population sector.

Importance of population policy in achieving development objectives: The population programme is a necessary element in Indonesia's overall socio-economic development. Indonesia has a comprehensive planning process which recognizes that population variables must be considered in all sectoral planning. The present five-year plan - REPELITA IV (1985/86-1989/90) - calls for a holistic and integrated approach to population issues and assigns considerable importance to the community and non-governmental institutions in initiating and implementing population programmes. To meet the challenges posed by population growth, the Government believes that the principal solution lies in implementing a population-oriented development pattern in which population is both the subject and object of development.

INSTITUTIONAL FRAMEWORK

Population data systems and development planning: The major sources of demographic data have been censuses and surveys. In 1960 the Central Bureau of Statistics (CBS) became responsible for overall development and the co-ordination of statistical data collection. Censuses were taken in 1961, 1971 and 1980. A national socio-economic survey (SUSENAS) is taken annually. Although vital registration has a long history in Indonesia and efforts have recently been made to improve and expand the system, coverage remains inadequate. Four five-year development plans have been issued since 1969. The most recent is REPELITA IV for 1985/86-1989/90. The National Development Planning Board (BAPPENAS), established in 1967, has a broad mandate for directing and co-ordinating the formulation and implementation of development plans.

Integration of population within development planning: The National Development Planning Board (BAPPENAS) is responsible for overall population policy development and integration with other development policies. The Ministry of Population and Environment was created in 1983 to carry out the following duties: formulate policies regarding population and environmental management; co-ordinate all population activities; co-ordinate and handle all activities of environment management; and provide relevant reports, information and advice to the President.

INDONESIA

POLICIES AND MEASURES

Changes in population size and age structure: The Government's policy is to reduce the rate of population growth, chiefly by lowering fertility. The target is to reduce the annual population growth rate to 1.5 per cent by 1990. The Government has also formulated policies focusing on rural development, promoting the status of women and raising the age at marriage, in an effort to resolve problems of high population growth. In order to achieve population and family planning objectives, the fourth five-year plan has identified youth as a target group. Youth are seen as a major source of human capital and a focal point to improve the quality of the population required for Indonesia's ambitious economic and social development targets. In rural areas and poor urban communities, the aged make significant contributions to farm labour and are treated as a productive labour force with special needs. Under the pension scheme, coverage is gradually being expanded to include establishments smaller than those currently covered (firms with 100 or more employees or a payroll of 5 million rupiahs or more a month).

Mortality and morbidity: Reducing rates of morbidity and mortality is part of the Government's welfare policy. It includes strengthening the health infrastructure so as to expand health service coverage and developing local community participation in providing preventive and curative care through the primary health care system. Primary health care is being developed throughout the country under the technical guidance of the government health services and is closely linked with the government referral system. The Government has called for intensified efforts to lower the crude death and infant and child mortality rates. Quantitative targets are to reduce the crude death rate to 10 per thousand and the infant mortality rate to 35 per thousand by 1990. Children under age five and pregnant women in rural areas are of special policy concern. The fourth five-year plan calls for trained personnel to assist 60 per cent of all deliveries by 1989, and for 65 per cent of pregnant women to have an average of four pre-natal visits to a health facility. Health services continue to be expanded, particularly in transmigration, border and remote areas.

Fertility and the family: The major policy objective is to modify the effect of fertility on the rate of population growth and to improve maternal and child health and family well-being. Direct intervention includes family planning programmes and measures to improve the status of women. A goal of achieving a crude birth rate of around 23 per thousand by 1990 has been specified. The diffusion of information and access to all modern methods of contraception are both permitted by law. To curb the level of fertility, high priority is given to the National Family Planning Programme, which has gained popularity and established roots in rural areas, especially in the high-density areas of Java and Bali. It is being integrated with the nutrition programme. Abortion is permitted only on medical grounds. Sterilization is legal.

International migration: International migration as such has not been a major concern in Indonesia. Since 1975 Indonesia has provided temporary asylum to more than 100,000 Indo-Chinese refugees, mostly Viet Namese. Temporary emigration of workers is encouraged. Emigration of skilled Indonesians, however, is to a certain degree restricted since they are scarce and are

needed for national development. The aims of expanding overseas employment
are to strengthen the existing relations between sending and receiving
countries, to reduce unemployment, under-employment and income inequality, to
improve the welfare of workers and their dependents, and to increase foreign
currency remittances from those working abroad.

Spatial distribution/urbanization: Though the urban share of Indonesia's
population is still relatively low, the absolute size and annual growth is
significant enough to warrant serious concern among policy makers. Realizing
that spontaneous migration would never be of sufficient volume to offset
overcrowding or stimulate the development of relatively unpopulated areas, the
Government established a large-scale resettlement programme, the
Transmigration Programme, which seeks to improve population and manpower
distribution and develop new areas. The number of people involved has
increased markedly over the past 15 years. Under the fourth five-year plan it
is expected that approximately 4 million persons will be moved. It was
reported, however, in November 1986, that the Transmigration Programme would
be curtailed for budgetary reasons and that the Government will now encourage
private Indonesian and foreign companies to help finance the plan.

Status of women and population: A Ministry on the Role of Women has been
established, and the Convention on the Elimination of All forms of
Discrimination Against Women has been ratified. The minimum legal age at
marriage for women is 16 years.

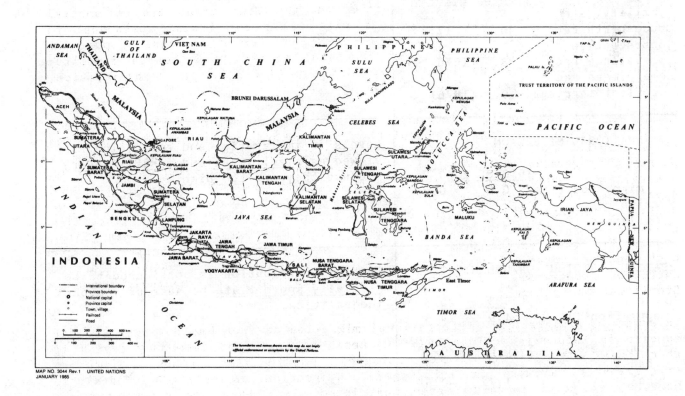

MAP NO. 3044 Rev.1 UNITED NATIONS
JANUARY 1985

IRAN (ISLAMIC REPUBLIC OF)

DEMOGRAPHIC INDICATORS	CURRENT PERCEPTION

SIZE/AGE STRUCTURE/GROWTH

Population:	1985	2025
(thousands)	44 632	97 011
0-14 years (%)	42.7	25.3
60+ years (%)	5.1	10.2

Rate of:	1980-85	2020-25
growth	2.9	1.2
natural increase	28.8	11.8

The Government perceives the current growth rate as satisfactory.

MORTALITY/MORBIDITY

	1980-85	2020-25
Life expectancy	57.3	72.0
Crude death rate	12.0	6.0
Infant mortality	115.0	38.0

The Government views mortality as unacceptable. Concerns include the reduction of infant and maternal morbidity and mortality.

FERTILITY/NUPTIALITY/FAMILY

	1980-85	2020-25
Fertility rate	5.6	2.2
Crude birth rate	40.8	17.8
Contraceptive prevalence rate	23.0 (1978-79)	
Female mean age at first marriage	19.7 (1976)	

Current levels and trends are considered to be satisfactory.

INTERNATIONAL MIGRATION

	1980-85	2020-25
Net migration rate	0.0	0.0
Foreign-born population (%)	0.5 (1976)	

Levels of immigration and emigration are viewed as significant and unsatisfactory because they are too high.

SPATIAL DISTRIBUTION/URBANIZATION

Urban	1985	2025
population (%)	51.9	74.6

Growth rate:	1980-85	2020-25
urban	4.0	1.8
rural	1.7	-0.6

Spatial distribution is considered to be partially appropriate because of regional inequalities.

GENERAL POLICY FRAMEWORK

Overall approach to population problems: The Government does not have an explicit policy to modify fertility or population growth, mainly because it believes that the solution to economic and social problems does not lie in fertility control but in balanced growth. The Government wishes to reduce immigration and emigration as well as to encourage the return of skilled Iranians living abroad. It also seeks to modify the spatial distribution of population, largely as a means of achieving national economic integration and development.

Importance of population policy in achieving development objectives: The Government views population policies passively and has not assigned major importance to population policy and programmes. There has been no active attempt to achieve development objectives through the implementation of population policies.

INSTITUTIONAL FRAMEWORK

Population data systems and development planning: The most recent population census was taken in 1986 by the Statistical Centre of Iran. The system of vital registration is considered incomplete. Population projections for planning purposes are prepared by the Population and Manpower Planning Division. The Institute of Social Studies and Research of Tehran University undertakes special demographic surveys and provides information on population/development interrelationships. Development since the Second World War has been guided by a series of five development plans under the auspices of the semi-autonomous plan organization established in 1948. An outline of the first five-year development plan of the Revolutionary Government, 1983/84-1988/89, was published in 1983, but few of the projects were implemented. A new plan is to begin in 1988. In 1987 the Government launched the first household survey ever conducted in the country, which was to be carried out over a three-year period in all 24 provinces. The objectives of the survey are to analyse demographic trends and the socio-economic characteristics of the population.

Integration of population within development planning: Since 1973 the Population and Manpower Planning Bureau of the Plan and Budget Organization has been the governmental agency charged with taking into account population variables in development planning.

POLICIES AND MEASURES

Changes in population size and age structure: The Government does not consider population growth to be a major problem. Hence, there is no explicit policy with regard to population size and age structure. However, the Government does not restrict individuals' practice of birth control and family

IRAN (ISLAMIC REPUBLIC OF)

planning, provided it is implemented within the framework of the Islamic laws of the country. Some concern has been expressed over the rate of population growth, which has been boosted by the influx of refugees from Afghanistan. In 1986 the Prime Minister suggested that the issue should be addressed with appropriate measures. Under the social security scheme, coverage is limited to employed persons in urban areas.

Mortality and morbidity: Within the framework of the overall socio-economic development plan, a National Health Plan was formulated for the period 1983-1987. To improve co-ordination in the delivery of healthy care, approval was granted for the creation of a new ministry, the Ministry of Health and Medical Education. In early 1983 the High Council of Co-ordination and Supervision was established. The Government's main priority is to reduce infant and maternal morbidity and mortality through the provision of primary health care, with emphasis on hygiene, safe drinking water, improved nutrition and immunization against infectious diseases. The goal was to immunize 80 per cent of infants by 1985 and 100 per cent by 1988. Two new categories of health workers will be trained to work in urban and rural health centres. Female family health workers will be responsible for maternal and child health, family planning, nutrition, immunization and school health; while male workers will deal with disease control. Students will be reoriented to serve in their communities. Recent legislation requires that all newly graduated physicians serve for from three to five years in rural areas.

Fertility and the family: The Government has no explicit policy to influence fertility. However, the Supreme Council for Policy Making in Health, Curative Services and Medical Education has recommended child-spacing, health education, and the use of legitimately approved methods of contraception aimed at improving the welfare of women and children. According to the Islamic Shariat and the decree of Iman Khomeini, all contraceptive methods except sterilization are acceptable, particularly on medical grounds or to save the life of the mother, unless they harm the health of the couple.

International migration: Government policies seek a reduction in immigration. However, no quantitative target has been set. The Government has implemented policies and programmes for the resettlement of refugees and displaced persons who have fled to Iran. It is estimated that, as of early 1987, there were almost 2.3 million Afghanis and 400,000 refugees of other nationalities in Iran, making it host to the world's second largest refugee population. Registered refugees have access to the same food subsidies and educational and medical services as nationals, and for the most part have been integrated. The economic difficulties facing the country and the growing refugee population have strained national services. Declining oil revenues, the impact of the regional conflict on the economy, and increased competition for jobs led in 1985 to the introduction of restrictive regulations concerning the employment of refugees. Emigration policy aims at reducing the brain drain and encouraging the return of skilled Iranians from abroad.

Spatial distribution/urbanization: To decelerate rural-to-urban migration and to redress regional imbalances, programmes of decentralization, regional investment and various economic and social policies favouring rural and disadvantaged areas have been implemented. The Government has indicated that as of 1984 about 1.5 million persons have been forced to migrate from the western and south-western parts of the country to other areas because of regional conflict.

Status of women and population: The status of Iranian women is influenced to a large degree by Islamic laws and teachings. For example, practices relating to marriage, divorce and inheritance are consistent with Islamic law. The minimum age at marriage for women is reported to have been lowered to 13 years.

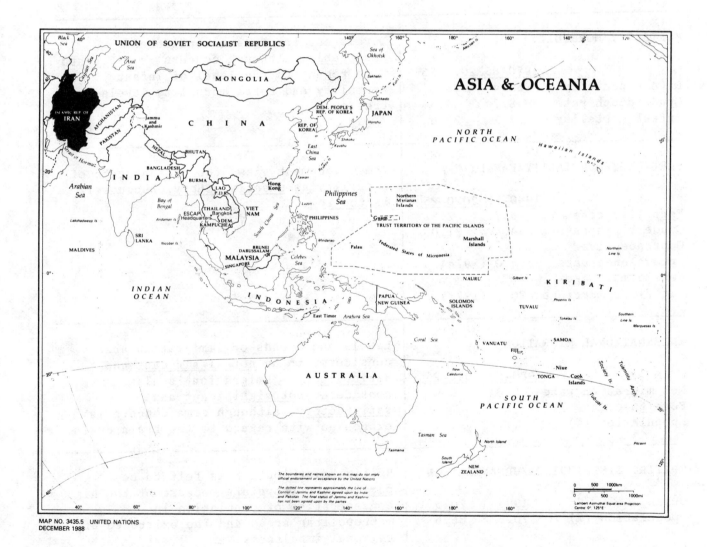

IRAQ

DEMOGRAPHIC INDICATORS	CURRENT PERCEPTION

SIZE/AGE STRUCTURE/GROWTH
 	
Population: 1985   2025
  (thousands)   15 898   43 520
   0-14 years (%)   46.9   29.5
   60+ years (%)   4.3   7.6
 	
Rate of: 1980-85   2020-25
 growth   3.6   1.6
 natural increase   35.7   16.4
	The rate of growth is considered <u>unsatisfactory</u> because it is <u>too low</u>. A sustained increase in population is considered desirable so as to achieve development objectives through an adequate supply of manpower and maintain national identity.

MORTALITY/MORBIDITY 1980-85 2020-25 Life expectancy 62.4 73.8 Crude death rate 8.7 4.5 Infant mortality 77.1 20.6	Levels and trends are considered <u>acceptable</u>, although concern is expressed with regard to the level of infant mortality and rural mortality levels and trends.
FERTILITY/NUPTIALITY/FAMILY 1980-85 2020-25 Fertility rate 6.7 2.5 Crude birth rate 44.4 21.0 Contraceptive prevalence rate 14.0 (1974) Female mean age at first marriage 20.8 (1977)	The Government views the present rate of fertility as <u>unsatisfactory</u>, because it is <u>too low</u>.
INTERNATIONAL MIGRATION 1980-85 2020-25 Net migration rate 0.0 0.0 Foreign-born population (%)	Levels and trends of immigration are considered to be <u>not significant</u> and <u>satisfactory</u>. Emigration is also considered <u>not significant</u> and <u>satisfactory</u>, although some concern is expressed with regard to the brain drain.
SPATIAL DISTRIBUTION/URBANIZATION Urban 1985 2025 population (%) 70.6 86.6 Growth rate: 1980-85 2020-25 urban 4.8 1.9 rural 0.9 -0.1	Spatial distribution is felt to be <u>partially appropriate</u> because of the high concentration of population in metropolitan areas and the existence of regional imbalances.

GENERAL POLICY FRAMEWORK

Overall approach to population problems: The Government considers the
continuous growth of the population to be desirable. Its official policy
is to increase population size, lower mortality, and raise fertility
through programmes of maternal and child health care, family welfare and
free medical care.

Importance of population policy in achieving development objectives: The
Government recognizes the importance of population policy in development
planning. Its policy of promoting a sustained increase in population size
is geared towards making adequate manpower available for economic growth
and development.

INSTITUTIONAL FRAMEWORK

Population data systems and development planning: The most recent
published population census was taken in 1977, and another took place in
1987. A curfew was imposed while it took place, with all foreigners
resident in the country included in the count. The system of vital
registration is considered to be incomplete. The national development
plan, 1976-1980, outlined a number of policies for development, but their
implementation has been hampered by the military conflict in the region.
In 1982 the Government acknowledged that it had discontinued all
development projects that were not essential to the war effort. The
Government noted, however, that, in spite of difficulties arising from the
war, Iraq has continued its economic and social development activities, as
evidenced by progress in the field of health and improvements in life
expectancy. According to government reports in late 1987, the Planning
Board is to be replaced by another body which will be chaired by the
Minister of Planning and will act in a consultative role to the Council of
Ministers. It will prepare five-year and annual development plans.

Integration of population within development planning: Attempts to
integrate population factors within development planning started in 1969
with the establishment of the Department of Demography and Manpower
Statistics. In 1972, a National Committee for Population Policies was
established. It is responsible for planning and implementing national
programmes in the field of population and for advising the Government on
population matters. In 1973, an Agency for Demographic Studies was
established within the Central Statistical Organization. It is charged
with co-ordinating basic demographic research and analysis in order to
meet the requirements of development planning.

POLICIES AND MEASURES

Changes in population size and age structure: Because of the country's
perceived economic advantages, such as large agricultural tracts, abundant
water supplies and mineral resources, which permit it to absorb additional

IRAQ

population, Government policy consists of boosting population growth by raising fertility and lowering mortality. Among the measures undertaken to achieve these objectives are raising the standard of living and implementing maternal and child health programmes and free medical care. While social security coverage excludes agricultural and temporary employees, domestic servants and family labour, the intention is to achieve eventually full coverage for all workers.

Mortality and morbidity: While the Government considers levels of morbidity and mortality to be acceptable, it has paid increased attention to preventive health care measures, with emphasis on rural areas. Two national immunization campaigns have been launched, one in 1985 and the other in 1986. In addition, the Government has concentrated on maternal and child health care and family welfare, as well as the control of diarrhoeal diseases. Iraq's President has ordered that a five-year health plan be implemented specifically to reduce infant mortality. Studies on the birth weight of newborns were planned for 1986. While most health services and pharmaceuticals had been provided free of charge, a very small charge is now imposed in order to discourage unnecessary visits. A health insurance scheme has been organized, and benefits are progressively being improved, particularly in rural areas.

Fertility and the family: The Government has intervened to increase fertility by means of various pro-natalist measures such as family allowances and benefits, child allowances for salaried workers, and paid maternity leave for working women, including 100 per cent of earnings payable for at least 10 weeks. In 1986, the President of Iraq announced that women would be encouraged to have at least four children. He also indicated that female employment should not hinder child-bearing, since it could threaten the country's development and defence. The Government has begun to limit access to modern methods of contraception. Abortion is permitted only to save the life of the mother. Information on the status of sterilization is not available.

International migration: Both immigration and emigration are regarded by the Government as not significant and satisfactory. While the country has traditionally been an importer of labour and has regarded all Arab migrants as Iraqi citizens in terms of rights and obligations, the number of foreign workers was reduced by 30 per cent in 1987, according to government reports. This resulted in a saving of $50 million. The Government has implemented measures to reduce the emigration of skilled personnel, and it encourages the repatriation of Iraqis living abroad.

Spatial distribution/urbanization: Policies are in effect to decelerate the excessive migration from rural areas. In 1978, the Government reported that it had formulated plans for the industrialization of third-order urban towns, development of medium-sized regional towns and market centres, implementation of agrarian reform and collectivization and expansion of physical infrastructure, all aimed at equitable population distribution. Concerned with the rapid growth and size of Baghdad, the Government has adopted steps to reduce migration there, including limiting the purchase of property in the Baghdad municipality.

<u>Status of women and population</u>: The Government pays constant attention to the development and improvement of the role of women in national development. The General Federation of Iraqi Women advises and participates in formulating national policy. To encourage the participation of women in the labour force, policies focus on training women to acquire the skills required in industrial and rural production and on providing appropriate conditions for increasing employment opportunities for women. In addition, the Government has been concerned with developing policies that counter the tendency for women to be employed in traditional, low-paying jobs. The promotion of women's participation in decision-making and the introduction of patterns of part-time employment for women with family responsibilities are also advocated. The minimum legal age at marriage for women is 18 years.

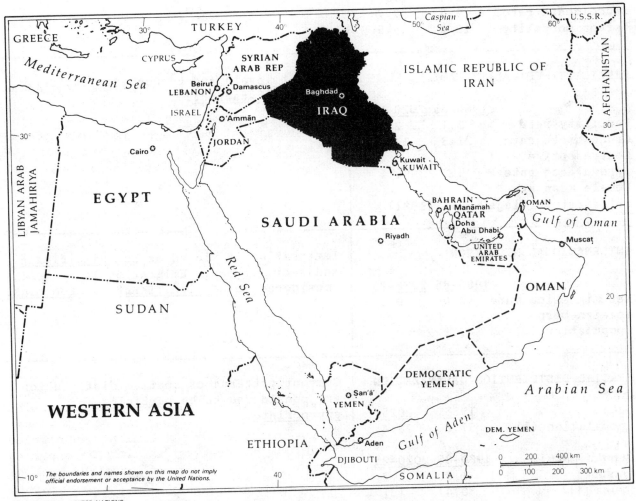

MAP NO. 3434.1   UNITED NATIONS
DECEMBER 1988

IRELAND

DEMOGRAPHIC INDICATORS	CURRENT PERCEPTION
SIZE/AGE STRUCTURE/GROWTH	The Government perceives the current rate of growth as <u>satisfactory</u>.
Population: 1985 2025	
(thousands) 3 608 5 326	
0-14 years (%) 29.6 21.0	
60+ years (%) 14.4 17.0	
Rate of: 1980-85 2020-25	
growth 1.2 0.6	
natural increase 11.8 6.5	
MORTALITY/MORBIDITY	Levels and trends of mortality are viewed as <u>acceptable</u>.
1980-85 2020-25	
Life expectancy 73.0 77.3	
Crude death rate 9.5 7.7	
Infant mortality 10.2 5.5	
FERTILITY/NUPTIALITY/FAMILY	Current levels and trends are considered to be <u>satisfactory</u>.
1980-85 2020-25	
Fertility rate 3.1 2.0	
Crude birth rate 21.3 14.2	
Contraceptive prevalence rate	
Female mean age at first marriage 23.4 (1981)	
INTERNATIONAL MIGRATION	Immigration is viewed as <u>not significant</u> and <u>satisfactory</u>. Emigration is considered to be <u>significant</u> and <u>too high</u>.
1980-85 2020-25	
Net migration rate 0.0 0.0	
Foreign-born population (%)	
SPATIAL DISTRIBUTION/URBANIZATION	Current patterns of spatial distribution are considered to be <u>partially</u> <u>appropriate</u>.
Urban 1985 2025	
population (%) 57.0 76.4	
Growth rate: 1980-85 2020-25	
urban 1.8 1.2	
rural 0.4 -1.1	

GENERAL POLICY FRAMEWORK

Overall approach to population problems: The main goals of the Government's policy are to maintain the current rates of population growth and fertility, adjust patterns of spatial distribution and stem the flow of emigration. In recognition of the high rate of emigration, a committee has been charged with advising on emigration welfare services.

Importance of population policy in achieving development objectives: There is no reported comprehensive population policy to date.

INSTITUTIONAL FRAMEWORK

Population data systems and development planning: Census-taking is the responsibility of the Central Statistics Office. Censuses were conducted in 1951, 1956, 1961, 1966, 1971, 1979, 1981. The most recent census was conducted in 1986. Vital registration is considered to be complete. The 1984-1987 plan for growth, entitled "Building on reality", is currently in effect.

Integration of population within development planning: There is no government agency charged with integrating population within development planning.

POLICIES AND MEASURES

Changes in population size and age structure: The Government has not adopted any explicit policies to influence the size, growth, or age structure of the population. Currently, Ireland has one of Europe's youngest populations, with 30 per cent under the age of 15.

Mortality and morbidity: The country does not have a comprehensive health-care policy, although a short-term strategy was included in the national plan for 1984-1987. Measures have been directed towards prevention, with emphasis on community care and primary health care, while shifting away from institutional care and keeping down health expenditures through increased efficiency. Scarce resources are being focused on those in greatest need. Emphasis is placed on a sectoral approach towards health promotion, and positive steps have been taken to promote healthy living, such as the imposition of new controls on tobacco-smoking. In addition, self-care and family care are being emphasized. On the local level, health awareness is being promoted through schools, women's groups and occupational health services. Another approach to encourage healthier life-styles has been the imposition of a 2 per cent tax on cigarette advertising, with the proceeds going to programmes of health education. Most services provided through the public health care system are free of charge. A working party created by the Minister of Health in 1986 was made responsible for suggesting measures to improve the medical care and living conditions of the elderly.

Fertility and the family: The Government has pursued a policy of intervention to maintain the rate of fertility. As announced in the national plan for 1984-1987, "Building on reality", a new child-benefit scheme was implemented, effective April 1986. Under the scheme a child benefit of 15 Irish pounds (Ir 0.81 = $US 1) was payable for each of the first five children, increasing to Ir 22 a month for each subsequent child. The child tax allowance was abolished. Other pro-natalist incentives, such as maternity grants and maternity leave, are also available. In view of the need for family planning services, amendments to the Health Bill have eased restrictions on the availability of contraceptives. In 1985 the sale of "non-medical contraceptives" was legalized to all those over 18 years of age without a prescription. Previously, contraceptives were available only to married couples with a prescription. Since 1979, a license has been required for the manufacture and importation of contraceptives. Birth control pills are available as menstrual-cycle regulators. Abortion and abortion counselling are illegal as a result of a constitutional amendment passed in 1983. Sterilization is not legally regulated. In 1986 a referendum to legalize divorce was defeated. A parliamentary committee set up a pilot Family Conciliation Service in 1986, which intends to resolve marital disputes such as those involving parenting, living arrangements, the family home, financial support and division of property.

International migration: The Government has not reported any policy concerning immigration. As regards the country's substantial level of emigration, in June 1984 the Minister for Labour appointed a new committee with particular responsibility for advising on emigration welfare services and charged with making recommendations on the allocation of state financial assistance towards the employment of professional workers dealing with the welfare problems of Irish emigrants in Great Britain. Between 1983 and 1985, the Government nearly trebled the grant for emigration advisory services. The substantial flow of emigrants, particularly of the young and educated, is expected to continue in the near future, given the persistence of high unemployment.

Spatial distribution/urbanization: To combat problems associated with an inappropriate pattern of spatial distribution as a result of migration to Dublin and the continuing outflow of population from the agricultural sector, a regional development policy has been implemented under the auspices of the Industrial Development Authority. Policy objectives are the development of the capital city to accommodate the natural increase of the present population, the expansion of eight other major urban centres, the development of other large towns of strategic importance in each region, and the continuation of special measures for the development of the Gaeltacht (Irish-speaking areas).

Status of women and population: There have been substantial measures to improve female employment in the public sector, while other initiatives have been taken to diminish the differences for men and women, for example, in social security. After the Government approved proposals for the adoption of a statement of policy on equality of opportunities between men and women in employment in 1984, a number of initiatives were taken in 1985, including creation of a working party under the Minister of Labour to monitor the effectiveness of equal opportunity initiatives in State-sponsored bodies. The overall development plan concerning women in the next decade is contained in the report entitled <u>Irish Women: Agenda for Practical Action</u>, produced in 1985 by a working party chaired by the Minister of State for Womens' Affairs. The minimum legal age at marriage for women is 16 years.

<u>Other issues</u>: In 1986 Parliament was considering a Children's (Care and Protection) Bill, which would provide for a system of statutory registration of day-care services for children, to be administered by local health boards. The boards would be given the task of improving the well-being of children in their area of responsibility and of adopting the necessary measures to help parents raise their children.

ISRAEL

DEMOGRAPHIC INDICATORS	CURRENT PERCEPTION
SIZE/AGE STRUCTURE/GROWTH	The Government considers the rate of population growth to be <u>unsatisfactory</u> because it is <u>too low</u>.

Population:	1985	2025
(thousands)	4 252	6 865
0-14 years (%)	31.7	22.9
60+ years (%)	12.4	16.6

Rate of:	1980-85	2020-25
growth	1.8	0.8
natural increase	15.9	8.4

MORTALITY/MORBIDITY

The Government views the mortality and morbidity rates as <u>acceptable</u>.

	1980-85	2020-25
Life expectancy	74.4	77.7
Crude death rate	7.2	7.5
Infant mortality	14.2	7.2

FERTILITY/NUPTIALITY/FAMILY

Trends and levels of fertility are perceived as <u>unsatisfactory</u> because they are <u>too low</u>.

	1980-85	2020-25
Fertility rate	3.1	2.3
Crude birth rate	23.2	15.9
Contraceptive prevalence rate	...	...
Female mean age at first marriage	23.5 (1983)	

INTERNATIONAL MIGRATION

Immigration levels and trends are viewed as <u>not significant</u> and <u>too low</u>. Emigration is considered <u>significant</u> and <u>too high</u>.

	1980-85	2020-25
Net migration rate	2.5	0.0
Foreign-born population (%)	...	...

SPATIAL DISTRIBUTION/URBANIZATION

Spatial distribution is considered to be <u>partially appropriate</u>.

Urban	1985	2025
population (%)	90.3	95.6

Growth rate:	1980-85	2020-25
urban	2.2	0.9
rural	-1.4	-0.4

GENERAL POLICY FRAMEWORK

Overall approach to population problems: The main goals of population policy in Israel are to increase the size of the population and to adjust the geographical distribution of population to better conform to national needs. Higher growth rates are encouraged through measures aimed at increasing fertility and immigration rates. The Government has instituted direct measures to change the spatial distribution pattern which focus on strategies to disperse the population.

Importance of population policy in achieving development objectives: The Government is keenly aware of the importance of demographic problems, particularly because the population has increased several-fold in the past several decades. The Government acknowledges the interrelationships between population and development and considers the achievement of national goals to be for the mutual benefit of the population and the State. National services directed towards general welfare, housing and education aim to promote an egalitarian and integrated society.

INSTITUTIONAL FRAMEWORK

Population data systems and development planning: The first Israeli census was conducted in 1948; the most recent census was held in 1983. The Statistics Ordinance of 1972 provides the legal framework for the census; however, formal census planning is lacking. Registration of vital events is considered virtually complete. The Economic Planning Authority within the Ministry of Finance prepares the National Economic Plan.

Integration of population within development planning: In 1968 the Demographic Centre was established in the Prime Minister's Office. At present, within the Ministry of Labour and Welfare, the Centre is responsible for proposing, developing, and assisting in the implementation of demographic policy. It commissions and monitors demographic research. The Centre devotes special interest to research on determinants of fertility. The Central Bureau of Statistics also has a demographic section and is responsible for demographic projections and censuses. The Ministry of the Interior maintains a Population Registry which also serves as a source of demographic information.

POLICIES AND MEASURES

Changes in population size and age structure: The governmental objective of increasing the growth rate and size of the population is coupled with the goal of protecting the family and its well-being. The decline of immigration is considered partially responsible for the lower-than-expected population growth rate. The Government views intervention appropriate to raise growth,

ISRAEL

fertility, and immigration rates. The Government has stated that the changing
age structure of the population has necessitated new investment and resources
to cope with the growing population of the aged.

Mortality and morbidity: The policy is to improve health conditions for the
entire population, with specific attention given to reducing regional
disparities and differentials due to socio-economic inequalities. Health
agencies and related organizations implement the Government's comprehensive
health policy. Recent changes in the health system include the integration of
preventive and curative services and the expansion of maternal and child
health centres into family health centres in order to provide for the elderly
and the handicapped. The system stresses services for the mentally ill and
the training of new health personnel. The Well-Child Care Project supports a
broad immunization programme. Safe water and fluoridation of public drinking
water projects aim at improving general health standards. The changing age
structure has focused attention on the increasing incidence of chronic and
debilitative diseases.

Fertility and the family: The Government actively promotes a policy of
raising the fertility rate. Although fertility differentials among social
groups appear to have diminished, the Government encourages the increase of
fertility rates and has recently called for an optimum of four children per
family. Concern over infertility has prompted the Government to allocate
funds to help infertile couples. The Government's social welfare policies
encourage couples to maximize the size of their families. Free medical
services are available to pregnant women as well as a 12-week post-natal
maternity leave. The National Insurance Institute administers benefits,
including one-time birth grants, child allowances, and special allowances for
the third and subsequent children. The Government offers special tax
exemptions to working mothers. Maternal and child health centres provide
necessary education on child-care, nutrition and hygiene. The Government
provides family planning in Well-Child Clinics. Abortion is available only
for broad health reasons. Sterilization is permitted for health reasons only.

International migration: Government policy advocates boosting the level of
immigration, which in recent years has fallen sharply. The Government cites
the decrease in the Jewish diaspora as the reason for the reduced
immigration. Israel aims to integrate immigrants and refugees into the
country's culture and economy. The 1950 Law of Return guarantees the right of
any Jew to immigrate to Israel and to receive government assistance for
settlement. The Ministry of Absorption aids all immigrants and refugees with
special services for employment, day-care, and Hebrew language instruction.
In 1987 the Minister of Immigrant Absorption indicated that his Ministry was
preparing for a possible large influx of immigrants. Although the Government
does not have an emigration policy, serious concern has been expressed over
the significant level of out-migration. The Central Bureau of Statistics
reports that return migration accounts for a large portion of recent
emigration from Israel.

Spatial distribution/urbanization: Government policy is to decelerate
internal migration and to disperse population to specified regions. Policy
objectives include reducing regional inequalities, creating a balanced urban

hierarchy, and improving urban/rural linkages. National security is an objective in regard to the dispersal of population to border and occupied territories. The creation of new towns and land colonization schemes comprise the focus of policy implementation. The Government subsidizes housing rents, social services, and the construction of industrial infrastructure. Disincentives aimed at controlling the growth of Tel Aviv include bans on the construction of immigrant housing and the conversion of agricultural land for urban land use in metropolitan areas.

Status of women and population: Legal measures guarantee equal rights, equal pay (1964), and equal opportunity regardless of sex, marital or parental status (1982). Government programmes furnish literacy and vocational training for women. In addition, within the Ministry of Education a Special Consultant on the Status of Women is responsible for eliminating sexual stereotyping in school curricula and textbooks and expanding training opportunities for women. The minimum legal age at marriage for women is 16 years.

ITALY

DEMOGRAPHIC INDICATORS	CURRENT PERCEPTION
SIZE/AGE STRUCTURE/GROWTH	The Government considers the rate of population growth to be <u>satisfactory</u>.

Population: 1985 2025
 (thousands) 57 300 57 178
 0–14 years (%) 19.4 16.9
 60+ years (%) 18.6 26.8

Rate of: 1980–85 2020–25
 growth 0.1 −0.1
 natural increase 0.8 −1.1

MORTALITY/MORBIDITY — Mortality and morbidity levels are perceived as <u>unacceptable</u>.

 1980–85 2020–25
Life expectancy 74.5 77.6
Crude death rate 10.4 13.0
Infant mortality 12.7 6.6

FERTILITY/NUPTIALITY/FAMILY — Levels and trends of fertility are viewed as <u>satisfactory</u> by the Government.

 1980–85 2020–25
Fertility rate 1.6 2.0
Crude birth rate 11.2 11.9
Contraceptive
 prevalence rate 78.0 (1979)
Female mean age
 at first marriage 23.2 (1981)

INTERNATIONAL MIGRATION — Immigration is considered <u>significant</u> and <u>too high</u>. Emigration levels are perceived as <u>not significant</u> and <u>satisfactory</u>.

 1980–85 2020–25
Net migration rate 0.0 0.0
Foreign-born
 population (%) 2.0 (1981)

SPATIAL DISTRIBUTION/URBANIZATION — The Government considers spatial distribution to be <u>partially appropriate</u>.

Urban 1985 2025
 population (%) 67.4 75.8

Growth rate: 1980–85 2020–25
 urban 0.3 0.2
 rural −0.5 −1.0

GENERAL POLICY FRAMEWORK

<u>Overall approach to population problems</u>: The Government believes that population policy objectives can be achieved through careful and effective governmental activity. Italy has established several governmental bodies since the 1970s to deal with the collection and analysis of demographic data. The Government regards recent legislation and socio-economic policy, such as the legalization of abortion and the restructuring of health services, as measures that affect population but do not constitute a demographic policy.

<u>Importance of population policy in achieving development objectives</u>: Measures which affect population are viewed as important in coping with problems of economic, social, and demographic development. Measures are needed to improve the quality of life of individuals, regardless of ideological and cultural systems. The Government believes that direct and specific interventions to alter population trends are inappropriate for Italy, but that social policies may affect demographic variables indirectly.

INSTITUTIONAL FRAMEWORK

<u>Population data systems and development planning</u>: The most recent census was conducted in 1981. Vital registration is considered to be complete. No comprehensive planning apparatus is reported. However, the Interministerial Committee for Economic Planning functions as an advisory board for budget planning.

<u>Integration of population within development planning</u>: The National Committee on Population Problems, subordinate to the Chairman of the Council of Ministers, was created in 1976 to formulate and co-ordinate population policies. The Central Statistical Institute (ISTAT), established in 1928, prepares population projections and special demographic inquiries. The National Research Council and the Population Research Institute, established in 1980 and 1981, respectively, share responsibility with ISTAT for furnishing the Government with information on population matters. The Council campaigns for the promotion of demographic research and co-ordinates working groups dealing with demographic studies. It also provided support for the first National Fertility Survey, held in 1979.

POLICIES AND MEASURES

<u>Changes in population size and age structure</u>: Official policy is to study population trends but not to alter them directly by means of a comprehensive population policy. The Government considers to be particularly important: aging, the improvement of health conditions, and imbalances in the pattern of spatial distribution. Italy considers the short-, medium- and long-term effects of the aging of population to be of primary concern.

ITALY

Mortality and morbidity: Official policy is to improve health care and health conditions, especially for infants and the aged. In 1978, the Government reorganized health care services into a nationalized system, the National Health Service. The basic aim was to provide free and homogeneous medical services throughout the country. The system has provided unified health services integrated with social services and is regionally decentralized to increase access. The Government hopes that decentralization will result in an improved distribution of medical resources, while shifting resources from hospitals to primary health care facilities. The system stresses preventive medicine and education in sanitation. Priorites include aiding the handicapped, preventing drug abuse and assisting addicts, and combating cancer. Vaccination against diptheria, measles, poliomyelitis, and tetanus are compulsory.

Fertility and the family: The Government maintains an explicit policy not to intervene to modify levels and trends of fertility. However, Government objectives are to improve the status of women and to protect the family. Family allowances based on family income are available for one or more children and other dependents. Women are entitled to materniety leave of three months following the birth of a child with an allowance equivalent to 80 per cent of wages and the option of an additional unpaid leave of up to six months before the child's first birthday. After the Second World War, and during the 1970s, the Government passed legislation liberalizing access to contraception. The Government has stated that the new laws granting greater access to contraception indicate its support of individual liberties, rather than a demographic policy. The Government now provides direct support and access to modern methods of contraception through family planning clinics. Laws forbidding the advertising of contraceptives were repealed in 1971. In 1978 legislation decriminalized sterilization and legalized abortion. Abortion is available upon request during the first three months of pregnancy. Parental permission is necessary for abortions for women under 18 years of age. A waiting period of seven days is required between the application for and the performance of the abortion.

International migration: Immigration policy is aimed at curbing future immigration while maintaining the present immigrant population. Permanent immigration is considered to be undesirable. In 1982, the Government instituted a programme to regularize undocumented immigrants who had been in Italy prior to 30 September 1981 and had been working for at least six months as of that date. Italy has traditionally been a country of emigration; however, between 1970 and 1984, Italy experienced net in-migration. The positive net-migration flow is a matter of concern to the Government, especially the influx of undocumented immigrants from developing countries. ISTAT is preparing its first survey of foreigners in Italy, which indicates the importance the Government places on this issue. Because of the disappointing numbers of undocumented immigrants who came forward to regularize their situation under a new law passed in December 1986, the Government was forced to extend its amnesty programme until June 1987. The Government has fostered the return migration of Italians by making available resettlement aid in the form of grants and scholarships. The Government pursues a policy of further reducing the current low level of emigration.

Spatial distribution/urbanization: The Government professes the lack of a specific policy but states that its objective is to reduce the economic disparities between the mezzogiorno (South) and the central and northern regions. Recent administrative decentralization measures have given more responsibility to regions to direct their own development. The Central Government has passed legislation to promote the development of the south. The measures include requiring state-controlled companies to devote at least 80 per cent of new investment or 60 per cent of total investment to projects in the south. The Government also provides substantial subsidies for companies locating in areas suffering from population losses. Additional measures include public infrastructure subsidies and grants, loans, and tax incentives to new industry. Other measures include housing and social services, human resource investment, and job training. The former investment fund for the mezzogiorno has been abolished. A new approach, with flexible funding designed to encourage individual and co-operative enterprise, was being debated as of 1986.

Status of women and population: Government policy is to improve the status of women and guarantee equal rights for men and women. A 1970 law legalized divorce and emphasizes equality in marriage between spouses. A 1977 law provides for equal treatment of men and women in the work place. The National Commission for the Realization of Equality between Men and Women produced an outline in 1986 of a national action programme for equality. The programme deals with information and training, women and politics, equality in the constitution and legislation, women and health, and women and new technology. The minimum legal age at marriage for women is 16 years.

JAMAICA

DEMOGRAPHIC INDICATORS	CURRENT PERCEPTION
SIZE/AGE STRUCTURE/GROWTH	The rate of growth is viewed as unsatisfactory and too high because it contributes to chronic unemployment and other serious economic problems.

Population: 1985 / 2025 (thousands) 2 336 / 3 704; 0-14 years (%) 36.7 / 21.6; 60+ years (%) 8.6 / 15.7

Rate of: 1980-85 / 2020-25; growth 1.5 / 0.9; natural increase 22.5 / 9.2

MORTALITY/MORBIDITY

Present levels and trends of mortality are considered to be unacceptable, since problems exist concerning deficiencies in health care and nutrition.

1980-85 / 2020-25; Life expectancy 73.0 / 77.2; Crude death rate 5.6 / 5.7; Infant mortality 21.0 / 9.0

FERTILITY/NUPTIALITY/FAMILY

Current fertility levels are considered unsatisfactory because they are too high.

1980-85 / 2020-25; Fertility rate 3.4 / 2.1; Crude birth rate 28.1 / 14.9; Contraceptive prevalence rate 52.0 (1983); Female mean age at first marriage 25.2 (1982)

INTERNATIONAL MIGRATION

Immigration is not significant and satisfactory. Emigration is significant and too high.

1980-85 / 2020-25; Net migration rate -8.0 / 0.0; Foreign-born population (%) 1.0 (1982)

SPATIAL DISTRIBUTION/URBANIZATION

The pattern of spatial distribution is considered to be inappropriate because it contributes to unemployment in urban areas and stagnation of rural areas.

Urban population (%) 1985 53.8 / 2025 76.8

Growth rate: 1980-85 / 2020-25; urban 3.0 / 1.5; rural -0.2 / -0.8

GENERAL POLICY FRAMEWORK

Overall approach to population problems: The Government wishes to lower
population growth by reducing fertility, in order to foster demographic
trends that will make the best contribution to satisfying human needs.
Official policy seeks to establish favourable conditions for economic and
social development, promote a continued improvement in the health status
of the country, ensure access to high-quality family planning services,
create new and additional employment opportunities, promote balanced
rural, urban and regional development and improve the satisfaction of
basic human needs and quality of life.

Importance of population policy in achieving development objectives:
Jamaica was one of the first countries in Latin America and the Caribbean
to become actively concerned about population issues. In 1983 the
Parliament adopted a National Population Policy which established a
coherent set of national population goals and set out priorities in terms
of optimal size and growth consistent with sustained economic and social
development.

INSTITUTIONAL FRAMEWORK

Population data systems and development planning: The most recent
population census was conducted in 1982. Vital registration is considered
to be complete. A National Fertility Survey was conducted in 1974, and
Jamaica also participated in the World Fertility Survey during 1975/76.
The Central Planning Unit and the Central Statistics Department are under
the same portfolio, thereby facilitating the flow of information needed
for planning.

Integration of population within development planning: Population policy
is an essential part of planning for Jamaica's social and economic
development. The Government has implemented a formalized and
comprehensive National Population Policy which is consistent with
development goals. It emphasizes that population policy and related
activities are integral parts of development planning. The strategy for
achieving population goals is to involve all areas of government as well
as the public sector. Specific responsibility for implementing and
monitoring rests with a co-ordinating and advisory population policies
committee, working in co-operation with the Population Unit established
within the Government's Planning Institute. The committee reports
directly to the Minister of Finance and Planning, who is also the Prime
Minister. The Planning Institute has received international assistance
for a project to incorporate demographic variables into the country's
macro-economic planning model.

POLICIES AND MEASURES

Changes in population size and age structure: The National Population Policy
seeks to establish a coherent set of national goals and objectives for the
future and sets out priorities in terms of optimal size and growth of the

JAMAICA

population, consistent with sustained socio-economic growth and development. It aims at decreasing population growth through decreasing fertility levels, and adjusting economic and social factors. The multifaceted strategy combines family planning, mass media and outreach programmes. A goal has been set to have a population of not more than 3 million in the year 2000. Under the social security scheme created in 1958, coverage is given to all employed workers; casual workers earning below a certain amount and unpaid family workers are excluded.

Mortality and morbidity: The main focus is on the delivery of primary health care, particularly in rural areas, through a network of health centres backed up by community health teams composed of multipurpose health workers. Special attention is devoted to health education, in particular to the need for the immunization of all children and to the health and nutritional advantages of breast-feeding. Emphasis is given to maternal and child care and to the delivery of health care to the neediest strata of the population and to persons living in remote rural areas. The provision of clean drinking water and solid waste disposal is considered vital. As a means of achieving the goal of adequate nutrition levels, the Government promotes local production and distribution of food for newly weaned infants and supplemetary food for pregnant and lactating women, provides intensive nutrition education and communication programmes to encourage breast-feeding, and strengthens school lunch programmes. As a result of severe austerity measures, basic fees for certain health services were instituted for the first time in 1985. The target is to increase life expectancy at birth from 70 to 73 years by the year 2000.

Fertility and the family: In order to reduce fertility rates, the family planning programme has been expanded by opening a number of full-time clinics, introducing an outreach programme to recruit new acceptors and to follow up on drop-outs, and training field workers and other paramedical personnel. Family planning is integrated into programmes of maternal and child health, nutrition and general health care. The Government has developed a number of information, education and communication programmes and other innovative approaches to increase awareness of techniques for the spacing of births and the limitation of family size. Among the programmes that have been implemented are family life and sex education curricula in primary and secondary schools; a workers' population education programme; radio, television and billboard advertising of family planning services; commercial marketing of contraceptives; and the use of male family-planning motivators. The Government has also implemented a number of social measures such as mass literacy campaigns, free secondary-school tutors, equal pay for working women etc., which are expected to affect fertility indirectly. Sterilization is legal and widely practiced. Abortion, though technically illegal, is available.

International migration: Migration policy in effect restricts immigration by requiring a prospective immigrant to obtain a work permit prior to employment in Jamaica. It seeks to reduce the number of emigrants, since much of the outflow consists of highly skilled personnel whose departure involves a loss of both human and financial capital. The Government is attempting to create additional employment opportunities. It has sought (and received) assurance from the United States that there will be no mass deportation of Jamaicans residing in the United States without proper entry documents under the Immigration Reform and Control Act of 1986.

Spatial distribution/urbanization: Since most urban growth in Jamaica has taken place in the Kingston metropolitan area, the Government has formulated policies of industrial deconcentration and rural development, with special emphasis on rural medical and social services. The Government has focused on improving the quality of life in rural areas by revitalizing agriculture and implementing programmes of agrarian reform and integrated rural development. Efforts are made to improve rural communities by providing the necessary amenities, such as housing, access roads, water, electricity and community services. Measures are being taken to alleviate urban problems in the Kingston metropolitan area and to develop alternatives to it. With respect to regional planning, the Urban Development Corporation has initiated integrated development projects aimed at job creation, local resource allocation and provision of physical facilities.

Status of women and population: The development strategy incorporates policies to improve the status of women and increase employment opportunities for women. The Bureau of Women's Affairs of the Ministry of Youth and Community Affairs has been responsible for such activities since 1975. A home extension unit has been developed within the integrated rural development programme to assist women in small-scale agriculture. The minimum legal age at marriage for women is 16 years.

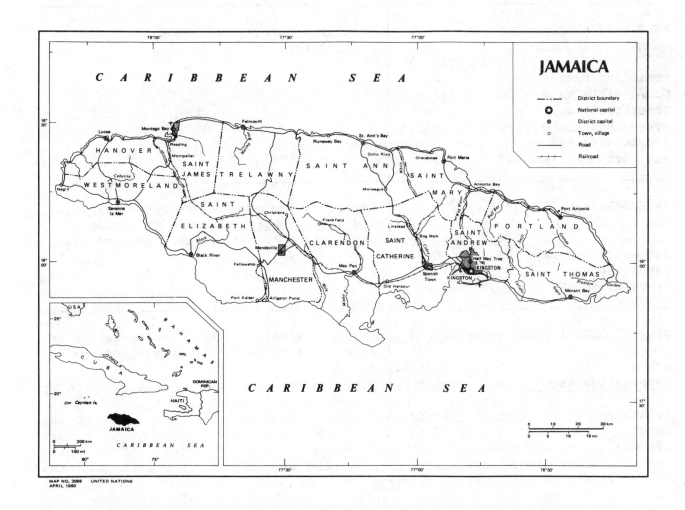

JAPAN

DEMOGRAPHIC INDICATORS	CURRENT PERCEPTION

SIZE/AGE STRUCTURE/GROWTH

Population:	1985	2025
(thousands)	120 742	132 082
0-14 years (%)	21.8	18.0
60+ years (%)	14.5	26.0

Rate of:	1980-85	2020-25
growth	0.7	-0.1
natural increase	6.6	-0.8

Population growth is viewed as satisfactory by the Government.

MORTALITY/MORBIDITY

	1980-85	2020-25
Life expectancy	76.9	78.2
Crude death rate	6.5	13.2
Infant mortality	6.5	4.8

The Government considers the present conditions of health, levels of mortality and life expectancy to be acceptable. However, there is concern over geriatric diseases such as cardio-vascular-renal diseases and cancer.

FERTILITY/NUPTIALITY/FAMILY

	1980-85	2020-25
Fertility rate	1.8	2.1
Crude birth rate	13.1	12.4
Contraceptive prevalence rate	64.0 (1986)	
Female mean age at first marriage	25.1 (1980)	

Fertility levels are viewed as being satisfactory.

INTERNATIONAL MIGRATION

	1980-85	2020-25
Net migration rate	0.0	0.0
Foreign-born population (%)	...	...

Levels of immigration are not significant and satisfactory. Emigration levels are unsatisfactory because they are too low.

SPATIAL DISTRIBUTION/URBANIZATION

Urban	1985	2025
population (%)	76.5	80.6

Growth rate:	1980-85	2020-25
urban	0.7	0.1
rural	0.4	-0.7

The spatial distribution of population is considered to be partially appropriate.

GENERAL POLICY FRAMEWORK

Overall approach to population problems: The Government's overriding population concerns are the rapid aging of the population and the inappropriate distribution of population. Efforts are under way to effect a more balanced population distribution and to improve the welfare of the aged.

Importance of population policy in achieving development objectives: The Government recognizes the need for integrating population and economic policies. Although it has called for "harmony between the population policies and the economic and social development policies within each country", it has not formulated any policies to influence demographic events in Japan.

INSTITUTIONAL FRAMEWORK

Population data systems and development planning: The most recent population census data were taken in October 1985. Vital registration is considered to be complete. The basic objectives of development planning have recently been articulated in the Fourth National Development Plan (1983-1990), which integrates various economic policies.

Integration of population within development planning: The Policy Planning and Evaluation Division, Minister's Secretariat, Ministry of Health and Welfare, is the sole governmental agency responsible for the formulation and co-ordination of population policies. The Economic Planning Agency and National Land Agency, established in 1952 and 1974, respectively, are responsible for taking into account population variables in planning. The Institute of Population Problems, Ministry of Health and Welfare, prepares population projections used in development and programme planning. It is also charged with the responsibility of special demographic surveys to meet specific planning needs.

POLICIES AND MEASURES

Changes in population size and age structure: The Government has no explicit policy to influence population growth. However, it is concerned with the consequences of the increasing number of the aged, and is, therefore, seeking effective solutions. Socio-economic policies have been formulated with the purpose of improving pension schemes and welfare benefits of the aged. Measures have also been undertaken to promote vocational training and employment exchange services for the middle-aged and elderly. Policy is aimed at revising upwards the mandatory retirement age. Reluctant to increase spending on social security programmes because of budget deficits, the Government is investigating the possibility of encouraging the aged to move overseas to retirement settlements, built and managed by private Japanese companies.

JAPAN

<u>Mortality and morbidity</u>: A comprehensive health care programme, <u>Kenko-Kanri</u>, has been implemented. Its multiple approach aims at integrating public health and clinical medicine. Special attention is paid to high-risk groups, among which are pregnant women with toxemia, premature or abnormally low-weight babies and those with tuberculosis. The activities of the health centres, of which there were 855 in 1980, include health consultation clinics, chest examinations, home visits, community health education, sanitation supervision, the promotion of family planning, maternal and child health, and counselling services on mental health. In view of the growing importance attached to the control of malignant neoplasms and cerebro-cardiovascular diseases, mass screening programmes for the early detection of stomach and uterine cancer and for the prevention of circulatory diseases have been intensified.

<u>Fertility and the family</u>: No policy has been formulated regarding fertility, because the Government believes that child-bearing should be a matter of individual choice. Nevertheless, through better housing, longer maternity leave and nurseries, the Government tries to improve conditions for young couples who wish to have children. The Government family planning programme has been in effect since 1952, and there is also support for the family planning activities of non-governmental organizations, such as the Japan Family Planning Association. While contraception is widely practised, hormone pills are generally illegal and may only be prescribed to control menstrual disorders. The Ministry of Health and Welfare is examining the possibility of lifting the ban on birth control pills. Women have been able to receive abortion on demand since 1948. Sterilization is permitted on certain grounds.

<u>International migration</u>: Immigration is not an active policy concern of the Government, given the insignificant number of foreigners in the country. The Government, nevertheless, has begun a crackdown on undocumented Asian immigrants working in Japan. Emigration policy is geared towards increasing the level of emigration in the future.

<u>Spatial distribution/urbanization</u>: Official policy is aimed at decreasing in-migration to the largest metropolitan areas, increasing in-migration to other urban areas; and decreasing out-migration from rural areas. The Third Comprehensive National Development Plan also intends to decentralize industry, promote well-balanced land distribution, and stabilize the rural population by encouraging modernization of agriculture and increasing job opportunities in the rural non-agricultural sector. The law of Emergent Counter-measures for Depopulated Communities, enacted in 1970 and revised in 1980, aims to provide assistance to communities suffering the adverse consequences of excessive depopulation.

<u>Status of women and population</u>: The role of women in the solution of population problems, particularly in family planning, is fully recognized by the Government; and the enhancement of women's status and the promotion of their social participation have been very strongly advocated. The Office of Planning and Promotion of Policies Relating to Women, chaired by the Prime Minister, has as its mandate promoting the implementation of policy relating to women and integrating it into national policy. The Equal Employment Opportunity Law, which went into effect in April 1986, promotes equal

opportunity and treatment of male and female workers. The law covers job advertising, hiring, placement, training, promotion, fringe benefits, retirements and dismissals. The minimum age at marriage for women is 16 years.

<u>Other issues</u>: The Government, as a donor country, anticipates the need for international co-operation in the form of technical or financial assistance in the field of population.

PREFECTURES OF JAPAN

1 Aichi	25 Miyazaki
2 Akita	26 Nagano
3 Aomori	27 Nagasaki
4 Chiba	28 Nara
5 Ehime	29 Niigata
6 Fukui	30 Oita
7 Fukuoka	31 Okayama
8 Fukushima	32 Okinawa
9 Gifu	33 Osaka
10 Gunma	34 Saga
11 Hiroshima	35 Saitama
12 Hokkaido	36 Shiga
13 Hyogo	37 Shimane
14 Ibaraki	38 Shizuoka
15 Ishikawa	39 Tochigi
16 Iwate	40 Tokushima
17 Kagawa	41 Tokyo
18 Kagoshima	42 Tottori
19 Kanagawa	43 Toyama
20 Kochi	44 Wakayama
21 Kumamoto	45 Yamagata
22 Kyoto	46 Yamaguchi
23 Mie	47 Yamanashi
24 Miyagi	

JAPAN

- –·–·– International boundary
- –––– Prefecture boundary
- National capital
- Prefecture capital
- Town
- International airport
- Bullet Train
- Railroad
- Expressway
- Main road

The boundaries and names shown on this map do not imply official endorsement or acceptance by the United Nations.

MAP NO. 3487   UNITED NATIONS
JUNE 1988

JORDAN

DEMOGRAPHIC INDICATORS	CURRENT PERCEPTION
SIZE/AGE STRUCTURE/GROWTH	The Government perceives current growth rates as <u>satisfactory</u>.

Population: <u>1985</u>   <u>2025</u>
 (thousands)   3 515   13 611
  0-14 years (%)   48.2   35.9
  60+ years (%)   4.1   5.0
 	
Rate of: <u>1980-85</u> <u>2020-25</u>
 growth   3.7   2.4
 natural increase 36.8 23.7	

MORTALITY/MORBIDITY	The level of mortality is regarded as <u>unacceptable</u>.
<u>1980-85</u> <u>2020-25</u> Life expectancy 63.7 74.6 Crude death rate 7.9 3.2 Infant mortality 54.1 14.4	
FERTILITY/NUPTIALITY/FAMILY	The level of fertility is viewed as <u>satisfactory</u>.
<u>1980-85</u> <u>2020-25</u> Fertility rate 7.4 3.1 Crude birth rate 44.7 26.9 Contraceptive prevalence rate 26.0 (1983) Female mean age at first marriage 22.6 (1981)	
INTERNATIONAL MIGRATION	The level of immigration is considered <u>significant</u> and <u>satisfactory</u>, while the level of emigration is considered <u>significant</u> and <u>too high</u>.
<u>1980-85</u> <u>2020-25</u> Net migration rate 0.0 0.0 Foreign-born population (%)	
SPATIAL DISTRIBUTION/URBANIZATION	The spatial distribution of the population is considered to be <u>partially appropriate</u>.
Urban <u>1985</u> <u>2025</u> population (%) 64.4 83.2 Growth rate: <u>1980-85</u> <u>2020-25</u> urban 5.1 2.7 rural 1.4 0.6	

GENERAL POLICY FRAMEWORK

Overall approach to population problems: The Government recognizes that population variables are directly linked to socio-economic development, and that there is a need to address demographic and socio-economic objectives within a common framework. Major objectives of the Government's development plan include the reduction of disparities between the various regions of Jordan, achievement of a more balanced pattern of population distribution, and increasing female participation in the labour force.

Importance of population policy in achieving development objectives: Although the Government has not adopted an explicit population policy, it regards the link between population policies and economic development as of utmost significance. Population planning is encouraged as a major tool to help reach a satisfactory accommodation between available resources and the legitimate expectations of the people for a better present and a promising future.

INSTITUTIONAL FRAMEWORK

Population data systems and development planning: The Department of Statistics is responsible for conducting population censuses and surveys. There is a Population Division in the Department, comprising the Demographic Analysis and Research Unit, the Manpower and Employment Section and the Vital Statistics Section. The Demographic Analysis and Research Unit was established in 1983. Population censuses were undertaken in 1961 and 1979. The 1979 census was only for the east bank of the Jordan River. The next census has tentatively been scheduled for 1989. In addition, several surveys were conducted, including the 1972 National Fertility Survey, the 1976 Fertility Survey, the 1981 Demographic Survey, and the 1983 Fertility and Family Health Survey. The Civil Status Department was established in 1977 to take full responsibility for civil registration. Registration of births is virtually complete, whereas deaths are still under-registered. Jordan has completed two five-year development plan periods and has launched the third plan for the period 1986-1990.

Integration of population within development planning: The National Population Commission was established in 1973 to plan and promote a national population policy. The Commission is chaired by the Minister of Labour and Social Development. It is mandated to advise the Government on all population and population-related matters, and to undertake, promote, and assist in policy-oriented research studies, training, and assessment of data gaps and needs. Population projections are prepared by the Department of Statistics.

JORDAN

POLICIES AND MEASURES

Changes in population size and age structure: The Government has not adopted an explicit population policy. There is no intervention to affect the size of the population, either directly or indirectly. However, the Government has been considering strategies to reach a stable population growth rate by manipulating known fertility determinants. The aim is to create gradually and steadily the necessary infrastructure and proper conditions for enhancing human welfare. The pension scheme covers private, governmental and public-sector employees, while excluding agricultural employees, the self-employed and family labour. Efforts are being undertaken ultimately to extend coverage to all residents. There is also a supplementary assistance scheme for needy elderly couples. The National Association for the Elderly has been created, with representatives of public agencies and voluntary associations, to energize and co-ordinate public and private efforts in the field of aging.

Mortality and morbidity: The Government has identified infants and children as being of special policy concern. A target infant mortality rate of 27 per thousand live births by the year 2000 has been specified. The objectives for the health sector include strengthening primary health care and preventive services, extending coverage to all citizens, increasing the quality and supply of health personnel, and expanding medical research. There is a Primary Health Care Project financed jointly by the Government and the World Bank, whose objective is to implement new ways of providing health services to the population.

Fertility and the family: The Government has no policy of intervention to affect the level of fertility but acknowledges the right of parents to decide the number and spacing of their children. It has supported the establishment of the Jordan Family Planning and Protection Association. Since 1979 the Ministry of Health has made contraceptive services available in some of its facilities but does not promote their use. The Maternal and Child Health/Family Planning project educates mothers about breast-feeding, child-spacing and health, in classes conducted at Maternal and Child Health Clinics. In 1983, a rural women's development project and the integration of family planning into rural health education programmes were initiated. Abortion is permitted only on medical and juridical grounds. Voluntary sterilization is permitted only for medical or health reasons.

International migration: The Government wishes to keep the level of immigration more or less constant and reduce the level of emigration. It has called for co-operation between labour-exporting and labour-importing countries so as to strengthen complementarity among countries and regions for the benefit of all. Although accurate data on the emigration of Jordanians and the immigration of foreign workers are not available, the Government has clearly recognized the problems associated with a substantial outflow of Jordanian workers to other countries and the importation of manpower from Arab and other countries. In 1986, the Government convened a conference of expatriates. The objectives were to attract increased investment in Jordan by Jordanian expatriates, to stimulate greater remittances by bringing Jordanians living abroad into the social security system and to provide a forum for expatriates to air their grievances. Following a previous conference, the Government had increased the number of university places specifically earmarked for children of Jordanians working abroad.

<u>Spatial distribution/urbanization</u>: Minor changes from the present pattern, such as changes between regions, are considered desirable. The main goals are to increase in-migration into rural areas, decrease in-migration into Amman, the capital and largest metropolitan area, increase out-migration from the other large metropolitan areas, and decrease out-migration from rural areas. To stimulate economic activity and stem migration, the Government announced that it would spend over $1 billion on housing, education and public works projects.

<u>Status of women and population</u>: As part of the Ministry of Labour and Social Development, the Department of Women's Affairs is charged with developing and harnessing the full potential of Jordanian women to meet the country's development goals. In the non-governmental sector, the Queen Noor Foundation seeks to promote and support programmes aimed at providing training, education, and employment for rural and urban women. Similarly, the Women's Union Federation promotes women's participation in development activities. The Government has proposed the establishment of a Commission on Women's Affairs, among other things, to promote the adoption of policies relating to the status of women. The minimum legal age at marriage for women is 17 years.

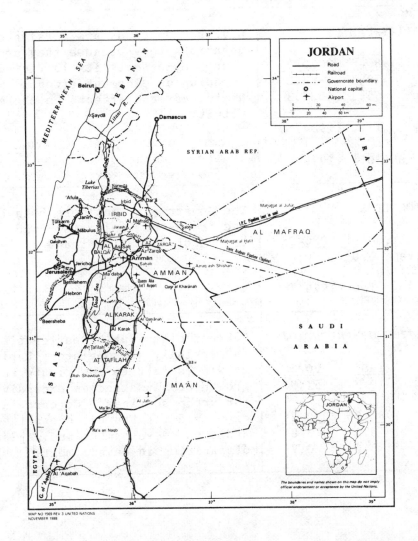

MAP NO 1569 REV 3 UNITED NATIONS
NOVEMBER 1988

KENYA

DEMOGRAPHIC INDICATORS	CURRENT PERCEPTION
SIZE/AGE STRUCTURE/GROWTH Population: 1985 / 2025 (thousands) 20 600 / 82 850 0-14 years (%) 52.5 / 37.3 60+ years (%) 3.0 / 4.2 Rate of: 1980-85 / 2020-25 growth 4.1 / 2.2 natural increase 41.0 / 22.2	The rate of growth is viewed as <u>unsatisfactory</u> because it is <u>too high</u> in relation to employment generation, the maintenance of the standard of living, the provision of social services, and resource availability.
MORTALITY/MORBIDITY 1980-85 / 2020-25 Life expectancy 52.9 / 68.1 Crude death rate 14.0 / 5.1 Infant mortality 80.2 / 27.8	Levels and trends are considered to be <u>unacceptable</u>. Of particular concern are infant and maternal mortality and the inadequacy of health services, especially in rural areas.
FERTILITY/NUPTIALITY/FAMILY 1980-85 / 2020-25 Fertility rate 8.1 / 3.2 Crude birth rate 55.1 / 27.3 Contraceptive prevalence rate 17.0 (1984) Female mean age at first marriage 20.4 (1979)	Levels and trends are considered to be <u>unsatisfactory</u> because they are too high. High fertility is viewed as impeding development efforts and as having adverse effects on the employment situation.
INTERNATIONAL MIGRATION 1980-85 / 2020-25 Net migration rate 0.0 / 0.0 Foreign-born population (%) 1.0 (1979)	The Government considers both the levels and trends of immigration and emigration to be <u>not significant</u> and <u>satisfactory</u>.
SPATIAL DISTRIBUTION/URBANIZATION Urban 1985 / 2025 population (%) 19.7 / 51.5 Growth rate: 1980-85 / 2020-25 urban 8.1 / 3.8 rural 3.2 / 0.7	Current distribution patterns are viewed as <u>partially appropriate</u>. Rapid urban growth is felt to contribute to the growth of slums and an excessive demand for urban services. Concern is also expressed for the balance between urban and rural development and regional disparities in development.

GENERAL POLICY FRAMEWORK

Overall approach to population problems: There is an official policy of direct intervention to modify demographic variables, combined with a policy of social and economic restructuring. Policies aim to decrease fertility, further reduce mortality and modify the spatial distribution of the population.

Importance of population policy in achieving development objectives: Population policy is seen as essential in meeting national development objectives and in serving the basic needs of the population. In recent years population has been a central concern in relation to resolving unemployment, rapid urbanization and other problems.

INSTITUTIONAL FRAMEWORK

Population data systems and development planning: The first complete census was conducted in 1948. Since 1969, censuses are conducted regularly every 10 years, the latest being held in 1979. Compulsory vital registration is considered incomplete. A formal system of development planning has existed since 1965, with the most recent plan being the development plan covering the period 1984-1988.

Integration of population within development planning: A Sectoral Planning Group on Population was established during preparation of the 1984-1988 development plan to ensure incorporation of demographic data into the development planning process. Under the plan, population policy and related matters are centralized in the National Council for Population and Development, which is based in the Office of the Vice-President and the Ministry of Home Affairs. Membership in the Council is drawn from government ministries and non-governmental agencies with population programmes and expertise in population matters.

POLICIES AND MEASURES

Changes in population size and age structure: Official policy is to decrease the rates of population growth and natural increase through direct governmental intervention. Central to this policy are the Government's efforts to decrease fertility levels, mainly by expanding and improving family planning services. Equally important are many socio-economic development programmes which are expected to reduce the rate of growth. These include decentralized planning and implementation of projects at the district level, so as to increase rural production and income, and expanding educational opportunities for women, in order to raise their status and reduce fertility rates. Finally, measures to adjust spatial distribution are expected to affect population growth. The official target was a 3.3 per cent rate of growth by 1988. The national pension scheme covers employed workers but excludes casual workers.

Mortality and morbidity: Official policy is to reduce the morbidity and mortality of the more vulnerable groups (especially infants, children and pregnant women) and to achieve a more equitable distribution of services between urban and rural areas. The Government has adopted a primary health care approach within a community-based health care system. Preventive and promotive health services are being emphasized. Specific measures include increasing the number of rural health and family planning centres and trained workers, improving methods for the early detection of communicable and vector-borne diseases, with an emphasis on mothers and children, and setting up community water supply and waste water projects. The official target is to increase life expectancy at birth to 60 years by the year 2000.

Fertility and the family: Official policy is to decrease fertility levels so as to decelerate the rapid population growth and improve family well-being. The President of Kenya stated in 1985 that women should have only four children and that maternity leave would not be granted for the fifth child and subsequent children. Family planning activities were introduced in Kenya in 1952, and the Government initiated the National Family Planning Programme in 1967. Fertility-related measures include maternal and child health care, the training of family planning personnel, population information and, indirectly, measures to raise the status of women and improve overall health, nutrition and education status. To expand the availability of contraceptives, the Government intends to increase the number of maternal and child health/family planning delivery points from 850 in 1986 to 1,550 by 1990. In 1984 two laws were passed facilitating access to contraception. The Sales Tax Act eliminated the sales tax on contraceptives, while the Customs and Excise Act removed the duty on the importation of contraceptives. Access to contraception is not limited and receives direct support from the Government. Abortion is illegal except for certified health reasons. Sterilization is legal. The Government's targets are to recruit more than 2.9 million family planning acceptors by 1988 and to reduce the total fertility rate to 5.2 by the year 2000.

International migration: The Government has not outlined an explicit policy with regard to the low levels of immigration and emigration. Citing an upsurge of unrest, the President of Kenya in March 1987 ordered the expulsion of undocumented migrants from neighbouring African countries residing in Kenya. To alleviate problems associated with the brain drain, skilled Kenyans are encouraged to return to Kenya.

Spatial distribution/urbanization: Official policy is to modify the pattern of spatial distribution by raising agricultural productivity and by developing certain regions in order to improve the rural/urban balance. An integrated rural development strategy is being pursued, partly in order to curb rural-to-urban migration. The Government has implemented an extensive variety of rural-oriented direct measures to modify spatial distribution. These include provision of agricultural credit, improvement of agricultural marketing, rural co-operatives, infrastructure development, communications and transport expansion, regional development, and housing and environmental improvement. Other relevant measures include export-oriented industralization and the planned location of industrial centres.

Status of women and population: The Government recognizes that expanding the educational and employment opportunities available to women is essential if fertility levels are to decrease, and it has begun taking measures to promote those opportunities. The minimum legal age at marriage for women varies between nine and 18 years, depending on major administrative division and religious and ethnic group.

Other issues: Programmes are being considered for population education and communication in the formal and non-formal sectors and for strengthening the technical capacity of the National Council for Population and Development.

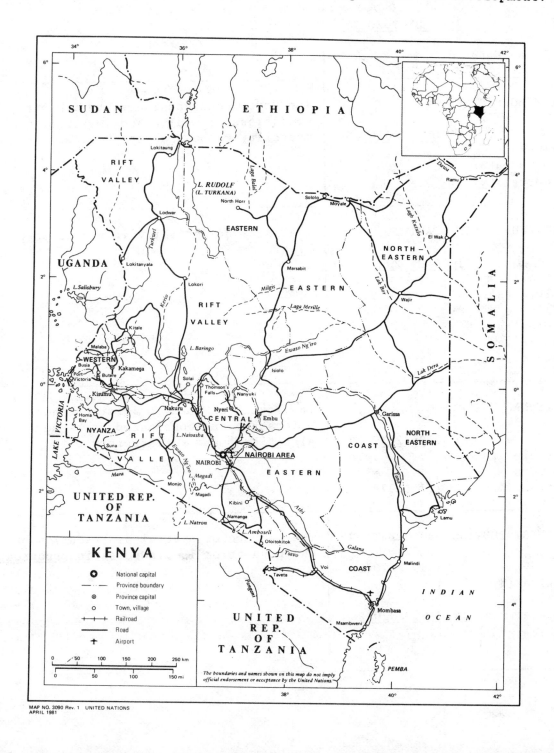

KIRIBATI

DEMOGRAPHIC INDICATORS	CURRENT PERCEPTION
SIZE/AGE STRUCTURE/GROWTH Population: 1985 2025 (thousands) 56 89 0-14 years (%) ... ... 60+ years (%) ... ... Rate of: 1980-85 2020-25 growth 1.6 ... natural increase	The present rate of population growth is considered to be <u>too high</u>.
MORTALITY/MORBIDITY 1980-85 2020-25 Life expectancy ... ... Crude death rate ... ... Infant mortality	The Government considers the present conditions of health and levels of mortality to be <u>unacceptable</u>.
FERTILITY/NUPTIALITY/FAMILY 1980-85 2020-25 Fertility rate ... ... Crude birth rate ... ... Contraceptive prevalence rate ... ... Female mean age at first marriage	The level of fertility is viewed as <u>too high</u>.
INTERNATIONAL MIGRATION 1980-85 2020-25 Net migration rate ... ... Foreign-born population (%) 2.7 (1978)	The levels of both immigration and emigration are considered to be <u>not significant</u> and <u>satisfactory</u>.
SPATIAL DISTRIBUTION/URBANIZATION Urban 1985 2025 population (%) 34.0 ... Growth rate: 1980-85 2020-25 urban ... ... rural	The pattern of spatial distribution of the population is viewed as <u>inappropriate</u>.

GENERAL POLICY FRAMEWORK

Overall approach to population problems: The Government's overall objective is to decrease the rate of population growth, provide for the health of individuals and reduce mortality, with particular emphasis on infant mortality, and improve the pattern of spatial distribution.

Importance of population policy in achieving development objectives: Although there is no explicit population policy, national development plans have stressed the importance of taking into account population variables for achieving development objectives. A National Population and Development Co-ordinating Committee has been formed, signalling the Government's awareness of the importance of population policy.

INSTITUTIONAL FRAMEWORK

Population data systems and development planning: Data collection is the responsibility of the Statistics Unit, which is under the Ministry of Finance and Development. Population censuses have been held since 1921, the last two being in 1978 and 1985. A population and housing census is provisionally planned for 1990. The Registrar's Office, which is in the Ministry of Home Affairs, is responsible for the registration of vital statistics. Vital registration is incomplete. There is no formal co-ordination reported between the Statistics Unit and the Registrar-General's Office. The Immigration Office collects information on arrivals. The Ministry of Planning and Development is responsible for planning and co-ordinating development activities. Two four-year national development plans have been undertaken since the country's independence in 1979. The latest available plan is for the period 1983-1986.

Integration of population within development planning: A National Population and Development Co-ordinating Committee was set up in 1980 to develop population policies, priorities and programmes, and to implement and monitor such programmes. Population projections have been prepared by the Statistics Unit since 1982. The Ministry of Health and Family Planning is also responsible for the integration of population variables in planning.

POLICIES AND MEASURES

Changes in population size and age structure: The Government's objective was to achieve an annual population growth rate of 1.6 per cent by the end of 1986 and of 0 by the year 2000, chiefly by means of family planning programmes. Measures include providing education and advice on family planning methods, and referral systems for vasectomies and tubectomies. The Government has indicated its commitment to maintaining the balance between population and natural resources; the special geographical circumstances of the islands

KIRIBATI

impose limits on the size of the population that can be accommodated. The social security system includes pension benefits for employees earning at least $10 a month.

Mortality and morbidity: The Government intends to implement the strategy of "Health for All by the Year 2000". By 1986 health services were expected to cater to 85 per cent of the population in order to prevent and control 13 specified priority problems. Infant and child mortality are of special policy concern in reference to current levels of mortality. Among the major diseases that are given priority are respiratory tract diseases, diarrhoeal diseases, communicable (tuberculosis/leprosy) diseases and non-communicable diseases. Health services, including drugs, are free. The first national health system for the years 1982-1986 reorganized health services on the basis of the primary health care approach. Programmes were redefined and integrated into an overall strategy focusing on rural health improvement, based on village welfare groups receiving support from the health services. The second national health system plan for 1987-1991 continues the same strategy. The Health Education Unit of the Ministry of Health and Community Affairs is responsible for increasing public awareness of good health practices.

Fertility and the family: The Government intends to reduce the level of fertility, both to modify the effect of fertility on the rate of population growth and to improve maternal and child health and family well-being. Family planning programmes and measures for the improvement of the status of women are designed to achieve a total fertility rate of 2.0 by the year 2000. Dissemination of information on, and access to, all methods of contraception are permitted by law. Eighty-five per cent of the population was expected to have access to family planning services by 1986. The family planning goal for the use of contraception by women was 85 per cent of those in child-bearing ages by 1986. Family planning services are integrated with maternal and child health. The main non-governmental family planning activity has been carried out since 1981 by the Christian Family Life Centre, which promotes "natural family planning". The Federation of Women's Organizations includes family planning education in its programmes. Abortion is legal if there is any risk to a woman's life. There is no information readily available on the status of sterilization.

International migration: Immigration and emigration are not active policy concerns of the Government.

Spatial distribution/urbanization: The primary goal is to modify the urban/rural balance by decreasing in-migration to the urban areas and decreasing out-migration from rural areas. Measures that have been taken include rural development, decentralization and resettlement. The Government has pointed out the shortage of land in the Gilbert Island group while huge areas of land, lagoon and coastal waters are being under-exploited or not used at all in the Line and Phoenix groups. The latter two groups are targets for resettlement. The aims of decentralization have been to strengthen local governmental councils so that they may become self-reliant in meeting the internal needs of the islands. Budgetary aid in the form of support grants will continue to be disbursed to island councils on the basis of population as a proportion of the national recurrent budget. Alternative methods of local revenue collecting, more in keeping with rural practices, are encouraged. In 1983, 63 families were settled on land on Kiritmati, as part of a plan to develop the island, which comprises more than half of the total land area of Kiribati, as an alternative economic centre to South Tarawa. In early 1988 the Government was studying the possibility of launching an integrated rural development project on one of the outer islands.

Status of women and population: The Community Affairs Division of the Ministry of Health and Community Affairs was established in 1976 to co-ordinate government efforts in community work. The Women's Interest Section of the Division assists the Government in all matters pertaining to women. The National Women's Federation, a non-governmental organization, plays an important part in stimulating community activity and social and economic progress, and in recreational and sports activities. There is no information readily available on the minimum legal age at marriage for women.

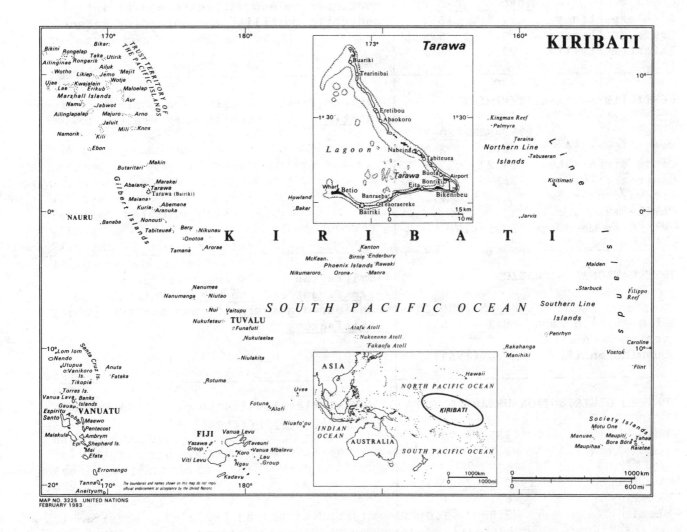

MAP NO. 3225 UNITED NATIONS
FEBRUARY 1983

KUWAIT

DEMOGRAPHIC INDICATORS	CURRENT PERCEPTION

SIZE/AGE STRUCTURE/GROWTH

Population:	1985	2025
(thousands)	1 811	4 828
0-14 years (%)	40.0	28.3
60+ years (%)	2.5	11.4

Rate of:	1980-85	2020-25
growth	5.5	1.4
natural increase	36.0	13.9

The Government considers current growth rates to be unsatisfactory because they are too low. The high growth rate is perceived as a positive contribution to socio-economic development.

MORTALITY/MORBIDITY

	1980-85	2020-25
Life expectancy	71.6	76.9
Crude death rate	3.3	5.5
Infant mortality	23.0	8.7

Levels and trends are considered acceptable; however, the Government continues to express concern over infant and child mortality and morbidity issues.

FERTILITY/NUPTIALITY/FAMILY

	1980-85	2020-25
Fertility rate	6.1	2.5
Crude birth rate	39.2	19.4
Contraceptive prevalence rate	...	...
Female mean age at first marriage	20.5 (1975)	

Current fertility rates are perceived as unsatisfactory because they are too low.

INTERNATIONAL MIGRATION

	1980-85	2020-25
Net migration rate	18.8	0.0
Foreign-born population (%)	59.8 (1985)	

Immigration levels are considered significant and too high. Emigration is considered not significant and satisfactory.

SPATIAL DISTRIBUTION/URBANIZATION

Urban	1985	2025
population (%)	93.5	99.2

Growth rate:	1980-85	2020-25
urban	6.2	1.4
rural	-2.8	-1.0

Spatial distribution is perceived as partially appropriate.

GENERAL POLICY FRAMEWORK

Overall approach to population problems: The main goal of Kuwait's population policy is to achieve a balance between the size of population and economic resources in order to maintain an acceptable standard of living and to improve the well-being of individuals. A major problem is the lack of trained, native workers. Because of concern over the small proportion of native Kuwaitis in the population, the Government has opted to raise fertility among the nationals. Concern over the extreme concentration of the urban population has also prompted the Government to adopt strategies to deconcentrate the population.

Importance of population policy in achieving development objectives: The Government of Kuwait has designated population policy as an important and integral component of economic and social planning. The Government sees an organic link between population trends and socio-economic development and believes that social and economic change should serve as the basis for solving problems associated with demographic characteristics.

INSTITUTIONAL FRAMEWORK

Population data systems and development planning: The first modern Kuwaiti census was taken in 1957. At independence in 1961 the Government held a census; subsequent censuses have been conducted at regular five-year intervals beginning in 1965, with the most recent census having been conducted in 1985. The registration of births and deaths was made compulsory in 1964. Vital registration is considered relatively complete. The Government only recently decided to formalize development planning with a new economic plan for 1985/86-1989/90. Prior to that, the Government had established sets of economic guidelines for 1967/68-1971/72 and 1975/76-1980/81.

Integration of population within development planning: No single governmental agency is responsible for formulating population policies. However, since 1972, the General Department for Planning Affairs within the Ministry of Planning has been responsible for taking into account population variables in planning. Since 1964, the Ministry of Planning has prepared population projections for use in the planning process. The Central Statistical Office is charged with conducting censuses and special demographic surveys to meet planning needs.

POLICIES AND MEASURES

Changes in population size and age structure: The Government's policy consists of encouraging an increase in the native-born population through the use of social measures and an emphasis on improved health care. The Government wishes to limit the size of its immigrant population. The social security scheme covers employed and self-employed workers.

KUWAIT

Mortality and morbidity: The Government's policy is to provide the population with a well-developed, free health-care system. The goals are to promote and maintain the health of the population, improve their physical, mental, and social well-being, and reduce mortality, morbidity, and disabilities. The introduction of comprehensive health-care planning in 1979 was followed by the General Frame of Policies and Strategies to the Year 2000, which identified areas and problems for further study. In 1982, the Government introduced the Kuwait Health Plan to the Year 2000 and enunciated issues to be dealt with and targets to be reached. The Government established programmes for public health, licensing and training of medical service personnel, and health education. Morbidity issues for children are specified as infectious diseases, infant pneumonia, and intestinal diseases. Additional morbidity and mortality concerns are motor vehicle accidents and heart disease. The Government aims to reduce infant mortality to 10 per 1,000 and child mortality from mumps, rubella, and tuberculosis by 20-30 per cent every two years, and from intestinal diseases by 25 per cent every 10 years. Additional targets include reducing the rate of home and traffic accidents by 15 per cent every five years and reducing cardio-vascular diseases by 25 per cent every 10 years.

Fertility and the family: The Government has a policy to boost fertility rates among the national population. Government objectives are to improve the status of women and create conditions conducive to child-birth and parenting. The Government provides cash benefits by means of child allowances, maternity benefits and housing subsidies to families with a male Kuwaiti in government service. Since 1980, Kuwaitis marrying for the first time have been entitled to a marriage allowance. In 1986 the Government required both the public and the private sector to grant paid leave to employees marrying for the first time. The provision of family planning services is not considered a priority. Access to contraception is permitted, but without government support for information or access to methods. Abortion and sterilization are permitted only for medical or health reasons. In 1984, the highest religious authority in Kuwait gave approval to test-tube fertilization for married couples.

International migration: Immigration policy is to maintain the inflow of labour resources to alleviate shortages but to reduce the level in the future. The policy favours the migration of males, while discouraging the entry of dependents. The immigrant population in 1985 comprised approximately 60 per cent of Kuwait's total population and about 70 per cent of the labour force. Formal legislation regulates the employment of foreign workers. A 1979 decree requires work permits for foreigners in the private sector. Attempts are under way to encourage the replacement of non-nationals in important positions with Kuwaitis. In 1982 a new citizenship law was enacted which tightened restrictions on obtaining Kuwaiti citizenship. Arab nationals residing in Kuwait for at least 20 years, or 15 consecutive years, may qualify for citizenship, provided other eligibility requirements are met. Concerning emigration, there is a desire to prevent a brain-drain by retaining migrant labour with important skills and expertise.

Spatial distribution/urbanization: The Government's policy is to influence directly the pattern of urban settlement in order to resolve problems of urban overcrowding. The highly urbanized population is concentrated on 6 per cent of the land area, while 30 per cent of the total population resides in the capital city agglomeration. Policy objectives are to redistribute the urban population and continue to provide a high level of public service. The basic strategy is the promotion of small towns and intermediate cities, supplemented by the creation of new towns. In recent years, the Government has invested in three large industrial zones, a new port, and the reconstruction of Kuwait City. Additional measures include public infrastructure subsidies, financial incentives to new industry, the provision of housing and social services, human resource investment, and job training.

Status of women and population: Government policy consists of improving the status of women and encouraging greater female labour-force participation. The Women's Committee within the Government discusses women's problems and carries out research to promote the abilities of women. The Committee co-ordinates its work with the Women's Centre for Training. The mean age at marriage for Kuwaiti women is reportedly rising. Information on the minimum age at marriage for women is not readily available.

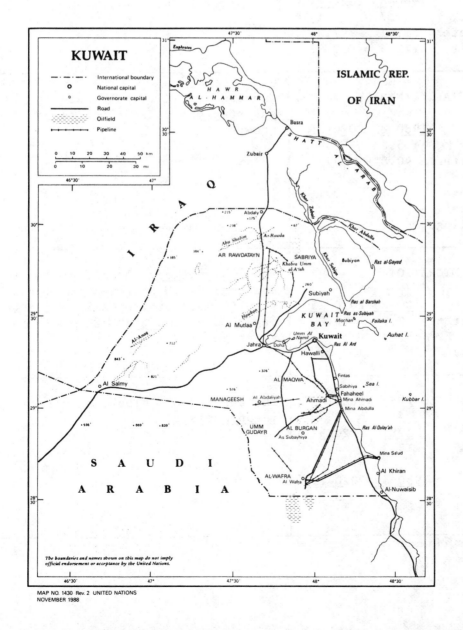

LAO PEOPLE'S DEMOCRATIC REPUBLIC

DEMOGRAPHIC INDICATORS	CURRENT PERCEPTION
SIZE/AGE STRUCTURE/GROWTH	The Government perceives current rates of population growth as <u>unsatisfactory</u> and <u>too low</u>.

Population:	1985	2025
(thousands)	4 117	8 576
0-14 years (%)	42.5	27.4
60+ years (%)	5.1	8.2

Rate of:	1980-85	2020-25
growth	2.2	1.2
natural increase	25.1	12.0

DEMOGRAPHIC INDICATORS	CURRENT PERCEPTION
MORTALITY/MORBIDITY	Health conditions and mortality levels are regarded as <u>unacceptable</u>.

	1980-85	2020-25
Life expectancy	49.7	67.1
Crude death rate	15.7	7.3
Infant mortality	122.5	39.8

DEMOGRAPHIC INDICATORS	CURRENT PERCEPTION
FERTILITY/NUPTIALITY/FAMILY	Current fertility rates are considered <u>satisfactory</u> in relation to population growth.

	1980-85	2020-25
Fertility rate	5.8	2.3
Crude birth rate	40.8	19.3
Contraceptive prevalence rate	...	...
Female mean age at first marriage	...	...

DEMOGRAPHIC INDICATORS	CURRENT PERCEPTION
INTERNATIONAL MIGRATION	The <u>insignificant</u> levels of immigration are considered <u>satisfactory</u>. The <u>significant</u> level of emigration is regarded as <u>too high</u> because of manpower shortages.

	1980-85	2020-25
Net migration rate	-2.9	0.0
Foreign-born population (%)	...	...

DEMOGRAPHIC INDICATORS	CURRENT PERCEPTION
SPATIAL DISTRIBUTION/URBANIZATION	The spatial distribution is regarded as <u>inappropriate</u>.

Urban	1985	2025
population (%)	15.9	44.5

Growth rate:	1980-85	2020-25
urban	5.5	3.1
rural	1.7	-0.2

GENERAL POLICY FRAMEWORK

Overall approach to population problems: The Government perceives its rate of population growth not as problematic, but rather as necessary for the effective utilization of the country's resources. Informal policies exist to modify the rate. Policies are also in effect which aim at reducing mortality and morbidity and socio-economic restructuring.

Importance of population policy in achieving development objectives: Although the role of population policy in the achievement of national development objectives is widely recognized, the Government has not yet formulated a comprehensive policy, because of the lack of demographic data. The 1985 census results are expected to provide insight into the relationships between population and development variables.

INSTITUTIONAL FRAMEWORK

Population data systems and development planning: Population data have been scanty. The first complete census of population was conducted in March 1985. The vital registration system is considered incomplete. An infrastructure for the collection of demographic data was initiated in 1984. A sample fertility and mortality survey was carried out in 1986 in order to approximate the rate of natural increase. The Second Five-Year Economic and Social Development Plan, 1986-1990, is currently in effect.

Integration of population within development planning: The lack of demographic data, coupled with problems of transport and communication has hindered the planning process. The Government is gradually integrating population matters into development planning, but at present there is no specific institution responsible for doing so. The 1985 census is expected to provide an important input into the 1986-1990 Development Plan. The State Statistics Centre within the State Planning Committee is the central unit for the collection of statistical data from ministries and from the provinces.

POLICIES AND MEASURES

Changes in population size and age structure: Although there is no formulated policy of intervention with regard to population size and age structure, there exist some informal policies that may affect demographic variables. Family planning services are available on a limited basis as a means of child-spacing but not for the purpose of reducing population growth. They are viewed as a way of reducing health risks, while maintaining an acceptable rate of population growth. As a result of the 1985 census, the official estimate of the average annual rate of population growth has been revised upwards to 2.9. Information on the status of pension schemes is not readily available.

LAO PEOPLE'S DEMOCRATIC REPUBLIC

Mortality and morbidity: Governmental policy aims at the reduction of morbidity and mortality through improved medical services available to the entire population. The policy orientation is to integrate fully primary health care into the socio-economic development plans of the country. The main objectives of the health care strategy are to control and eradicate endemic diseases, provide maternal and child health care throughout the country, and improve nutrition, hygiene and sanitation in the rural areas. The other priorities are to renovate and re-equip referral hospitals and to increase the number of doctors and other health personnel and the training for health workers, village nurses and traditional birth attendants. The Government is working towards a goal of universal child immunization.

Fertility and the family: Since the Government supports an increase in population size in the long run, it favours the current levels of fertility. The official policy is to maintain the fertility levels so as to have a steady population growth. At the same time, the official policy encourages child-spacing as a means of reducing the possible health risks faced by mothers and children. There is no official family planning programme. Contraceptives are available through pharmacies, but the Government does not promote the use of contraceptives through the health care system or any government agencies. Spacing of pregnancies for reasons of health is encouraged by the Government, and couples are free to determine the size of their families. Prescriptions for contraceptives are available only from physicians. The Government provides maternity leave and child allowances. Abortion and sterilization are permitted only with the special approval of the Ministry of Health.

International migration: There is no officialy formulated policy in regard to immigration and emigration. In recent years there has been no immigration into the country. During the long period of war, however, a significant number of people fled to neighbouring countries as refugees. As of mid 1986, approximately 90,000 Laotians were in Thailand under the care of the United Nations High Commissioner for Refugees. A programme of voluntary repatriation is in effect which, since the programme's initiation in 1980, has repatriated about 3,000 Laotians. Though there is no specific policy on the matter, the Government, which has urgent labour force shortages, welcomes the return of Laotians who left the country after 1975. The Government also wishes to control emigration, in order to meet labour force requirements for the country's reconstruction and development.

Spatial distribution/urbanization: Although there is no officially stated policy with regard to the spatial distribution of the population, the Government does have some programmes aimed at resettling certain populations and at eliminating slash-and-burn cultivation. Redistribution and relocation of the population for economic and demographic reasons is not a major concern, nor are problems related to high urban concentration. The main concerns of the Government are in regard to the resettlement of war-related displaced persons and the mountain people. In the absence of explicit regional development policies, the Government has programmes in the areas of agriculture and rural development, industrialization, transportation and infrastructure development. Development plans include modernization of agriculture, irrigation and water control, soil and plant protection, rural electrification etc. The Government encourages agro-based industries which utilize local raw materials and primary-sector production.

<u>Status of women and population</u>: The Government has extensive policies aimed at improving the status of women. There are policies to encourage full-time participation of women in the labour force. Employment opportunities are equally available to men and women, with equal pay for both and no legal restriction for women. Sons and daughters have been officially declared equal by the Government, and equal education opportunities are provided. The Lao Patriotic Women's Association is actively participating in government programmes for the improvement of women's status. The Association also works to raise the political consciousness of women, to eradicate illiteracy, and to strengthen health and sanitation facilities. There is no information readily available on the minimum legal age at marriage for women.

LEBANON

DEMOGRAPHIC INDICATORS	CURRENT PERCEPTION
SIZE/AGE STRUCTURE/GROWTH	Current rates of population growth are considered to be satisfactory.
Population: 1985 2025	
(thousands) 2 668 5 221	
0-14 years (%) 37.5 25.7	
60+ years (%) 7.8 11.4	
Rate of: 1980-85 2020-25	
growth 0.0 1.3	
natural increase 20.5 12.9	
MORTALITY/MORBIDITY	Current mortality levels are considered to be unacceptable.
1980-85 2020-25	
Life expectancy 65.0 75.1	
Crude death rate 8.8 5.6	
Infant mortality 48.0 13.2	
FERTILITY/NUPTIALITY/FAMILY	Current fertility rates are viewed as satisfactory.
1980-85 2020-25	
Fertility rate 3.8 2.4	
Crude birth rate 29.3 18.5	
Contraceptive prevalence rate 53.0 (1971)	
Female mean age at first marriage	
INTERNATIONAL MIGRATION	The levels of immigration and emigration are believed to be significant and considered to be unsatisfactory.
1980-85 2020-25	
Net migration rate -20.6 0.0	
Foreign-born population (%)	
SPATIAL DISTRIBUTION/URBANIZATION	The Government views the pattern of spatial distribution as inappropriate.
Urban 1985 2025	
population (%) 80.1 91.8	
Growth rate: 1980-85 2020-25	
urban 1.4 1.4	
rural -4.7 0.5	

GENERAL POLICY FRAMEWORK

Overall approach to population problems: In order to alleviate demographic problems, which have been greatly affected by the severe economic and political situation, the Government has given security and national reconstruction programmes its highest priority. National goals are to improve the living standard of all citizens through national reconstruction projects in the social services. A specific population programme is viewed as not likely to succeed at present due to ethnic, religious, psychological and political differences, which in the past have created obstacles and barriers to the formation of a population policy acceptable to all concerned. An appeal to the international community by the Government has been made for experts to devise ways of solving the population problems.

Importance of population policy in achieving development objectives: The Government recognizes that overall socio-economic development is the most effective way to resolve demographic problems. The present unstable economic and political conditions, however, do not permit the initiation of large-scale development projects. Government priorities therefore are to restore public services and repair damage to structures.

INSTITUTIONAL FRAMEWORK

Population data systems and development planning: A population census has not been taken since 1932. A sample survey was conducted in 1970. Vital registration of births and deaths is considered to be incomplete. In 1977 the Government established the Council for Development and Reconstruction to replace the former Ministry of Planning. An eight-year reconstruction plan was prepared in 1978 and later revised in 1983. Due to a renewed outbreak of fighting, the reconstruction and development plan was interrupted and has now become outdated. A new revision is anticipated.

Integration of population within development planning: A National Population Council has been established, the objectives of which are to monitor population trends and their impact on development, create public awareness of population issues, prepare a national census including studies and surveys and creating links with relevant regional and international, governmental and non-governmental agencies. The Council so far lacks funding to carry out its programme, given other priorities brought about by the country's political turmoil.

POLICIES AND MEASURES

Changes in population size and age structure: Events in Lebanon since 1975 have influenced population size and growth. Since the onset of war there have been increases in the number of refugees arriving, and in the number of Lebanese emigrating. It is estimated that over 50,000 people have been

LEBANON

killed, and the number of orphans has risen to 75,000. A pension scheme provides benefits to public employees and employees in industry, commerce and agriculture.

Mortality and morbidity: As a result of the current recession induced by the worsening security problem, there has been a general decline in living standards. Education, health, water supply and housing facilities have experienced enormous physical damage to structures and equipment. Public health services have also been paralysed due to the large-scale emigration of personnel. Consequently, infant mortality rates have increased. In order to remedy the deteriorating situation, the Government has implemented national reconstruction projects with priorities in the areas of housing, education, road construction, drinking water and waste management, electricity and health. With international assistance an expanded programme of immunizaion began in 1986 for 150,000 children and is designed to reach full immunization by 1990.

Fertility and the family: Although there is no official policy concerning fertility rates, the Government acknowledges that among certain population groups demographic problems are associated with large families and inadequate spacing of children. Family planning services are, in part, provided in clinics of the Ministry of Labour and Social Welfare and by the Lebanese Army. The Lebanese Family Planning Association receives government support for improving maternal and child health and family welfare. Because of the current situation, the Association is one of the few organizations still able to provide social services to the population. In 1983 provisions of the Penal Code restricting the sale, acquisition and use of contraceptives were repealed. Maternity benefits consist of maternity leave of up to 40 days and cash benefits covering 100 per cent of wages, paid by the social security scheme. As of 1983, sterilization was included among the family planning services provided by the Ministry of Health. Abortion is only permitted in order to save the life of the mother.

International migration: The Government has not expressed any explicit policies concerning immigration or emigration. It is aware, however, that the levels of international migration have been drastically affected by the tension and conflict. With the influx of refugees - their numbers at times equal to a quarter of the indigenous population - social services have been placed under enormous strain. Hundreds of thousands of Lebanese have been displaced both within the country and abroad. Emigration has taken place on a large scale, drastically affecting the operation of public health services.

Spatial distribution/urbanization: The Government is concerned with the inappropriate concentration of population in Greater Beirut and southern Lebanon. The advent of the war, however, has made it impossible to implement any specific development plan to remedy the overcrowded situation in Beirut. The internal migration flow of dislocated families to southern Lebanon is also the result of the hostilities and has created severe over-population in the region. Owing to the deterioration of living conditions in urban areas, a substantial migration towards rural areas has taken place. In a study prepared for the Council of Development and Reconstruction, an organization created by the Government of Lebanon in 1977, 450,000 persons were estimated to have been displaced. Due to the political turmoil, Government policies concerning internal migration accord high priority to basic relief needs and projects dealing with repair and rehabilitation.

Status of women and population: In 1983, a national conference was held by the Lebanese Family Planning Association to evaluate the status of women. A proposal to create a National Council for Women's Affairs was also addressed. The legal minimum age at marriage for women varies between 12-18 years, according to the practices of the major religious and ethnic groups.

LESOTHO

DEMOGRAPHIC INDICATORS	CURRENT PERCEPTION

SIZE/AGE STRUCTURE/GROWTH
 	
Population: 1985   2025
 (thousands)   1 520   3 877
  0-14 years (%)   42.3   33.1
  60+ years (%)   5.7   7.1
 	
Rate of: 1980-85 2020-25
 growth   2.5   1.6
 natural increase   25.3   16.2
	The rate of population growth is felt to be <u>too high</u>. The Government has indicated that the growth rate far exceeds the rate at which it can deliver basic services.

MORTALITY/MORBIDITY 1980-85 2020-25 Life expectancy 49.3 65.2 Crude death rate 16.5 7.5 Infant mortality 111.1 35.5	The present conditions of health and levels of mortality are regarded as <u>unacceptable</u>. Children under five years of age and mothers are identified as being of special policy concern.
FERTILITY/NUPTIALITY/FAMILY 1980-85 2020-25 Fertility rate 5.8 2.9 Crude birth rate 41.8 23.6 Contraceptive prevalence rate 5.0 (1977) Female mean age at first marriage 20.5 (1977)	The level of fertility is viewed as <u>unsatisfactory</u> and <u>too high</u>.
INTERNATIONAL MIGRATION 1980-85 2020-25 Net migration rate 0.0 0.0 Foreign-born population (%)	The level of immigration is considered to be <u>not significant</u> and <u>satisfactory</u>, while the level of emigration is considered to be <u>significant</u> and <u>too high</u>.
SPATIAL DISTRIBUTION/URBANIZATION Urban 1985 2025 population (%) 16.7 47.6 Growth rate: 1980-85 2020-25 urban 6.7 3.3 rural 1.8 0.2	The pattern of spatial distribution of the population is considered to be <u>partially appropriate</u>.

GENERAL POLICY FRAMEWORK

Overall approach to population problems: Lesotho has shifted its policy from a position of caution on population issues to one of recognizing the need to moderate and effectively manage population growth so as to keep pace with the country's economic growth. The main goals of Lesotho's demographic policy are to reduce population growth by decreasing fertility levels and through a programme of economic and social restructuring, to provide for the health of all individuals, to enhance job opportunities and living conditions, and to improve the pattern of spatial distribution. The Government stresses the importance of the religious and cultural traditions of the Basotho in designing population programmes.

Importance of population policy in achieving development objectives: The Government has adopted population management as an integral part of overall national development policies and strategies, hoping to ensure improvement in the quality of life of the people. As a result, the Government wants to bring Lesotho's population into line with economic growth rates.

INSTITUTIONAL FRAMEWORK

Population data systems and development planning: Lesotho has conducted decennial population censuses since 1926. The last population and housing census was conducted in April 1986. The Central Bureau of Statistics has been responsible for conducting censuses and surveys since 1966. As part of its integrated programme of collecting relevant data for the formulation of a comprehensive population policy, the Central Bureau of Statistics conducted the Lesotho Fertility Survey in 1977 and the Migration and Manpower Survey in 1978/79. Vital registration is incomplete. Since 1969, Lesotho has completed three five-year planning periods. The latest five-year development plan was for 1980/81-1984/85. The change of government in January 1986 caused a delay in issuing the fourth development plan, for the period 1986-1991.

Integration of population within development planning: There is no special unit established for the integration of population into development planning. The Government has assigned several ministeries, particularly the Ministry of Health, to formulate policies and implement programmes to achieve that objective. The Central Planning and Development Office, of the Ministry of Planning, Employment and Economic Affairs, is the governmental agency responsible for co-ordinating development projects and programmes.

POLICIES AND MEASURES

Changes in population size and age structure: The Government has a policy of decreasing the rate of growth, chiefly by means of reducing fertility levels. Although no target date is specified, the Government is committed to reducing the population growth rate to 2.0 per cent and has emphasized the importance of family planning as a means of achieving the target. No information is readily available on the status of pension schemes.

Mortality and morbidity: The Government has accorded high priority to reducing the incidence of infant and childhood diseases, particularly communicable diseases such as diarrhoea, measles and tuberculosis, reducing malnutrition and promoting proper sanitation. Continuing efforts are under way to strengthen the primary health care approach by creating the necessary health infrastructure and training personnel. One of the strategies implemented to improve child survival has been to expand the programme of immunization and maternal and child health to cover all communities by the year 1990. The goal is to immunize fully 90 per cent of infants by the year 1990.

Fertility and the family: The major objective is to modify the effect of fertility on the rate of population growth and to improve maternal and child health and family well-being. The Government aims at reducing fertility levels chiefly by means of family planning programmes. The Government believes that it is a basic human right of individuals and couples to decide freely on the number and spacing of their children. The Government's role is to marshall all necessary educational information to enable couples to appreciate the need for population control consonant with prevailing cultural and religious values. The Government works hand in hand with non-governmental organizations, educating, training and advising women on family health and planning. Other programmes to reduce fertility aim at raising the status of women, improving women's health, nutrition and educational status; and increasing their employment opportunities. Abortion is prohibited by law except on health grounds. Sterilization is permitted in certain circumstances.

International migration: In January 1986, South Africa imposed a border embargo upon Lesotho which seriously affected the supply of basic commodities. A change in the Government of Lesotho in the same year necessitated the transfer of a considerable number of refugees to other countries. As of mid 1987, the Government estimated that there were about 2,500 South African exiles remaining in the country. Although emigration is believed to have contributed positively to the country's socio-economic development, the Government aims at reducing the level of future emigration. About one half of Lesotho's male working-age population is employed outside the country due to the lack of employment at home. In order to reduce the level of emigration, the Government aims at development of job opportunities at home rather than relying on neighbouring South Africa for the employment of its citizens.

Spatial distribution/urbanization: The Government has indicated that it would like to adjust the current urban-rural balance as well as the distribution between regions. Most services are concentrated in a few urban centres. The country has regional variations in resource endowments and population densities. To narrow the disparities, the Government has a policy of encouraging an equitable distribution of services and an improvement in living standards by integrating urban and rural development planning, concentrating on improving rural areas. The policies also encourage the development of regions that are economically deprived, such as the mountain zone and the drought-stricken lowlands of the southern region. Programmes include rural road construction, educational programmes, increased employment opportunities, nutrition, water supply and sanitation programmes, and support for the establishment of cottage industries. In 1986 the Government announced its intention to make Maseru, the capital, a municipality with its own council under the terms of the 1983 Urban Government Act. The spur to change is the desire to control the growth of Maseru's city limits and population and the subsequent depletion of available resources.

Status of women and population: As a result of the high proportion of men who have migrated from rural areas to work in South Africa, women in Lesotho head over 60 per cent of rural households. In 1979, the Government established a Bureau of Women's Affairs within the Directorate of Women and Youth Affairs of the Prime Minister's Office. Headed by a Commissioner for Women's Affairs, the dual goals of the Bureau are to improve the welfare of women in Lesotho and to influence government policy with regard to women. In recognition of the important role women play in overall national development, the Government has developed programmes to enhance women's overall status, and improve their health, nutritional and educational status. The minimum legal age at marriage for women is 16 years.

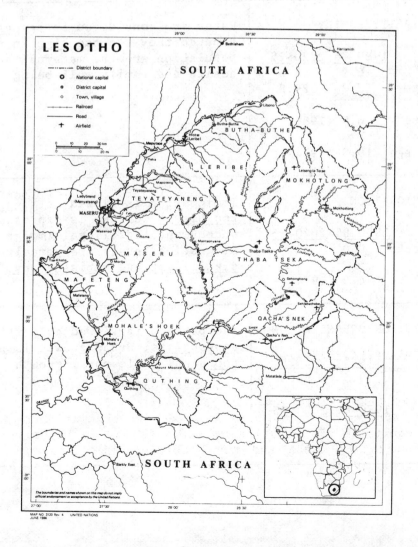

LIBERIA

DEMOGRAPHIC INDICATORS	CURRENT PERCEPTION

SIZE/AGE STRUCTURE/GROWTH
 	
Population: 1985   2025
 (thousands)   2 191   7 517
  0-14 years (%)   46.8   39.0
  60+ years (%)   4.9   4.9
 	
Rate of: 1980-85   2020-25
 growth   3.2   2.3
 natural increase   31.5   23.1
	Population size and growth are <u>unsatisfactory</u> because they are <u>too high</u>. There is concern that the rate of growth will strain the country's educational system, medical facilities, and housing supply, leading to high unemployment.

MORTALITY/MORBIDITY 1980-85 2020-25 Life expectancy 49.0 65.0 Crude death rate 17.2 6.7 Infant mortality 132.5 61.6	Current rates are considered to be <u>unacceptable</u>. The Government's primary concern is the reduction of high infant, child and maternal mortality rates.
FERTILITY/NUPTIALITY/FAMILY 1980-85 2020-25 Fertility rate 6.9 3.6 Crude birth rate 48.7 29.8 Contraceptive prevalence rate 6.5 (1986) Female mean age at first marriage 19.3 (1974)	Rates are considered to be <u>unsatisfactory</u> because they are <u>too high</u> in relation to population growth, maternal and child health and family well-being.
INTERNATIONAL MIGRATION 1980-85 2020-25 Net migration rate 0.0 0.0 Foreign-born population (%) 4.0 (1974)	Immigration is viewed as <u>significant</u>, and <u>too high</u>. Concern is expressed over undocumentated/illegal immigrants. Emigration levels are perceived as <u>not significant</u> and <u>satisfactory</u>.
SPATIAL DISTRIBUTION/URBANIZATION Urban 1985 2025 population (%) 39.5 68.3 Growth rate: 1980-85 2020-25 urban 5.6 3.2 rural 1.7 0.6	The pattern is viewed as <u>partially appropriate</u>. Urban growth is perceived as <u>too high</u>, while rural growth is <u>too low</u>.

GENERAL POLICY FRAMEWORK

Overall approach to population problems: There is an explicit policy of intervention to reduce the rates of population growth and fertility, morbidity and mortality rates and adjust the pattern of spatial distribution.

Importance of population policy in achieving development objectives: Socio-economic development and population policies are seen as complementary. Officially inaugurated in September 1986, the National Population Commission, which was given a permanent institutional framework was instrumental in drafting the country's first population policy, the "National Policy on Population for Social and Economic Development".

INSTITUTIONAL FRAMEWORK

Population data systems and development planning: The Population Division of the Ministry of Planning and Economic Affairs is responsible for conducting censuses. Population and housing censuses were held in 1962, 1974 and 1984. Vital registration of births and deaths is compulsory but is considered incomplete. A formal system of development planning has been in effect since 1976, the latest plan being the Second Four-Year National Socio-Economic Development Plan, 1981-1985. In 1986 the development plan was suspended in order to prepare the Economic Recovery Programme.

Integration of population within development planning: By expanding its scope, the National Committee on Population, established in 1983 to advise the Government on population matters, became the foundation for the National Population Commission. It was officially inaugurated in September 1986 with the Minister of Planning and Economic Affairs as the Chairperson and the membership composed of representatives from various ministries and international organizations. Among the terms of reference of the Commission are the co-ordination of all population activities and the integration of all population variables into socio-economic development planning. The newly formed Parliamentary Council on Population and Development pledged to work towards encouraging policies to promote family and sex education, improve child health, spearhead population awareness campaigns and improve the status of women.

POLICIES AND MEASURES

Changes in population size and age structure: In 1987 the Government formulated an explicit policy to reduce its high rate of population growth, which was felt to have an adverse effect on socio-economic development. An advisory committee on population activities, set up by the Government in 1983 was the first step in the development of a national population policy to reduce growth. Only public employees and employees of firms with at least 25 workers are covered under the social security scheme. Voluntary coverage is available for self-employed persons and those not covered by the law.

Mortality and morbidity: The Government has indicated that data on mortality and morbidity are extremely limited. Official policy is to reduce mortality by emphasizing maternal and child health services and preventive health care. A pyramidal health delivery system has been instituted, with rural health centres in villages forming the base, county medical centres further up, and the John F. Kennedy Medical Center in Monrovia at the apex. A new maternity hospital is being built near the Kennedy Center. Specific health measures include the provision of free inoculations, vaccinations, and examinations at prenatal clinics: health education in rural areas; training personnel in the control of malaria; and a yaws control and eradication project. A primary health care programme, due to begin in 1981 was postponed until 1983 due to serious financial constraints. The goal is to extend health coverage from 35 per cent to 90 per cent by the year 2000.

Fertility and the family: A policy of intervention was formulated in 1987 to reduce fertility. The Government now directly provides family planning services within the context of the maternal and child health programme, with the objective of improving maternal and child health and family well-being. Family planning services are also offered by the private Family Planning Association of Liberia. The Government conducts or supports projects to train paramedical personnel in family planning methods, promote natural family planning methods (through the International Federation of Family Life Promotion), reduce infertility, and improve community-based distribution of contraceptives. In April 1986 the National Population Commission conducted a seminar on the role of fertility regulation and national development. Direct support is provided for access to modern contraceptive methods and information. Abortion is permitted to save the life of the pregnant woman and on eugenic and juridical grounds. There are no known legal provisions concerning sterilization.

International migration: There is a policy to curb the significant level of immigration. In June 1986 the Minister of Labour announced that for the time being additional work permits would not be issued to foreigners, in order to promote the employment of Liberians. Businesses attempting to bypass the freeze on new permits would be fined. No policy statement is known concerning emigration, although the country suffers from problems associated with the brain drain.

Spatial distribution/urbanization: Official policy is to decelerate trends in internal migration and to adjust the urban and rural configurations of settlements, primarily by curbing rural-to-urban migration. To that end, government policy stresses integrated rural development, regional development, and the promotion of small towns and intermediate cities. The primary concern is migration to Montserrado County, where Monrovia is located, and the resultant problems - housing shortages, slums, unemployment, declining agricultural production.

Status of women and population: No permanent organization addressing women's issues exists in Liberia. A National Commission for the Review and Appraisal of the United Nations Decade for Women was disbanded after the Conference in 1985. The Parliamentary Council on Population and Development in its Plan of Action of 1987 aims to improve the status of women by initiating legislation in support of equal opportunities in employment and education and elimination of cultural beliefs and practices that discriminate against women. The minimum legal age at marriage for women is 16 years.

Other issues: Liberia enjoyed a relatively favourable balance, by African standards, between economic growth and population growth until the early 1980s. The Government's current policy efforts to modify population trends are largely a result of the country's declining economic performance in recent years.

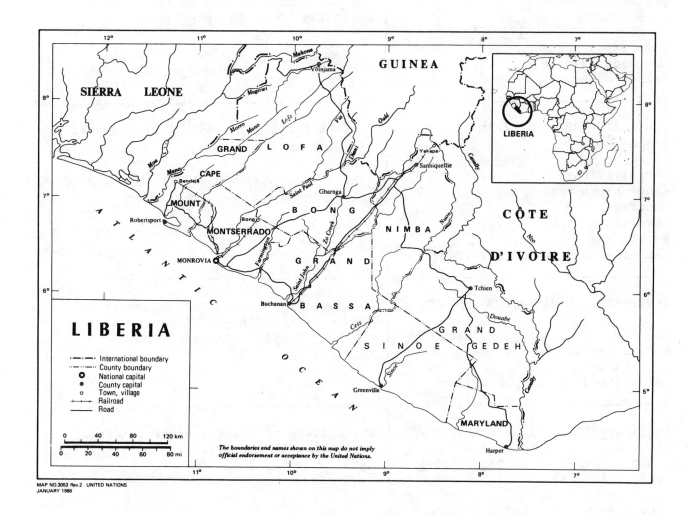

LIBYAN ARAB JAMAHIRIYA

DEMOGRAPHIC INDICATORS	CURRENT PERCEPTION
SIZE/AGE STRUCTURE/GROWTH	The Government perceives current growth as <u>satisfactory.</u>

Population:	1985	2025
(thousands)	3 605	11 090
0-14 years (%)	46.4	32.2
60+ years (%)	3.9	6.7

Rate of:	1980-85	2020-25
growth	3.9	1.9
natural increase	34.8	19.3

MORTALITY/MORBIDITY	The Government considers levels of mortality to be <u>acceptable</u>.

	1980-85	2020-25
Life expectancy	58.3	72.8
Crude death rate	10.9	4.7
Infant mortality	96.5	23.5

FERTILITY/NUPTIALITY/FAMILY	Current fertility rates are considered to be <u>satisfactory</u>.

	1980-85	2020-25
Fertility rate	7.2	2.8
Crude birth rate	45.6	23.9
Contraceptive prevalence rate	...	...
Female mean age at first marriage	18.7 (1973)	

INTERNATIONAL MIGRATION	The <u>significant</u> immigration levels are viewed as <u>too high</u>. Emigration is considered <u>not significant</u> and <u>satisfactory</u>.

	1980-85	2020-25
Net migration rate	3.6	0.0
Foreign-born population (%)	8.8 (1973)	

SPATIAL DISTRIBUTION/URBANIZATION	The pattern of spatial distribution of population is perceived as <u>inappropriate</u>.

Urban	1985	2025
population (%)	64.5	84.6

Growth rate:	1980-85	2020-25
urban	6.4	2.3
rural	-0.1	0.2

GENERAL POLICY FRAMEWORK

Overall approach to population problems: In order to alleviate population problems, the Government is committed to social welfare programmes, such as the expansion of educational, health and housing facilities. Government objectives are to continue economic growth aimed at maintaining fertility, encouraging the participation of women in the labour force and reducing both rural to urban and international migration.

Importance of population policy in achieving development objectives: Population measures are an integral part of the Libyan Arab Jamahiriya's socio-economic planning, due to the fact that a substantial amount of oil revenues has been used in the past to fund programmes aimed at enhancing standards of living and health conditions. Due to falling prices on the world oil market and its impact on the Libyan economy, the Government no longer includes foreign labour on such a large scale in its development plans.

INSTITUTIONAL FRAMEWORK

Population data systems and development planning: Census-taking falls under the responsibility of the Census and Statistics Department. The most recent population census was conducted in 1984. Vital registration of births is considered virtually complete, while registered data for deaths is considered to be incomplete. Development planning has been conducted by the People's Congresses. There have been four development plans, a three-year plan in 1973-1975 and two five-year plans in 1976-1980 and 1981-1985. Current development objectives are embodied in the Third Transformation Plan for the period 1986-1990, which was issued amid uncertainties concerning the future price of oil and government revenues. Among other objectives the Plan aims to further raise standards of living and promote "Libyanization" through the development of human resources.

Integration of population within development planning: The Directorate General of Demography and Manpower Planning, established in 1966, is the planning organization charged with taking into account population variables in development planning. It is responsible for the study and analysis of population trends and their relationship with development planning objectives. Population projections have been prepared since 1965 by the General Department of Demographic Planning. The Census and Statistics Department, established in 1952, is responsible for conducting special demographic surveys to meet specific planning needs.

POLICIES AND MEASURES

Changes in population size and age structure: Increased fertility levels are seen as vital for higher growth rates, which the Government favours, in order to increase the small native-born population. High birth rates and

LIBYAN ARAB JAMAHIRIYA

substantial levels of immigration, along with declining mortality, have caused growth rates to soar and have created a relatively young population in the Libyan Arab Jamahiriya. A pension scheme is available for employed persons.

Mortality and morbidity: Special emphasis is placed on maternal and child health, to further improve health conditions and increase life expectancy at birth. Oil revenues in the past greatly contributed to the achievement of government objectives in social services and the improvement and expansion of health care facilities. Oil revenues have also produced significant advances in construction projects, education and housing programmes. This, is turn, has contributed to the large decrease in infant mortality and overall improvements in the standard of living. Objectives include integrating therapeutic and preventive services, training health manpower and increasing the proportion of Libyan health workers.

Fertility and the family: Government policy regarding fertility is to maintain the current rates. Of principal concern is an improvement in the well-being of the family, with special emphasis on maternal and child health. Measures being implemented include child welfare allowances, family benefits, maternity leave of up to three months, and a birth grant known as a "delivery aid". While maternal and child health projects receive government support, family planning does not, and the importation of modern contraceptives is illegal. Contraceptives are only available privately, on special request. Abortion is legal only to save a woman's life. Information on the status of sterilization is not readily available.

International migration: The size of immigration flows to the Libyan Arab Jamahiriya has fluctuated drastically due to recent economic developments such as the fall in world oil prices. While in the past the Government encouraged immigration to alleviate severe labour shortages, now in order to reduce the number of expatriates employed, government policy concerning foreign Arab labour consists of requiring that the immigrants become Libyan citizens. Due to the current economic recession in the country, several new measures have been introduced, aimed at slowing down international migration. Since 1985 a policy of return migration aimed at workers from selected countries has been put into effect, in an attempt to reduce the drain on hard currency caused by worker remittances. Largely as a result of government restrictions on remittances, over one-half of the migrant workforce has left the country. This comes at a time when the Libyan Arab Jamahiriya's need to employ large numbers of expatriates has been greatly reduced.

Spatial distribution/urbanization: Traditionally, the population has concentrated along the coast, with 90 per cent of the population living on less than 25 per cent of the land area. Rural-to-urban migration has exacerbated this unbalanced distribution. Therefore, current policy aims to slow down rural-to-urban migration, with the objective of achieving an appropriate pattern of spatial distribution of population. To co-ordinate spatial planning, a National Physical Perspective Plan, 1981-2000, was prepared, to guide future development at the national, regional and local levels. While no limits have been placed on the growth of Tripoli and Benghazi, which will continue to dominate the urban system, some restructuring is planned. The Plan calls for the development of the central coastal area between Misurata and Benghazi by placing industrial development projects in small towns. Comprehensive rural development strategies have also been implemented.

Status of women and population: The Government has taken a leadership role in its efforts to change the status of women and expand their access to educational and employment opportunities. Women receive basic military training and are subject to the draft. There is no information readily available on the minimum legal age at marriage for women.

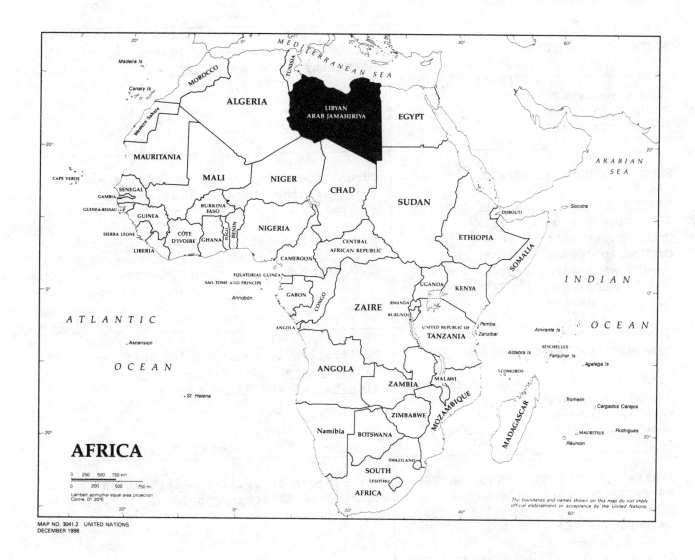

AFRICA

MAP NO. 3041.2 UNITED NATIONS
DECEMBER 1988

LIECHTENSTEIN

DEMOGRAPHIC INDICATORS	CURRENT PERCEPTION
SIZE/AGE STRUCTURE/GROWTH	The Government perceives current growth rates as <u>too low</u>.

Population:	1985	2025
(thousands)	28.0	44.0
0-14 years (%)	...	...
60+ years (%)	13.0	...

Rate of:	1980-85	2020-25
growth	1.5	...
natural increase	8.0	...

MORTALITY/MORBIDITY

The Government considers levels of mortality to be <u>acceptable</u>.

	1980-85	2020-25
Life expectancy	...	...
Crude death rate	6.0	...
Infant mortality	...	...

FERTILITY/NUPTIALITY/FAMILY

Curent fertility rates are considered <u>unsatisfactory</u> because they are <u>too low</u>.

	1980-85	2020-25
Fertility rate	1.3	...
Crude birth rate	14.0	...
Contraceptive prevalence rate	...	...
Female mean age at first marriage	...	...

INTERNATIONAL MIGRATION

Immigration is considered <u>significant</u> and <u>satisfactory</u>. Emigration is <u>not</u> <u>significant</u> and <u>satisfactory</u>.

	1980-85	2020-25
Net migration rate	...	...
Foreign-born population (%)	36.9 (1981)	

SPATIAL DISTRIBUTION/URBANIZATION

The pattern of spatial distribution is considered to be <u>appropriate</u>.

Urban	1985	2025
population (%)	24.0	...

Growth rate:	1980-85	2020-25
urban	...	...
rural	...	...

GENERAL POLICY FRAMEWORK

Overall approach to population problems: Although Liechtenstein has no explicit population policy, government goals in regard to population include increasing the rate of fertility, curbing future immigration flows, and preserving rural areas.

Importance of population policy in achieving development objectives: No information is readily available.

INSTITUTIONAL FRAMEWORK

Population data systems and development planning: The most recent population census was taken in 1981. In 1982 the Government indicated that it had encountered some problems in producing demographic statistics, since it was difficult to assess annual fluctuations given the country's small population. No information is available on whether there is a single government agency charged with the responsibility of development planning.

Integration of population within development planning: No information is readily available.

POLICIES AND MEASURES

Changes in population size and age structure: While Liechtenstein considers its rate of population growth to be too low, no policy exists to intervene or influence growth rates. Government policy towards the aged includes a pension plan and old-age and survivors' insurance schemes covered by Social Security.

Mortality and morbidity: A Health Commission, headed by a state medical officer, exists to investigate and establish controls regarding public health care. The Liechtenstein Red Cross has built up a comprehensive infant welfare service. Liechtenstein's modest medical facilities are supplemented by the neighbouring Swiss medical services, to which the Principality contributes support.

Fertility and the family: Government objectives are to raise current fertility rates. Government policy concerning maternity benefits entitles women to six weeks paid leave before and after confinement. Government policy also includes child allowances and an overall family allowance scheme covered under Social Security. No government support is provided for modern methods of fertility regulation. Abortions and the use of contraceptives are limited.

LIECHTENSTEIN

International migration: The policy aims at curbing immigration flows in the future while maintaining the already established immigrant population, which represents more than one third of the total population. An additional 4,300 workers cross the border each day from Austria and Switzerland to work in Liechtenstein. No policies concerning emigration have been implemented.

Spatial distribution/urbanization: The acceleration of industrialization and urbanization have posed new problems for land distribution, primarily in rural areas. Government policy includes improved allocation of land and the creation of a "national agricultural zone" with priority given to consolidating land suited for agricultural exploitation. Government concerns include the preservation of a healthy rural community with emphasis on long-term planning of natural resources for the conservation of nature. Regarding internal migration, Government policy favours non-intervention.

Status of women and population: A proposal to extend the franchise to women was approved by referendum in July 1984, but women were not permitted to vote on communal issues in three of Liechtenstein's 11 communes until April 1986. A proposal to add a clause in the Constitution concerning equality between the sexes was defeated by a large majority in a referendum in December 1985.

Other issues; In order to improve health conditions, and in particular to lower the incidence of respiratory illness, the Government has adopted a variety of measures to reduce atmospheric pollution, including an exemption from car tax for five years (until 1989) for all cars that are fitted with a catalytic converter to reduce noxious emissions or that do not exceed certain emission standards.

– 137 –

LIECHTENSTEIN

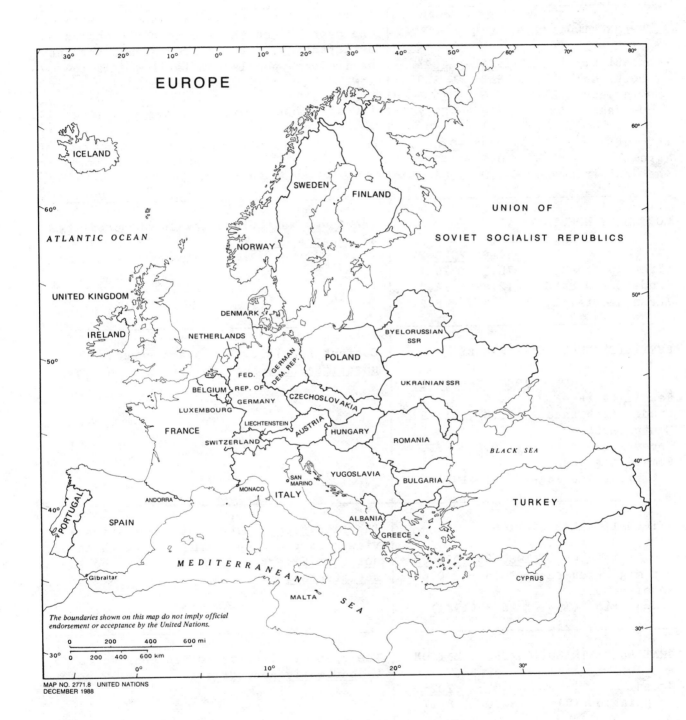

EUROPE

ICELAND

ATLANTIC OCEAN

SWEDEN

FINLAND

NORWAY

UNION OF

SOVIET SOCIALIST REPUBLICS

UNITED KINGDOM

DENMARK

IRELAND

NETHERLANDS

BYELORUSSIAN
SSR

POLAND

GERMAN
DEM. REP.

FED.
REP. OF
GERMANY

BELGIUM

UKRAINIAN SSR

CZECHOSLOVAKIA

LUXEMBOURG

LIECHTENSTEIN

AUSTRIA

HUNGARY

FRANCE

SWITZERLAND

ROMANIA

BLACK SEA

SAN
MARINO

YUGOSLAVIA

MONACO

ITALY

BULGARIA

ANDORRA

TURKEY

SPAIN

ALBANIA

PORTUGAL

GREECE

MEDITERRANEAN

SEA

CYPRUS

Gibraltar

MALTA

*The boundaries shown on this map do not imply official
endorsement or acceptance by the United Nations.*

0	200	400	600 mi
0	200	400	600 km

MAP NO. 2771.8   UNITED NATIONS
DECEMBER 1988

DEMOGRAPHIC INDICATORS	CURRENT PERCEPTION
SIZE/AGE STRUCTURE/GROWTH	The overall growth rate is perceived as satisfactory, but the growth rate for the native-born population is viewed as _too low_.

Population:	1985	2025
(thousands)	363	339
0-14 years (%)	17.6	16.6
60+ years (%)	17.8	28.7

Rate of:	1980-85	2020-25
growth	0.0	-0.2
natural increase	-1.0	-3.0

MORTALITY/MORBIDITY

The Government views levels of mortality as _acceptable_.

	1980-85	2020-25
Life expectancy	70.8	76.7
Crude death rate	12.8	14.3
Infant mortality	9.3	5.2

FERTILITY/NUPTIALITY/FAMILY

Current fertility rates are perceived as _unsatisfactory_ because they are _too low_.

	1980-85	2020-25
Fertility rate	1.5	2.1
Crude birth rate	11.8	11.3
Contraceptive prevalence rate	...	...
Female mean age at first marriage	23.1 (1981)	

INTERNATIONAL MIGRATION

The _significant_ levels of immigration are viewed as _too high_. Emigration, which is _not significant_, is considered to be _satisfactory_.

	1980-85	2020-25
Net migration rate	0.5	0.6
Foreign-born population (%)	26.3 (1981)	

SPATIAL DISTRIBUTION/URBANIZATION

The spatial distribution is considered to be _partially appropriate_.

Urban	1985	2025
population (%)	81.0	87.7

Growth rate:	1980-85	2020-25
urban	0.8	-0.3
rural	-3.4	-0.1

GENERAL POLICY FRAMEWORK

Overall approach to population problems: The main goals of the Government
concerning demographic issues are to increase the population growth rate
of nationals, curb future immigration flows, and provide progressive
family allowances in order to encourage higher fertility.

Importance of population policy in achieving development objectives:
Population measures are considered significant in achieving development
objectives because the large contingent of foreign-born labour in
Luxembourg is regarded as crucial for the country's development. In order
to maintain economic growth while simultaneously limiting future
immigration levels, higher birth rates among nationals are being
encouraged through specific family planning measures and allowances.

INSTITUTIONAL FRAMEWORK

Population data systems and development planning: Conducting censuses
falls under the responsibility of the Office of Statistics and Economic
Studies. The most recent population census was taken in 1981. Vital
registration of births and deaths is considered to be virtually complete.

Integration of population within development planning: There is no
government agency responsible for the formulation and co-ordination of
population policies. Population projections have been prepared by the
Office of Statistics and Economic Studies since 1975.

POLICIES AND MEASURES

Changes in population size and age structure: Government policy is to
increase fertility rates, with the ultimate goal of raising the level of
fertility to replacement level. This policy is seen as vital for higher
population growth rates and is aimed specifically at Luxembourg nationals.
Social legislation has been put into effect covering maternal and child health
care. Recent legislation covers domiciliary care for the elderly, chronically
sick, and handicapped. Because of demographic pressures on the national
pension scheme, the method of financing the system was changed in 1984 in
order to rescue the system from bankruptcy.

Mortality and morbidity: The Government's priority since 1984 has been
preventive medicine, with a policy aimed at expanding facilities for the early
detection of certain diseases. The national health policy guarantees all
citizens of Luxembourg preventive, curative, and rehabilitative health
services. Health policies and strategies are planned and administered by the
Ministry of Public Health and Social Security. Of particular concern are
cardio-vascular diseases and malignant neoplasms, which are the principle
causes of death.

LUXEMBOURG

Fertility and the family: The main concerns of the Government are the
declines in marriages and fertility levels. In order to remedy the situation,
the Government's priority is a family policy which, by creating favourable
social and economic conditions, will boost the fertility rate to replacement
level. Government policy promotes progressive child and birth allowances,
which are administered by the National Fund for Family Benefits. In 1986,
family and child allowances were raised to 1,748 Luxembourg francs (LuxF 50.4
= $US 1 as of 1985) per month for the first child, 3,582 LuxF monthly for the
second child, 6,398 LuxF for the third child, and 5,246 LuxF for each
additional child. Maternity benefits consist of up to 100 per cent of
earnings for 16 weeks of leave and four additional weeks in case of premature
or multiple births or if the mother nurses the child. In 1984, a new loan
system for young married couples was introduced, whereby the amount of the
loans reimbursed by the Government increases as a function of the number of
children the family has. To ease the burden on families of additional
expenses at the beginning of each school year, a new allowance went into
effect in July 1986 for families with at least two children. As of 1980, a
maternity allowance is payable for 16 weeks to women not gainfully employed.
Other benefits include nursing breaks during employment and prohibition of
dismissal during the leave. Access to modern methods of fertility regulation
is provided by private organizations with government funding. Counselling
centres, sex education, contraception and infertility treatment are provided
by the Government. Abortion is legal on health, juridical and socio-medical
grounds. Government health centres are required to provide sterilization
information and services.

International migration: The large numbers of immigrants in Luxembourg are
perceived as a threat to national identity, approximately 30 per cent of the
population is foreign-born. Projections imply that the foreign-born
population is likely to reach 34 per cent of the total population by the year
2000. In response to this situation, the Government has adopted a restrictive
policy of limiting the flow of new immigrants, while maintaining the already
established immigrant population. The policy includes tighter controls on
undocumented workers, strict limits on the issuance of work permits and the
imposition of a three-year residency requirement before a work permit can be
obtained if the immigrant entered the country under family reunification.
Immigration has a significant effect on economic development since foreign
labour represents about a third of the active population and is perceived as
an indispensable factor in increasing birth rates, which among nationals is
extremely low. The National Council of Immigration studies problems of
immigration and surveys the socio-economic conditions of immigrants. Social
action in favour of immigrants has been in place since 1972, helping
immigrants in adapting to social, economic and cultural conditions in
Luxembourg. There is no specific policy concerning emigration.

Spatial distribution/urbanization: Minor changes are desirable, such as
promoting the growth of lagging regions. Government measures offer
substantial incentives to new types of investment in rural areas.

Status of women and population: The minimum legal age at marriage for women
is 15 years.

Other issues: In 1986 the law on the acquisition of Luxembourg nationality was modified to permit children born of Luxembourg women and foreign-born fathers to automatically acquire Luxembourg nationality. Previously children of such marriages were considered to be foreigners. Also in 1986 a national guaranteed minimum income was introduced for those resident in the Grand Duchy for at least 10 years and who are at least 30 years of age and able to work, or at least 60 years and unable to work or a parent with a handicapped child.

MADAGASCAR

DEMOGRAPHIC INDICATORS	CURRENT PERCEPTION

SIZE/AGE STRUCTURE/GROWTH
 	
Population: 1985   2025
 (thousands)   10 012   28 120
  0-14 years (%)   44.2   34.7
  60+ years (%)   5.5   6.0
 	
Rate of: 1980-85   2020-25
 growth   2.8   1.7
 natural increase   27.9   17.4
	The rate of growth is viewed as <u>unsatisfactory</u> and <u>too high</u>.

MORTALITY/MORBIDITY 1980-85 2020-25 Life expectancy 49.6 62.7 Crude death rate 16.5 8.0 Infant mortality 67.0 22.7	Levels and trends are <u>unacceptable</u>. Concerns include high levels of infant and child mortality, malnutrition, the prevalence of infectious diseases (e.g., pneumonia, gastro-intestinal diseases) and the general level of morbidity.
FERTILITY/NUPTIALITY/FAMILY 1980-85 2020-25 Fertility rate 6.1 3.0 Crude birth rate 44.4 25.4 Contraceptive prevalence rate ... ... Female mean age at first marriage 20.3 (1975)	Rates are considered to be <u>unsatisfactory</u> and <u>too high</u>. They are felt to impose a short-run disequilibrium between demographic and economic growth.
INTERNATIONAL MIGRATION 1980-85 2020-25 Net migration rate 0.0 0.0 Foreign-born population (%)	Both immigration and emigration are <u>not significant</u> and <u>satisfactory</u>. There is concern with undocumented immigrants.
SPATIAL DISTRIBUTION/URBANIZATION Urban 1985 2025 population (%) 21.8 52.1 Growth rate: 1980-85 2020-25 urban 5.7 3.3 rural 2.1 0.2	The pattern of spatial distribution is viewed as <u>partially appropriate</u>. Major concerns are high population density in the plateau regions and low population density in the coastal regions.

GENERAL POLICY FRAMEWORK

Overall approach to population problems: There is no direct intervention to modify fertility and population growth, since it is felt that social and economic restructuring will adjust these factors appropriately. Policies are aimed at reducing morbidity and mortality levels and modifying spatial distribution.

Importance of population policy in achieving development objectives: Population policy is viewed within the context of the Government's socialist development strategy. Policy is to be based on economic growth and restructuring, social well-being and family welfare with the primary objective being to improve family welfare.

INSTITUTIONAL FRAMEWORK

Population data systems and development planning: A National Demographic Survey was undertaken in 1966, and the independent Government's first census was conducted in 1975. Since 1975, post-census and household budget surveys have taken place. The next census has been scheduled for 1990. Vital registration is considered incomplete. Post-Independence planning was begun in 1966, with the most recent plan being the Five-Year Plan for 1986-1990.

Integration of population within development planning: The Permanent National Population Committee was created in 1979 within the Population Directorate of the Ministry of Population and Social Welfare. The Committee has representation by all ministries and non-governmental agencies. It is planned to establish a population and development planning unit within the Directorate General of Planning.

POLICIES AND MEASURES

Changes in population size and age structure: There is no policy of intervention to modify growth, despite official acknowledgement of its negative consequences, such as poverty, unemployment, increased pressure on public services, a young population and a widening gap in income distribution. However, policies regarding the adjustment of the spatial distribution pattern are recognized to have an impact on population problems. More important to population growth have been the Government's attempts at social and economic restructuring (e.g., providing social services, combatting poverty, redistributing income). These measures are expected to influence size and growth patterns. Efforts have also been intensified recently to improve the collection of demographic and health statistics so as to improve policy formulation. The social security scheme covers employed persons and excludes temporary and casual workers.

MADAGASCAR

Mortality and morbidity: Health services are based on the primary health care approach, which is incorporated into socio-economic development strategies. The policy objective is to reduce morbidity and mortality in the most vulnerable groups - pregnant women, infants and young children, the rural population. Policy also aims to strengthen both preventive and curative services through a decentralized system to reach rural areas and to improve the training of medical personnel at all levels. Specific measures taken include the training and staffing of over 1500 primary health care units, expanding maternal and child health care centres, nutrition programmes aimed primarily at pregnant women and children and better use of medicine and traditional health attendants. In 1986 the Ministry of Health initiated, on an experimental basis, a child-spacing programme for women in high-risk groups as a means of reducing maternal morbidity and mortality. Since 1979 the Government has had a programme to improve the collection and transmission of health and demographic statistics throughout the country so as to improve family health. The Government has indicated that its health policies have suffered from a number of constraints such as limited financial resources, lack of equipment and an inadequate infrastructure. Quantitative targets that had been set for 1985 were an infant mortality rate of below 70 per thousand live births and a life expectancy at birth exceeding 50 years for both sexes.

Fertility and the family: There is no policy of intervention to modify rates. Measures improving the health of mothers and children and birth-spacing programmes are expected to indirectly affect fertility patterns. The Government has begun population information and education projects in and outside the formal sector and continues to explore the possibility of raising the minimum legal age for marriage for women. The National Family Planning Association of Madagascar (FISA) works to create an awareness among people and Government of the need for family planning services. Its efforts are increasingly being directed at involving young people in family planning. The Government provides direct support for access to modern contraceptive methods and information, but contraceptives are available only in pharmacies for adults with a physicians's consent. The French Anti-Contraception Law of 1920 is still in effect, but is not enforced. Abortion, which is a major concern of the Government, is strictly restricted in Madagascar. Sterilization is allowed only on specific conditions and not for contraceptive purposes.

International migration: No official policy statement is known concerning immigration. Although an emigration policy has not been officially formulated, the Government in the past has favoured monitoring the emigration of professional and skilled personnel.

Spatial distribution/urbanization: The official policy is to modify the urban-rural and regional balance, with the primary objective of correcting economic and social disparities within the population. Specifically, policies aim to reduce migration to the major metropolitan area, Antananarivo, to increase migration to rural zones and to voluntarily move people to less populated areas. The Government has vigorously pursued regional and rural development strategies, which are tied to the country's economic development goals. An example is the Government decree issued in 1974 to create a "fokonolona" (village communities) programme to mobilise the entire population, based on the country's traditional, decentralized socio-economic structures. In the 1986-1990 Development Plan, priority is given to the provision of low cost housing for the poor in cities.

Status of women and population: The Government has expressed the need to further incorporate women and youth in the country's development, including in population matters. Toward this end, the Ministry of Population contains a committee on the conditions of women and top priority has been given to educating women. Official concern with the early age at first marriage for women is in part related to concern with the status of women and with adolescent pregnancies and abortions. The Government acknowledges that for population policies to be effective women's participation is necessary. Measures to improve the social, economic, political and cultural status of women have already been undertaken. The minimum legal age at marriage for women is 14 years.

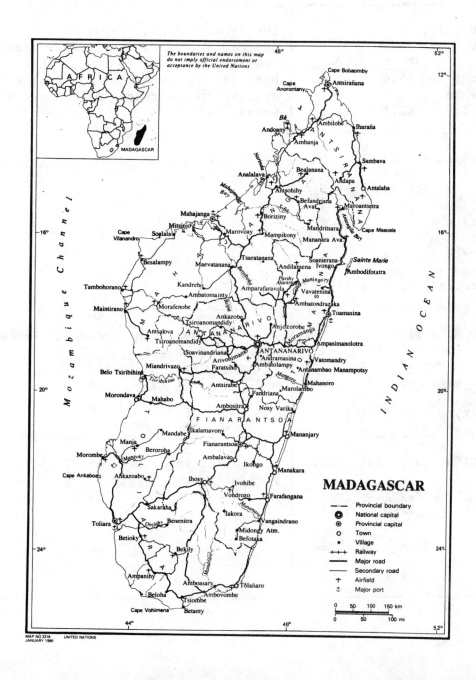

MALAWI

DEMOGRAPHIC INDICATORS			CURRENT PERCEPTION
SIZE/AGE STRUCTURE/GROWTH			The Government of Malawi considers its growth rate to be unsatisfactory and too high.
Population:	1985	2025	
(thousands)	6 944	21 855	
0-14 years (%)	46.0	36.3	
60+ years (%)	4.2	5.8	
Rate of:	1980-85	2020-25	
growth	3.1	2.0	
natural increase	31.8	19.5	
MORTALITY/MORBIDITY			Levels and trends are viewed as unacceptable. Particular concerns are low average life expectancy at birth, high infant mortality, maternal and child health, and shortages of trained health personnel.
	1980-85	2020-25	
Life expectancy	45.0	61.0	
Crude death rate	21.5	8.8	
Infant mortality	163.4	81.5	
FERTILITY/NUPTIALITY/FAMILY			Rates are considered to be unsatisfactory and too high.
	1980-85	2020-25	
Fertility rate	7.0	3.4	
Crude birth rate	53.2	28.4	
Contraceptive prevalence rate	...	...	
Female mean age at first marriage	17.8 (1977)		
INTERNATIONAL MIGRATION			Existing levels and trends of immigration are viewed as not significant and satisfactory. Emigration is significant and satisfactory.
	1980-85	2020-25	
Net migration rate	-0.9	0.0	
Foreign-born population (%)	5.2 (1977)		
SPATIAL DISTRIBUTION/URBANIZATION			Current patterns are perceived as partially appropriate.
Urban	1985	2025	
population (%)	12.0	39.7	
Growth rate:	1980-85	2020-25	
urban	7.5	4.1	
rural	2.6	0.7	

GENERAL POLICY FRAMEWORK

Overall approach to population problems: There is no direct intervention to modify population growth or fertility. However, there are policies of economic and social restructuring and of direct intervention to modify mortality and spatial distribution.

Importance of population policy in achieving development objectives: No explicit population policy has been formulated. Intervention in population-related areas is viewed as necessary only for achieving an improvement in living standards and an increase in gross domestic product.

INSTITUTIONAL FRAMEWORK

Population data systems and development planning: Since 1911, six pre-Independence and three post-Independence censuses have been conducted, the latest in 1987. Vital registration is considered incomplete. A formal system of development planning has existed since the mid 1960s. Although there is no current formal development plan, the Structural Adjustment Programme, currently in effect, provides a framework for major policy, institutional and investment decision-making.

Integration of population within development planning: While no special unit exists for this task, a project has ben undertaken with international assistance to establish a population planning unit within the Economic Planning and Development Division of the Office of the President, which is responsible for overall national planning. Population-related activities are carried out within other ministries and governmental institutions such as the Ministry of Health.

POLICIES AND MEASURES

Changes in population size and age structure: While there is no official policy of intervention, it is felt that rapid growth constrains the country's economic and social development efforts. However, there are official policies to decrease mortality, adjust spatial distribution, and adjust social and economic factors (including measures to improve the status of women), which will indirectly affect size and growth. The Government's efforts to promote child-spacing are also likely to have an effect on population growth. In general, though, all of these policies are aimed at improving general health and welfare rather than modifying specific demographic processes. Information on the status of pension schemes is not readily available.

Mortality and morbidity: The Government regards health improvement as essential for increased labour productivity and feels that health is an integral part of socio-economic development. The official policy is to reduce morbidity and mortality, with special emphasis placed on the health of the most vulnerable groups. Curative health care services in the past were the central focus of governmental health policy, but preventive services have recently been given increased priority. Primary health care has also recently received more attention. The maternal and child health programme is the channel for much of the health service delivery, and has been intensified. With the goal of reducing maternal morbidity and mortality, the Government began integrating child-spacing in maternal and child health programmes in 1985. These measures are not intended to influence the rate of population growth. Specific measures include the provision of affordable, safe drinking water for 70 per cent of the urban population and 30 per cent of the rural population; an expanded immunization programme; a diarrhoeal diseases-control programme, emphasizing the use of oral rehydration salts; an intensive nutrition programme and child welfare schemes; health manpower education and training; and the expansion of the health infrastructure. In the area of primary health care, coverage is being extended to three new districts each year and it is hoped that all districts will be covered by 1990.

Fertility and the family: There is no policy of intervention to modify fertility rates. However, there are fertility-related measures intended to improve family well-being. These include the creation of maternal and child health programmes (since 1982); child-spacing information and services within the maternal and child health programme; permitting contraceptive use for health and welfare purposes; and measures to improve the status of women. Family planning services are provided by the Ministry of Health through the maternal and child health programme, purely as a health measure; in general, family planning services are discouraged, except within private practice. Child-spacing is stressed as a method of reducing maternal and infant mortality and morbidity. The ban on the importation of contraceptives was lifted in 1983. Access to contraception is not limited, and the Government provides direct support. The advertising of contraceptives is still prohibited. There is no specific law regarding sterilization, which is allowed for contraceptive purposes. Abortion is illegal except to save the life of the pregnant woman.

International migration: In December 1986 an amendment to the Immigration Act was announced requiring all foreign residents within 24 months to apply either for a temporary employment permit or a permanent residence permit, register as a citizen of Malawi, or leave the country. Civil disturbancies in Mozambique in late 1986 led to a massive flow of Mozambicans into Malawi. The Government estimates that as of 1987, 300,000 Mozambicans may have entered the country. They have settled spontaneously in villages along the border and their immediate needs are being met by the Government and international donor organizations. As of mid 1987 official policy was to maintain emigration at the current levels. Emigration of workers on contract to South Africa, which was terminated by the Government of Malawi for some years during the 1970s, was resumed with a bilateral agreement in 1977, establishing an annual recruitment quota of about 2,400 workers.

Spatial distribution/urbanization: Official policy is to adjust spatial distribution by means of curbing rural-to-urban migration, modifying the rural and urban configuration of settlements, and redressing regional imbalances in economic development and population distribution. The national captial was moved in 1975 from Blantyre, in the southern region, to Lilongwe, in the central region, to promote more balanced economic development. Integrated rural development programmes and the creation of rural growth centres are intended to reduce migration to urban centres by improving the standard of living in the countryside. The National Rural Development Programme (NRDP) was adopted in 1978 to achieve that end.

Status of women and population: The Government of Malawi has been aware since the 1970s of the need to integrate women into development efforts and thereby raise their status. The League of Malawi Women was formed to help promote this process at the district, area and village levels of the country. The Government's functional literacy programmes have been targeted primarily at women, whose level of formal education is generally much lower than that of men. Training centres have been instituted for women, particularly in the fields of health, agriculture and community development. In 1987 the National Commission on Women and Development was in the process of preparing a family life education programme and compiling a review of laws affecting women. There is no information readily available on the minimum legal age at marriage for women.

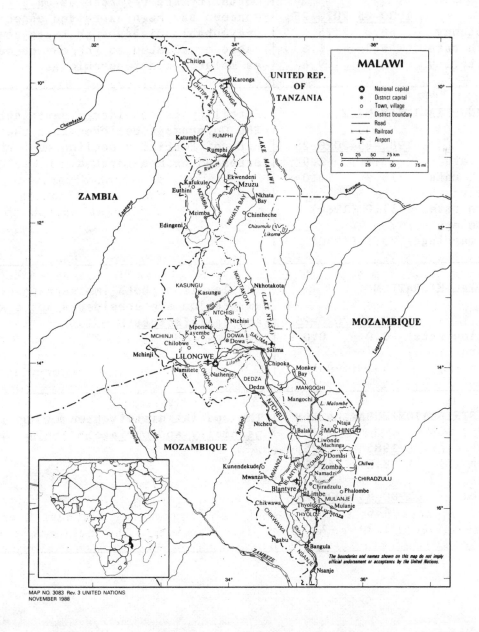

MAP NO. 3083 Rev. 3 UNITED NATIONS
NOVEMBER 1988

MALAYSIA

DEMOGRAPHIC INDICATORS	CURRENT PERCEPTION

SIZE/AGE STRUCTURE/GROWTH
 	
 Population: 1985   2025
 (thousands)   15 557   26 844
   0-14 years (%)   37.8   21.4
   60+ years (%)   5.7   14.4
 	
 Rate of: 1980-85   2020-25
   growth   2.4   0.7
   natural increase   24.5   7.3
	The present rate of population growth is considered <u>satisfactory</u>.

MORTALITY/MORBIDITY 1980-85 2020-25 Life expectancy 66.8 75.6 Crude death rate 6.5 6.6 Infant mortality 30.1 9.6	The conditions of health and levels of mortality are regarded as <u>unacceptable</u>. Concern has been expressed especially for preventable diseases that are communicable or related to the environment, such as malaria and tuberculosis.

FERTILITY/NUPTIALITY/FAMILY
 	
     1980-85   2020-25
 Fertility rate   3.9   1.9
 Crude birth rate   30.9   14.0
 Contraceptive
   prevalence rate   51.0 (1984)
 Female mean age
   at first marriage   23.5 (1980)
	Fertility is considered <u>satisfactory</u>. The Government believes that the present rate of fertility decline must be arrested or decelerated.

INTERNATIONAL MIGRATION
 	
     1980-85   2020-25
 Net migration rate   0.0   0.0
 Foreign-born
   population (%)   5.1 (1980)
	The levels of both immigration and emigration are considered <u>not significant</u> and <u>satisfactory</u>.

SPATIAL DISTRIBUTION/URBANIZATION
 	
 Urban   1985   2025
   population (%)   38.2   67.1
 	
 Growth rate: 1980-85   2020-25
   urban   4.6   1.6
   rural   1.2   -1.0
	The spatial distribution is considered <u>partially appropriate</u>.

GENERAL POLICY FRAMEWORK

<u>Overall approach to population problems</u>: After four national development plans and almost two decades of sustained efforts to reduce the population growth rate, the Government embarked upon a new population policy in 1984. The new policy calls for a population of 70 million people to be attained by the year 2100. The Government views the increase in population as necessary to alleviate a serious labour shortage. (Malaysia must now resort to the employment of foreign workers.) The Government recognizes the need for a comprehensive plan to ensure that the population is properly dispersed so that balanced development can take place.

<u>Importance of population policy in achieving development objectives</u>: The Government believes that a long-term and comprehensive population policy is an essential integral component of economic development plans. Population policy should provide for purposeful and planned growth in order to achieve a better quality of life. The Government has stated that establishing a fixed target of 70 million people by the year 2100 will facilitate the adjustment and monitoring of current and future economic and social development.

INSTITUTIONAL FRAMEWORK

<u>Population data systems and development planning</u>: The National Registration Department and the Department of Statistics are the key data collection agencies. Statistical units have been organized in various major federal ministries. Although Malaysia has had a relatively long history of census-taking during its colonial period, the first post-independence census was conducted in 1970. The latest census was conducted in 1980. Compulsory vital registration is virtually complete in Peninsular Malaysia but incomplete in Sabah and Sarawak. The Economic Planning Unit serves as the secretariat to the National Development Planning Committee which comprises heads of all major economic development ministries. Malaysia has undertaken four development plans and has entered into the fifth plan which covers the period 1986-1990.

<u>Integration of population within development planning</u>: The Economic Planning Unit in the Prime Minister's Department is responsible for the formulation and co-ordination of population policies. The Human Resources Section of the Economic Planning Unit is responsible for taking population variables into account in planning. Since 1965 population projections have been prepared by the Economic Planning Unit. The National Population and Family Development Board (NPFDB) and the Population Studies Unit of the University of Malaysia study population-development interrelationships. A National Population Advisory Committee was established, with the NPFDB as the secretariat, to monitor and evaluate the various programmes created as part of the new population policy.

MALAYSIA

POLICIES AND MEASURES

<u>Changes in population size and age structure</u>: In a significant shift in population policy, in 1984 the Government proposed a plan to boost the population to 70 million by the year 2100. The Government indicated that a population of 70 million could be attained with a population growth rate that was lower than the growth rate of the gross national product (GNP), so that efforts to improve living standards would not be nullified by population growth. Moreover, the time frame to achieve the target would be sufficiently long for social and economic development to take place to support 70 million people. The Government is investigating the various policy options to achieve a target of 70 million people. Under the Social Security Scheme, a fund exists for employed workers while domestic workers are entitled to voluntary coverage.

<u>Mortality and morbidity</u>: The Fifth Malaysia Plan places emphasis on preventive, promotive and curative health care for rural areas in particular, and the renovation, upgrading and refurbishing of existing health care delivery centres and institutions. Cost-effective methods for consolidating various health programmes will also be adopted in an attempt to reduce the country's financial burden. Of special policy concern are the disadvantaged, poverty-stricken mothers and children, including school children. No quantitative mortality or morbidity targets have been established.

<u>Fertility and the family</u>: In a significant policy reversal, the Government has discontinued its campaign of "two is enough" and is now encouraging families to have as many children as they can support. The strategy is to decelerate the declining rate of growth by delaying the onset of replacement level fertility from the year 2035 to 2075. Apart from extending paid maternity leave for public employees from three to up to five children, other measures are being explored, such as income tax benefits for families that have more children, better child care facilities for working mothers, maternity benefits and the encouragement of marriage at an earlier age. The Government also plans to build larger low-cost housing to help meet the needs of larger families. The Fifth Malaysia Plan indicates that efforts will be undertaken to increase awareness of family building patterns and the means of timing and controlling births, with special emphasis on family development and welfare. There are no legal restrictions concerning access to information on modern methods of contraception. Abortion is legal if there is a risk to a woman's life, or physical or mental health. Sterilization is permitted if the individual satisfies criteria pertaining to age and parity and if there is written consent from both spouses.

<u>International migration</u>: The Government does not report specific policies concerning immigration or emigration. The country suffers from serious labour shortages and has resorted to foreign workers. About 300,000 undocumented workers from Indonesia, Thailand and the Philippines are estimated to be employed in Malaysia. In 1987 the Governments of Malaysia and Indonesia agreed to explore the possibility of issuing border passes as a means of stemming the flow of undocumented immigrants from Indonesia to Malaysia. The country has also provided temporary asylum to substantial numbers of refugees. Between 1975 and 1985, almost all of the 200,000 boat people who landed in Malaysia have been resettled in other countries.

Spatial distribution/urbanization: The main policy goals are to lower migration to the largest metropolitan areas and to increase migration to other urban areas. One strategy consistently followed in the development plans is to narrow regional disparities in living standards by accelerating development in less developed regions. Among the various policy measures used to adjust the spatial distribution pattern have been the Federal Land Development Schemes (FELDA), industrial decentralization, the development of a viable hierarchy of urban centres, integrated rural development and urban restructuring. According to the Fifth Plan, new guidelines have been adopted for developing new townships in areas of the Regional Development Authority that will follow natural rather than artifically-stimulated growth. In addition, a rural urbanization programme will be implemented nationwide which will complement township development and infuse new vigour into rural areas.

Status of women and population: The Secretariat for Women's Affairs established in the Prime Minister's Department in 1983 is responsible for increasing female participation in the development process and ensuring that government programmes take into consideration the full integration of women by guaranteeing equal opportunities. The minimum legal age at marriage for women is 18 years of age for the non-Muslim population.

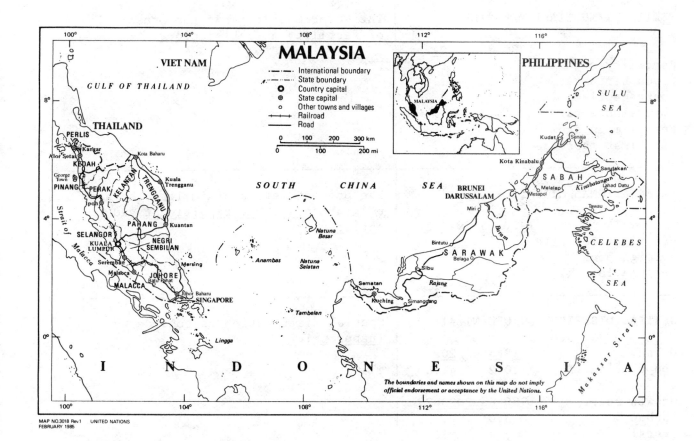

MAP NO.3018 Rev.1   UNITED NATIONS
FEBRUARY 1985

MALDIVES

DEMOGRAPHIC INDICATORS	CURRENT PERCEPTION
SIZE/AGE STRUCTURE/GROWTH	The Government views the present rate of population growth as <u>satisfactory</u>.

Population: <u>1985</u>   <u>2025</u>
  (thousands)   183   432
   0-14 years (%)   ...   ...
   60+ years (%)   ...   ...
 	
Rate of: <u>1980-85</u> <u>2020-25</u>
  growth   3.3   ...
  natural increase 32.0 ...	

MORTALITY/MORBIDITY <u>1980-85</u> <u>2020-25</u> Life expectancy 53.0 ... Crude death rate 12.0 ... Infant mortality 82.0 ...	Levels and trends are regarded as <u>unacceptable</u>.

FERTILITY/NUPTIALITY/FAMILY
 	
          <u>1980-85</u> <u>2020-25</u>
Fertility rate   ...   ...
Crude birth rate   44.0   ...
Contraceptive
  prevalence rate   ...   ...
Female mean age
  at first marriage   ...   ...
	The Government regards the present level of fertility as <u>satisfactory</u>.

INTERNATIONAL MIGRATION <u>1980-85</u> <u>2020-25</u> Net migration rate 0.0 0.0 Foreign-born population (%)	The present levels of immigration and emigration are <u>not significant</u> and <u>satisfactory</u>.

SPATIAL DISTRIBUTION/URBANIZATION
 	
Urban   <u>1985</u>   <u>2025</u>
  population (%)   20.2   41.8
 	
Growth rate: <u>1980-85</u> <u>2020-25</u>
  urban   3.0   ...
  rural   3.4   ...
	Spatial distribution is considered <u>inappropriate</u>.

GENERAL POLICY FRAMEWORK

Overall approach to population problems: The Government is concerned by
the trends in population growth but has not expressed an official position
with regard to the present population growth rate. Population policy aims
at improved family planning services along with improved health and
education facilities, overall economic development, and decreased urban
concentration on Male Island.

Importance of population policy in achieving development objectives: The
population policy of the Maldives is regarded as a part of the overall
socio-economic policy and aims at improving the living standards and
health conditions of the population. The policy aims at an overall
development of the population in general and, ultimately, the spiritual
and intellectual development of each individual. Finally, it aims at
enhancing the contribution of each individual, qualitatively and
quantitatively, to the development objectives of the country.

INSTITUTIONAL FRAMEWORK

Population data systems and development planning: The most recent
population census was taken in 1985. The vital registration system is
regarded as incomplete. Steps are being taken by the Government to
improve the quality and quantity of population statistics and the ability
to analyse them. The Statistical Section of the Ministry of Planning and
Development, established in 1980, has as its principal duties collecting
and analysing of population data and carrying out censuses. The National
Development Plan, 1980-1990, is the latest available.

Integration of population within development planning: In the Maldives no
single governmental agency is responsible for the formulation and
implementation of population policies. The Statistical Section of the
Ministry of Planning and Development is charged with incorporating
population variables into development planning.

POLICIES AND MEASURES

Changes in population size and age structure: The Government has not adopted
an explicit policy with regard to the rate of population growth. It has,
however, expressed increasing concern over population growth trends.
Currently, the Government takes no direct measures to influence changes in
population size and age structure. Maternal and child health programmes and
programmes to eradicate communicable diseases are expected to lead to a
further decline in the death rate and, therefore, an increase in the growth
rate of the population. There is no information readily available on pension
schemes.

- 156 -

MALDIVES

Mortality and morbidity: The Government gives priority to maternal and child health services and the eradication of water-borne diseases in order to bring down the high rates of morbidity and mortality. The policy seeks the equitable distribution of health services through the primary health care approach; greater emphasis is being given to preventive facilities in the outer-lying islands. It also seeks lower neo-natal, infant and maternal mortality through programmes of child-spacing, nutrition and growth monitoring. Additional objectives include reducing the incidence of tetanus, pertussis, measles, tuberculosis, leprosy and malaria, and of diarrhoeal epidemics, which regularly occur. Strategies to achieve "health for all" recognize the need to develop governmental services, on the one hand, and to mobilize the self-development capacity of the community, on the other. Other priorities include the provision of safe water and basic sanitary facilities, immunization against communicable diseases, the availability of essential medicines on each island and the provision of child-spacing programmes. A target has been set to reduce the rate of infant mortality to 60 per thousand by 1990 and lower maternal mortality by 20 per cent.

Fertility and the family: Although the Government does not intervene to modify the present levels of fertility, some of its health programmes may influence fertility levels, such as the maternal and child health programmes. The family planning programme aims to improve the health of mothers through birth-spacing. All methods of contraception are permitted by law. The Government provides direct support with respect to the use of modern methods of contraception. Efforts are being made to disseminate views on family planning at the community level, so as to foster a positive attitude towards the doctrine of small families for a better standard of living. Training programmes and mass media campaigns aim at improving couples' awareness of family planning. Abortion is legal if the woman's life is at risk. There is no information readily available on the status of sterilization.

International migration: There are no known policy statements concerning the levels of immigration and emigration, which are viewed as insignificant.

Spatial distribution/urbanization: The Government perceives the present pattern of population distribution between Malé, where more than one quarter of the population live, and the atolls as inappropriate. The policy aims at decreasing the level of migration to Malé, and at balancing the population density and socio-economic progress between Malé and the atolls. Priority is given to the development of atolls in order to attract migrants from over-crowded areas. The Government has formulated an overall development policy for the atolls. The Atolls Development Advisory Board implements development policies and allocates government resources and services to the atolls. The measures include provision of health, education and training services, construction of fisheries, implementation of agriculture development programmes, and the development of transport and communication systems. The Government had under consideration in 1985 a proposal to shift both population and economic activity to some of the nearby islands. For Malé itself, a town plan has been developed, establishing zoning standards and compatible land uses for housing and community services, including the utilization of reclaimed land.

<u>Status of women and population</u>: The measures taken by the Government to improve the socio-economic status of women are integrated into population policies, including family planning and population planning. Women in Maldives have a privileged status in society, enjoying equal pay with men and higher literacy rates. In 1977, the National Women's Committee was established to enhance the involvement of women in development activities. The activities of the Committee include encouraging women in leadership, training them in managerial, supervisory, income-generating and vocational skills, and involving them in development planning. There is no information readily available on the minimum legal age at marriage for women.

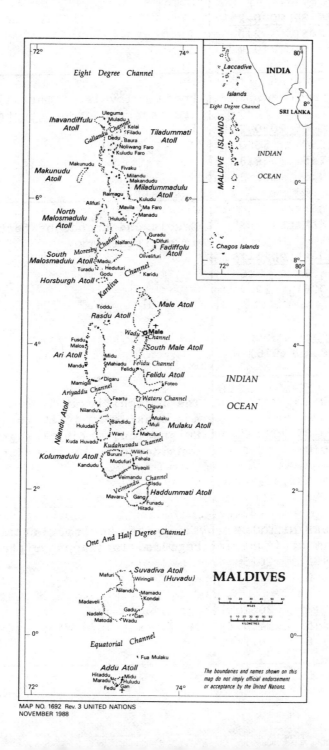

MAP NO. 1692 Rev. 3 UNITED NATIONS
NOVEMBER 1988

MALI

DEMOGRAPHIC INDICATORS	CURRENT PERCEPTION

SIZE/AGE STRUCTURE/GROWTH
 	
Population: <u>1985</u>   <u>2025</u>
(thousands) 8 082 24 142
  0-14 years (%) 46.3   38.0
  60+ years (%)   4.5   4.9
 	
Rate of: <u>1980-85</u> <u>2020-25</u>
 growth   2.8   2.0
 natural increase 28.0   19.9
	The Government considers the present rate of growth to be <u>satisfactory</u> with respect to the country's labour needs, low population density and under-utilized natural resources.

MORTALITY/MORBIDITY <u>1980-85</u> <u>2020-25</u> Life expectancy 42.0 58.0 Crude death rate 22.5 9.8 Infant mortality 179.5 107.3	Present levels of mortality and morbidity are regarded as <u>unacceptable</u>.
FERTILITY/NUPTIALITY/FAMILY <u>1980-85</u> <u>2020-25</u> Fertility rate 6.7 3.6 Crude birth rate 50.6 29.7 Contraceptive prevalence rate ... ... Female mean age at first marriage 18.1 (1976)	Levels and trends of fertility are viewed as <u>satisfactory</u>.
INTERNATIONAL MIGRATION <u>1980-85</u> <u>2020-25</u> Net migration rate 0.0 0.0 Foreign-born population (%) 2.3 (1976)	The insignificant levels of immigration are considered to be <u>satisfactory</u>. Emigration, which is <u>significant</u>, is considered to be <u>satisfactory</u>.
SPATIAL DISTRIBUTION/URBANIZATION Urban <u>1985</u> <u>2025</u> population (%) 18.0 41.7 Growth rate: <u>1980-85</u> <u>2020-25</u> urban 3.6 4.0 rural 2.6 0.7	The pattern of spatial distribution is regarded as <u>inappropriate</u>.

GENERAL POLICY FRAMEWORK

Overall approach to population problems: The Government has no explicit
policy with regard to population growth since it is felt that policies
centred on purely demographic objectives will inevitably be ineffective.
The Government's primary population concerns are the high rates of
morbidity and mortality. Specific governmental actions have been
undertaken in the areas of primary health care, maternal and child health,
education and family planning. Attention has also focused on improving
data collection.

Importance of population policy in achieving development objectives:
Although sectoral policies and action programmes exists, there is no
overall policy relating to the patterns of population change. The
Government, however, acknowledges the interdependence of population and
development. The Government has indicated the need to elaborate a
population policy aimed at overall socio-economic development. The
creation in 1983 of a Population Unit within the Human Resource Division
of the Ministry of Planning shows the increasing importance the Government
attaches to integrating demographic variables into development strategies.

INSTITUTIONAL FRAMEWORK

Population data systems and development planning: Demographic and related
socio-economic data sources for Mali are limited and inadequate. The
first modern census of Mali was conducted in December 1976. The most
recent census was held in 1987. Civil registration is considered
incomplete. Other data sources include annual agricultural surveys,
health, school and employment statistics, and a few demographic sample
surveys. The first five-year plan was executed for the period 1961-1966;
the most recent plan covers the period 1981-1985. The new development
plan for the period 1987-1991, which still was being drafted in early
1987, is expected to give top priority to agricultural development.

Integration of population within development planning: Though there is no
explicit population policy, the Government has expressed growing concern
about population-related matters and development on many occasions. In
1984 the Government indicated its intention to create an infrastructure to
integrate demographic variables and population policies into development
planning. The Government had stressed the importance of demographic
variables in its development strategy. The creation of a Population Unit
in the Human Resource Division of the Ministry of Planning is considered
to be the initial step in formulating appropriate population policies and
integrating them with the development programmes.

POLICIES AND MEASURES

Changes in population size and age structure: The Government does not
consider the country's population growth to be too high and has not adopted
any policy to alter growth on purely demographic grounds. The Government

MALI

considers Mali to be underpopulated relative to its natural resources. Nevertheless, policies in other areas, such as family planning, maternal and child health, and education, are expected to influence population growth. The Government supports family planning for reasons of health and for birth-spacing, but not for anti-natalist objectives. Under the social security scheme, voluntary coverage is available to the self-employed and their dependents.

Mortality and morbidity: The policy aims to reduce general and infant morbidity and mortality. The prevention of infectious and communicable diseases which cause a considerable proportion of all deaths, is a priority. The major policy orientations include primary health care in rural areas, maternal and child health care, and environmental sanitation. Mali has adopted the goal of "health for all by 2000". The Ministry of Public Health and Social Affairs has initiated the Ten-Year Plan for Social and Sanitary Development (1981-1990). Specific measures include programmes of curative and preventive medicine, health education, improvement of existing medical facilities, immunization campaigns, nutrition programmes, provision of adequate food and clean water, expansion of a rural health care network, and training of health personnel. The 1990 target is to reduce general and infant mortality by one half.

Fertility and the family: The Government maintains a policy of non-intervention towards fertility. Family planning is supported by the Government in the context of health services and for birth spacing. Contraceptive practices are legal, but there is no direct support from the Government in the distribution of contraceptives. Sterilization is permissible for medical reasons only, and abortion is illegal, except in cases where the life of the mother is in danger. The Government provides some pro-natalist benefits to mothers and children, including a birth grant and monthly allowance for each child, and a prenatal allowance for the mother.

International migration: There is no official policy with regard to immigration. The Government has indicated that it would seek to maintain the present significant levels of emigration. Fleeing the effects of the recent drought, thousands of Malians have gone across the border into southern Algeria. In 1986, it was reported that Algeria had expelled some 5,500 Tuareg refugees; they have since returned to the Gap Region of Mali.

Spatial distribution/urbanization: The Government has not formulated any explicit policy to limit the growth of urban centres, although it has expressed concern over the acceleration in rural-to-urban migration. The Government has received international assistance in order to formulate a population distribution policy and, eventually, a national plan for spatial distribution. The rural development programmes aim at narrowing the disparity between urban and rural areas, thereby decelerating migration to urban areas. They promote agricultural development and small-scale industries based on agricultural produce, improved irrigation and water supply, and better communication and transportation networks.

<u>Status of women and population</u>: In order to improve the status of women, the Government puts emphasis on women's education, maternal and child health and a reduction in polygamy. The Government has established a National Commission for the Advancement of Women which, in co-operation with the Union nationale de femmes maliennes (UNFM), implements programmes for the emancipation of women. The programmes aim at the promotion of women's status in the family and in society, efficient participation of women in gainful employment, and the overall economic, social and cultural development of women. Though the legal minimum age at marriage for females is 18 years, it is not very strictly enforced, and there are provisions for marriage at age 16 under certain circumstances.

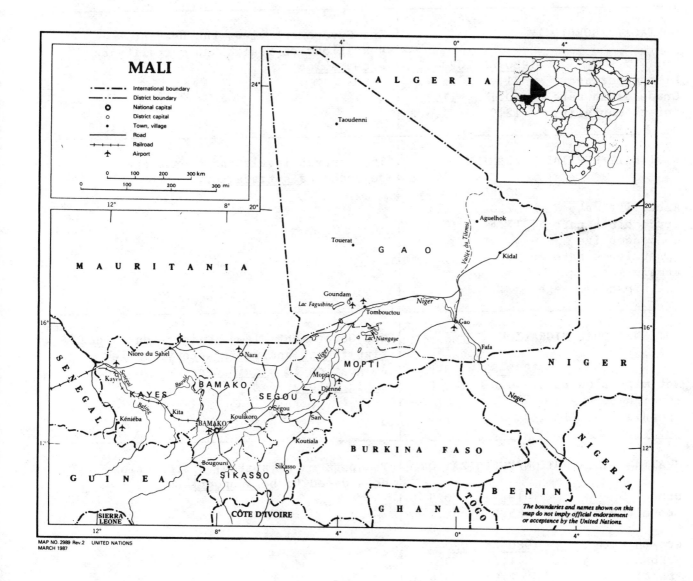

MALTA

DEMOGRAPHIC INDICATORS	CURRENT PERCEPTION
SIZE/AGE STRUCTURE/GROWTH	The Government perceives the current growth rate as <u>satisfactory</u>.

Population:	1985	2025
(thousands)	383	459
0-14 years (%)	23.9	19.5
60+ years (%)	13.8	23.7

Rate of:	1980-85	2020-25
growth	0.7	0.2
natural increase	7.3	1.8

MORTALITY/MORBIDITY	The Government views the present conditions of health and mortality as <u>acceptable</u>.

	1980-85	2020-25
Life expectancy	71.7	76.9
Crude death rate	10.1	11.2
Infant mortality	12.9	6.6

FERTILITY/NUPTIALITY/FAMILY	The current levels and trends are regarded as <u>satisfactory</u>.

	1980-85	2020-25
Fertility rate	2.0	2.1
Crude birth rate	17.4	13.0
Contraceptive prevalence rate	...	...
Female mean age at first marriage	...	...

INTERNATIONAL MIGRATION	The Government views immigration as <u>not significant</u> and <u>satisfactory</u>, while emigration is <u>significant</u> and <u>satisfactory</u>.

	1980-85	2020-25
Net migration rate	0.0	0.0
Foreign-born population (%)	...	...

SPATIAL DISTRIBUTION/URBANIZATION	The pattern of spatial distribution is considered to be <u>appropriate</u>.

Urban	1985	2025
population (%)	85.3	92.4

Growth rate:	1980-85	2020-25
urban	1.2	0.3
rural	-2.0	-0.8

GENERAL POLICY FRAMEWORK

Overall approach to population problems: The Government has no explicit population policy, but it recognizes the need to maintain a low birth rate. With regard to international migration, the policy of the Government is to maintain the levels of emigration. There are no plans to modify the population distribution pattern.

Importance of population policy in achieving development objectives: Even though the Government recognizes the adverse effects of uncontrolled population pressure, there is no statement on the importance of population policy in achieving development objectives.

INSTITUTIONAL FRAMEWORK

Population data systems and development planning: Censuses were conducted in 1948, 1957 and 1967. The most recent was held in 1985. Census-taking is the responsibility of the Central Office of Statistics. Vital registration is considered to be complete. The Government has switched from a five-year to a three-year cycle of development plans, since it feels that detailed, long-term projections are less meaningful for a small, open economy. A development plan for the period 1986-1988 is currently in effect. In 1987 the Government announced that it will be creating a National Development Council to draw up a new development plan and to monitor its implementation once it has been approved by Parliament.

Integration of population within development planning: The Government does not have a planning organization charged with the responsibility of taking into account population variables in planning. Population projections used in development and programme planning have been prepared by the Demographic Section of the Central Office of Statistics, founded in 1947.

POLICIES AND MEASURES

Changes in population size and age structure: There is no policy of intervention with regard to population growth, but the Government has expressed the need to maintain the low birth rate. Underscoring the importance the Government places on issues of aging, a National Commission on Aging was established in the Office of the Prime Minister to act as a co-ordinating body at the highest level. In 1986 the Government appointed a Parliamentary Secretary for the Aged within the Ministry of Social Policy.

Mortality and morbidity: The high incidence of diabetes and heart disease have been identified as being of special policy concern. Health services are provided free of charge, and there is an expanding network of polyclinics in the large urban areas for the provision of medical care. All hospitals are run by the Government. Through agreements of co-operation, those requiring

MALTA

medical care not available in Malta are transferred to hospitals in Belgium, Czechoslovakia and the United Kingdom, while foreign medical teams visit Malta to perform highly specialized surgery. In 1987 the Government announced its intention to establish special health centres in large industrial areas to focus on the health needs of workers. Concerned about the problems associated with drug abuse, the Government plans to take measures stressing both drug prevention and rehabilitation.

Fertility and the family: The Government does not intervene to influence the rate of fertility. Family policy aims at improving the living conditions of both parents and children. The care of children, greater opportunities for women, and social rehabilitation are the major concerns of the policies. Family allowances, first introduced in 1974, consist of 3.10 Malta lire (LM 0.43 = $US 1 as of 1985) a week for the first child, LM 2.45 for the second, LM 1.55 for the third, and LM 0.30 for each subsequent child. Maternity benefits of eight weeks before and five weeks after confinement, with the payment of full wages, are also provided for working women. To facilitate the choice between child-rearing and labour market activities, the Government plans to provide facilities for the care of young children during working hours and financial compensation for mothers who decide to stay at home. Housewives with grown children will be offered retraining services. Reflecting a significant change in the official attitude towards family planning, the Government has provided family planning services since 1981. In that year the Department of Health and Environment introduced family welfare centres as part of its plan to develop community services. Four such centres provide relationship counselling, child health care and gynaecological services as well as family planning facilities. All modern methods of contraception are permitted by law. A ban on the advertising of contraceptives was lifted in 1974, and the law prohibiting the importation of contraceptives was repealed in 1975. Abortion is illegal other than to save the mother's life. Information on the status of sterilization is not readily available.

International migration: The Government has no specific policy with regard to immigration and emigration. The traditional heavy outflow of Maltese emigrants to Australia, Canada, the United Kingdom and the United States was reversed in 1975. Since then, the amount of return migration has exceeded that of emigration. Through a 1977 law Malta discourages return migration, since an influx of predominantly working-age population would further aggravate the already strained labour market. Yet the Government has made various efforts, such as employing some 8,000 persons in its Emergency Labour Corps, to prevent high unemployment from becoming higher emigration.

Spatial distribution/urbanization: The Government has stated that problems usually arising from demarcating national, regional and municipal responsibilities are not present in Malta, since the entire group of islands is considered a single region, with urban and rural areas. Zoning projects, reserved areas and controlled growth to check urban sprawl are some of the means that have been used to strike a proper balance between the demands of urbanization, transport and industrial development, on the one hand, and the conservation of agricultural land and protection of the environment, on the other.

Status of women and population: A substantial increase has taken place in the labour-force participation of women in recent years.   In the public sector, for instance, restrictions on the continued employment of married women were modified in 1981, and paid maternity leave, in both the public and the private sectors, has been introduced.   However, the Government notes with concern that a large number of female workers withdraw from the labour force at marriage. It is, therefore, the intention of the Government to encourage greater employment participation of married women, without disruptive social consequences.   The minimum legal age at marriage for women is 14 years.

Other issues: Believing that the creation of an institute devoted to training and education on all aspects of aging can serve as a cultural bridge between north and south, the Government invited the United Nations to establish such an institute in Malta.   In 1987 the United Nations agreed to the establishement in Malta of the International Institute on Aging.

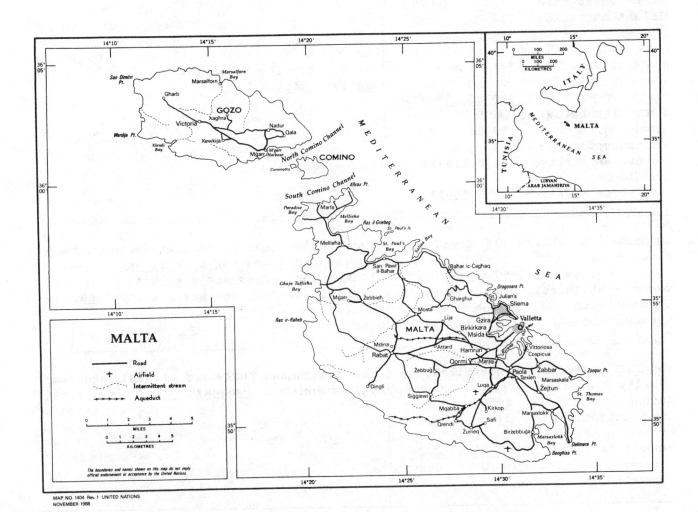

MAP NO. 1404 Rev. 1 UNITED NATIONS
NOVEMBER 1988

MAURITANIA

DEMOGRAPHIC INDICATORS	CURRENT PERCEPTION
SIZE/AGE STRUCTURE/GROWTH	Population growth is considered to be <u>satisfactory</u>.

Population:	1985	2025
(thousands)	1 888	5 780
0-14 years (%)	46.4	38.1
60+ years (%)	4.6	5.1

Rate of:	1980-85	2020-25
growth	2.9	2.1
natural increase	29.2	20.5

MORTALITY/MORBIDITY

Levels and trends of mortality and morbidity are viewed as <u>unacceptable</u>.

	1980-85	2020-25
Life expectancy	44.0	60.0
Crude death rate	20.9	8.9
Infant mortality	137.3	65.0

FERTILITY/NUPTIALITY/FAMILY

Fertility rates are viewed as <u>satisfactory</u>.

	1980-85	2020-25
Fertility rate	6.9	3.6
Crude birth rate	50.1	29.4
Contraceptive prevalence rate	1.0 (1981)	
Female mean age at first marriage	19.5 (1977)	

INTERNATIONAL MIGRATION

Immigration levels are considered to be <u>satisfactory</u> and <u>not significant</u>. Emigration levels are viewed as <u>significant</u> because they are <u>too high</u>.

	1980-85	2020-25
Net migration rate	0.0	0.0
Foreign-born population (%)	2.0 (1977)	

SPATIAL DISTRIBUTION/URBANIZATION

The Government perceives spatial distribution as <u>inappropriate</u>.

Urban	1985	2025
population (%)	34.6	69.5

Growth rate:	1980-85	2020-25
urban	8.0	2.9
rural	0.7	0.3

GENERAL POLICY FRAMEWORK

Overall approach to population problems: The Government has concentrated on the reduction of mortality and morbidity, rural development, and the deceleration of internal migration. Severe droughts in the 1970s and 1980s have hindered attempts to raise the quality of life of Mauritanians. The Government seeks a lasting solution to population problems by raising the economic, cultural, and social levels of its citizens.

Importance of population policy in achieving development objectives: Demographic variables are integrated into the development planning process. It appears that population policy, particularly in regard to the pattern of spatial distribution, figures prominently in the development strategy. Some official statements, in connection with the growth rate, fertility, and emigration, have indicated that a larger population may be desirable for development purposes, despite difficulties in feeding the present population.

INSTITUTIONAL FRAMEWORK

Population data systems and development planning: The first general census was held between December 1976 and April 1977. An attempt was made to enumerate both the sedentary and the nomadic populations. Additional information is available from an urban census taken in 1961/1962, a rural census in 1965, a demographic survey in 1961/1965, and a fertility survey in 1981. The Government announced plans to follow through with a census in 1988. The Government does not consider the available data to be adequate. Despite legal provisions for the registration of births, the Government believes that vital registration is not complete and plans to improve the registration system. Village registers, which were compiled at the time of the census, provide some demographic information. The fourth development plan covers the years 1981-1985. A medium-term economic and financial recovery plan for 1986-1988 was adopted in September 1985.

Integration of population within development planning: The Statistical Office and the Centre for Demographic and Social Research are responsible for the formulation and co-ordination of population policies. The Centre was initiated in 1980 but finally established in 1983. These two agencies also provide information on the relationships between population and development and conduct demographic surveys.

POLICIES AND MEASURES

Changes in population size and age structure: The Government has indicated that higher population growth would be favourable for socio-economic development. In the absence of a comprehensive population policy, it appears

MAURITANIA

that the strategy to increase population size focuses on a higher rate of natural increase brought about by lowered mortality rates. However, the Government has stated its intention to maintain emigration rates. The Government has reported that the only concrete conclusion to be drawn from the 1977 census is that the population is young. More and better information on population size and composition is desired. The National Social Security Fund administers old-age benefits for employed persons (excluding temporary or casual workers); a special system exists for public employees.

Mortality and morbidity: The reduction of mortality and morbidity is a principal concern of the Government. Its objectives are to improve primary health care, train personnel, and provide health education, especially on nutrition. Infants, children, and mothers warrant special attention and high priority. Morbidity issues include malnutrition, malaria, measles, tuberculosis, polio, tetanus, whooping cough, diarrhoea, and diptheria. The Government has received assistance to institute rehydration, immunization, and nutrition programmes. Begun in 1980, the strengthening of the national family well-being programmes was designed to reduce maternal and child mortality and improve health care facilities. Despite the expansion of Nutrition Rehabilitation and Education Centres for mothers and children, malnutrition is considered to be on the rise because of a high rate of relapse into previous habits and persistent food shortages. A project has been undertaken to train medical personnel and to extend health service to rural areas.

Fertility and the family: Official policy appears to be the maintenance of high fertility rates. Government efforts are directed towards improving maternal and child health for purely health objectives, and providing financial support for parents, children, and the aged. The National Social Security Fund administers maternity benefits which cover employed women, family benefits for employed women wih children under age 14, and lump-sum birth grants. The Government does not support access to contraception; a 1920 French anti-contraception law is still in effect. However, contraceptives are available by prescription. The 1981 fertility survey indicated that less than 10 per cent of the women surveyed had heard of family planning devices. Abortion is prohibited except for narrow medical reasons. Sterilization is available for medical reasons only.

International migration: Immigration is not an active policy concern. Although emigration is considered too high, official policy is to maintain the current rates in the future.

Spatial distribution/urbanization: The Government's policy is to halt the rural exodus, to modify the urban/rural population distribution pattern, and to reduce the growth rate of the capital city. In 1980, an estimated 40 per cent of the urban population lived in the capital, Nouakchott. Nouakchott and the principal secondary centres have been provided with urban master plans; an urban development code gives priority to the problems of squatters. Droughts, sedentarization, and mineral mining activities have caused major shifts in the pattern of population distribution. The Government hopes that the 1988 census will provide more information on them. The official strategy to control internal migration focuses on rural agricultural development and irrigation projects. Additional measures include public infrastructure subsidies, housing and social services, human resource development, and job training.

Status of women and population: Although the situation of women in Mauritania has improved in the past few years, the development of a strategy to improve their status has been constrained by inadequate data on women and the lack of women's involvement in the policy-making process concerning the promotion of women's status. This lack of participation may also be attributable to the absence of a national women's organization advocating the interests of women. The Ministry for the Protection of the Family aims to improve the status of women by creating conditions for economic and social independence. Information on the minimum legal age at marriage for women is not readily available.

Other issues: Due to droughts during the 1970 and 1980s, Government attention has necessarily focused upon food supply problems, subsequent malnutrition, and population movements stemming from harsh rural conditions.

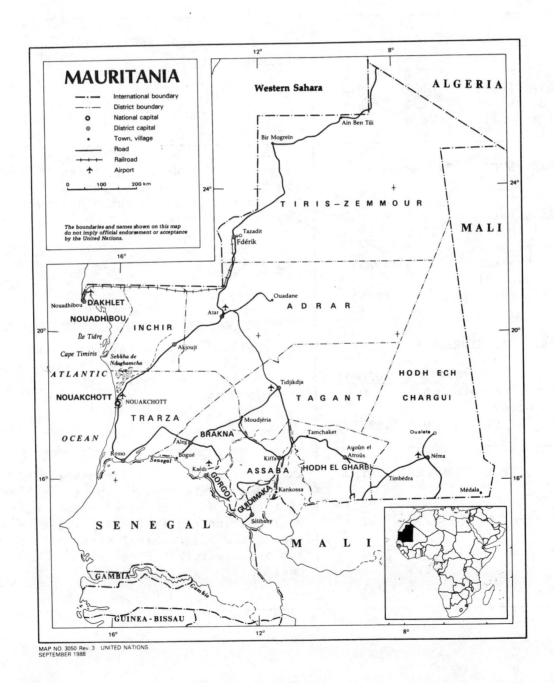

MAP NO. 3050 Rev. 3 UNITED NATIONS
SEPTEMBER 1988

MAURITIUS

DEMOGRAPHIC INDICATORS	CURRENT PERCEPTION
SIZE/AGE STRUCTURE/GROWTH	The rate of growth is perceived as unsatisfactory, and too high.

Population: 1985   2025

	1985	2025
Population: (thousands)	1 050	1 606
0–14 years (%)	31.6	21.2
60+ years (%)	5.7	17.8

Rate of:	1980–85	2020–25
growth	1.9	0.6
natural increase	19.5	5.9

MORTALITY/MORBIDITY	Levels and trends are considered unacceptable.

	1980–85	2020–25
Life expectancy	66.7	74.2
Crude death rate	6.0	8.6
Infant mortality	28.4	8.5

FERTILITY/NUPTIALITY/FAMILY	Rates are considered unsatisfactory and too high in relation to population growth, maternal and child health and family well-being.

	1980–85	2020–25
Fertility rate	2.8	2.1
Crude birth rate	25.5	14.5
Contraceptive prevalence rate	75.0 (1985)	
Female mean age at first marriage	21.7 (1983)	

INTERNATIONAL MIGRATION	Immigration is not significant and satisfactory. Emigration is significant and too low, due to high rates of unemployment.

	1980–85	2020–25
Net migration rate	-0.6	0.0
Foreign-born population (%)	0.5 (1983)	

SPATIAL DISTRIBUTION/URBANIZATION	The pattern of population distribution is viewed as inappropriate due to the lack of further development of towns, main villages and recreational facilities and inadequate geographical distribution of job opportunities in relation to place of residence.

	1985	2025
Urban population (%)	42.2	62.7

Growth rate:	1980–85	2020–25
urban	1.5	1.7
rural	2.2	-1.1

GENERAL POLICY FRAMEWORK

Overall approach to population problems: There is intervention to modify
demographic variables in combination with a policy of social and economic
restructuring. Official policy is to decrease population growth, chiefly
by means of modifying fertility. In recent years, increasing emphasis has
been placed on adjusting the pattern of spatial distribution.

Importance of population policy in achieving development objectives: The
Government considers population policy to be essential in achieving
development objectives, since it is acutely conscious of the fact that
unchecked population growth might dissipate many of the benefits accruing
from economic development, given the country's narrow resource base.

INSTITUTIONAL FRAMEWORK

Population data systems and development planning: The first census was
conducted in 1846 and the latest in 1983. Vital registration is almost
complete. The latest development plan is the two-year plan for economic
and social development (1984-1986).

Integration of population within development planning: The Ministry of
Economic Planning and Development is responsible for the formulation and
co-ordination of population policies. The Human Resources Section and the
Economic Analysis and Research Section are jointly responsible for
incorporating population variables in planning.

POLICIES AND MEASURES

Changes in population size and age structure: Although the Government's
policies are believed to have helped to lower significantly the rate of growth
since the early 1960s, officials are still aware of the problems posed by the
fact that Mauritius is one of the world's most densely populated countries.
Official policy is to decrease the rate of growth. This is to be accomplished
primarily by decreasing fertility levels through family planning, health
education, information programmes, improving the status of women, and
adjusting economic and social factors (e.g., creating employment, improving
income distribution, reorganizing the agricultural sector). The Government's
overriding policy objective is to intensify population limitation programmes
so as to make the growth rate compatible with the country's limited land area
and natural resources. Pension coverage exists for all residents.

Mortality and morbidity: Official policy is to provide more equitable health
services for the entire population. This is to be achieved by increasing the
number of health service delivery points in rural areas, and by bringing
together curative, promotive and preventive services. Emphasis is placed on
the primary health care approach. Specific measures include the extension and
enlargement of maternal and child health services by the Ministry of Health

MAURITIUS

and programmes in nutrition, environmental sanitation and clean water supply. A network of rural and urban health centres is to provide integrated services (e.g., family planning, maternal and child health, nutrition, health education). The Government had established the goal of completely eradicating malaria by 1987.

Fertility and the family: The Government has adopted a policy of intervention to modify the effects of fertility on the rate of population growth and maternal and child health and family well-being. Specifically, official policy aims to lower the rates of fertility through family planning services, measures to improve the status of women and changing the minimum legal age of marriage for females from 15 to 18 years. Other measures expected to affect rates include health education, communication and information programmes, improving educational attainment, increasing employment and improving income distribution. Access to contraception receives direct government support. Family planning service points increased from 90 to 158 between 1972 and 1983. Recently, population and family life education have been introduced into some secondary schools. Abortion is legal only to save the life of the mother. Sterilization is permitted for therapeutic, genetic and health reasons. A target of reducing the gross reproduction rate to 1.12 by 1987 was set.

International migration: Official policy is to maintain immigration at the current low levels. Various safeguards - e.g., work permits, restrictions on dependants' employment - have been implemented to contain the flow of immigrants. In the past, the Government has sought to maintain the level of emigration but with the current high rates of unemployment, officials now seek to increase levels of emigration in the future. The Government's policy might best be described as one favouring selective emigration since it is designed to retain the country's skilled workers while at the same time relieving the pressure for jobs. No quantitative targets have been set.

Spatial distribution/urbanization: Official policy is to decelerate internal migration. Since the island is very densely populated and urban areas already encompass the majority of the country's population, efforts have been made to cope with urban population growth. They include the adoption of a national housing policy and a national physical plan which have as objectives to promote a better distribution of housing and improve inter-urban and intra-urban traffic flows. Although the Government does not aim to adjust patterns of spatial distribution for demographic reasons, it does promote rural development and regional development policies for lagging regions with the specific objectives of preserving agriculturally productive land and developing towns and main villages. Public infrastructure subsidies have been directed towards enterprises, and individuals have benefited from social service and job training measures.

Status of women and population: The Government believes that women's participation in all population programmes has contributed to the programmes' effectiveness, and thus it has sought to further address women's status - education levels, reproductive rights, participation in decision-making - as a means of further improving the effectiveness of population policies. To promote the status of women, the civil code has been amended to provide additional civil rights to wives and raise their legal status to that of husbands. The minimum legal age at marriage for women is 18 years.

<u>Other issues</u>: The Government has emphasized the need to address its population problems in the context of international economic inequality (i.e., unequal trade patterns) and implied that future population policy efforts may be constrained by the country's overwhelming dependence on its sugar industry as a source of revenue.

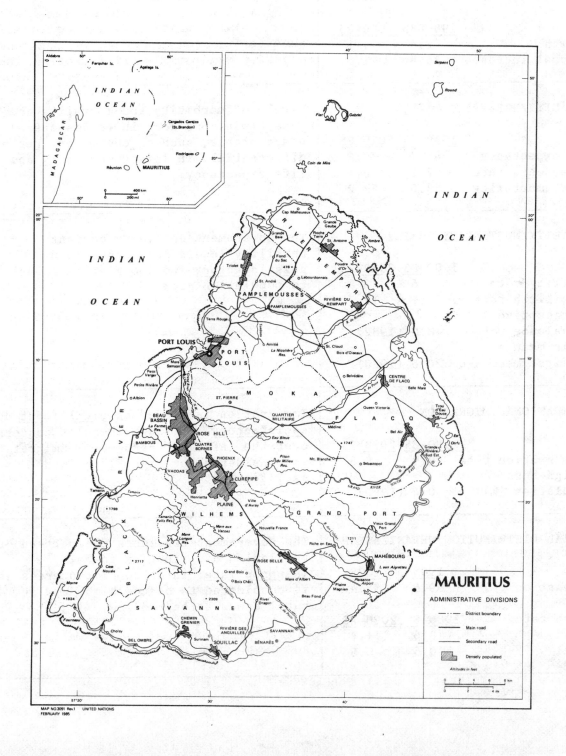

MAURITIUS

ADMINISTRATIVE DIVISIONS

District boundary
Main road
Secondary road
Densely populated

Altitudes in feet

MEXICO

DEMOGRAPHIC INDICATORS	CURRENT PERCEPTION

SIZE/AGE STRUCTURE/GROWTH
 	
Population: 1985   2025
 (thousands)   78 996   154 085
  0-14 years (%)   42.2   24.8
  60+ years (%)   5.4   11.6
 	
Rate of: 1980-85   2020-25
 growth   2.6   1.1
 natural increase   26.8   11.3
	The Government perceives the growth rate as <u>unsatisfactory</u> and <u>too high</u>, despite achievements in controlling growth.

MORTALITY/MORBIDITY 1980-85 2020-25 Life expectancy 65.7 73.2 Crude death rate 7.1 6.4 Infant mortality 53.0 22.2	Levels of morbidity and mortality are <u>acceptable</u>, but certain trends are unacceptable, such as continuing regional differentials in infant mortality and life expectancy.
FERTILITY/NUPTIALITY/FAMILY 1980-85 2020-25 Fertility rate 4.6 2.3 Crude birth rate 33.9 17.7 Contraceptive prevalence rate 48.0 (1982) Female mean age at first marriage 20.6 (1980)	The Government considers current fertility levels and trends to be <u>unsatisfactory</u> and <u>too high</u> in relation to population growth.
INTERNATIONAL MIGRATION 1980-85 2020-25 Net migration rate -0.9 -0.5 Foreign-born population (%) 0.4 (1980)	Immigration is viewed as <u>significant</u> and <u>satisfactory</u>, although there is concern over the influx of refugees. Emigration is considered <u>not significant</u> and <u>satisfactory</u>.
SPATIAL DISTRIBUTION/URBANIZATION Urban 1985 2025 population (%) 69.6 85.4 Growth rate: 1980-85 2020-25 urban 3.6 1.4 rural 0.5 -0.6	The Government considers the pattern of population distribution to be <u>inappropriate</u>; in metropolitan areas it is considered to be too high, and in rural areas to be too low.

GENERAL POLICY FRAMEWORK

Overall approach to population problems: The Government wishes to reduce substantially demographic growth, chiefly by modifying fertility. It combines direct intervention to modify demographic variables with economic and social restructuring. In addition, increasing importance has been assigned to adjusting patterns of spatial distribution, improving the status of women, the quality of life and social equity. The 1973 General Population Law promotes equilibrium between birth rates, population distribution and the distribution of socio-economic activity. In 1978, the Government formulated a regional demographic policy to adjust spatial distribution.

Importance of population policy in achieving development objectives: Population policy has been incorporated into development plans. The Population Policy of 1974 was established to regulate phenomenon that affect population structure, volume, dynamics and distribution. The Government has emphasized that regulating demographic variables is indispensable for accelerating economic and social development. Population policy serves to co-ordinate programmes in education, public health, investment, agrarian reform, rural development, employment etc. A National Population Programme, 1984-1988, has been formulated.

INSTITUTIONAL FRAMEWORK

Population data systems and development planning: Mexico has a long history of census-taking, with the 1980 census being the tenth conducted since 1895. A national demographic survey was conducted in 1982. In 1980, the Federal Statistics Law assigned responsibility to the National Population Council for co-ordinating statistics on demographic planning and development. Since 1976 the Ministry of Programming and Budget has been responsible for formulating, implementing and evaluating development plans. The national development plan for the period 1983-1988 is currently in effect.

Integration of population within development planning: The National Population Council (CONAPO), established under the 1974 Population Law, is an interministerial body headed by the Minister of the Interior. It is responsible for incorporating demographic variables into overall development plans. CONAPO integrates population policy into the socio-economic development plans of states and sectors and in 1985 issued the National Population Programme, 1984-1988.

POLICIES AND MEASURES

Changes in population size and age structure: In 1973 the Government made a dramatic turnaround in its population policy and stated that it sought to reduce population growth. Policies have included direct intervention such as

MEXICO

family planning, sex education, and communication and information programmes. Indirect measures have included raising educational levels and creating additional employment. The 1978 Regional Demographic Policy divided states into four regions based on fertility levels and population growth, and assigned targets and specific programmes to each to narrow regional differences. The National Population Council set a target of 1.8 per cent growth by 1988, and of 1.0 per cent by the year 2000. While social security coverage is currently available only to employees and members of certain co-operatives, coverage is gradually being extended to rural areas and to workers not yet covered.

Mortality and morbidity: The major objective is to create a single national health care system capable of meeting current and future needs. The right to health protection is guaranteed by the Constitution. The 1984 General Health Law stipulated the inclusion of the right to health in development plans. The Government has aimed at providing health services to all, particularly in the rural and urban fringes. The Ministry of Health has formulated strategies of decentralization - for example, giving states administrative responsibilities, modernizing information and evaluation systems. Goals include complete vaccination for those age six years and under; screening services; early detection for high-risk pregnancies; prenatal care; supplementary food during pregnancy and lactation; extension of basic services to marginal zones; lowering the incidence of malnutrition; and protecting the elderly and infants in rural and marginal zones. The target is to decrease the crude death rate from 8 per thousand in 1982 to 7 per thousand in 1988.

Fertility and the family: The official policy is to lower fertility. The National Family Planning Programme of 1985-1988 employs a three-pronged approach based on provision and improvement of maternal and child health and family well-being. Direct measures include family planning, sex education, and communication and information programmes. The Government emphasizes the interdependence of such measures with indirect action, such as raising educational levels, increasing employment and improving women's status. Abortion is illegal except to save the woman's life or in cases of rape or incest. Sterilization is legal.

International migration: The policy is to maintain current low immigration levels. In response to the large influx of political refugees from neighbouring countries seeking asylum in Mexico, the Government created the Mexican Commission for Assistance to Refugees (COMAR). It is estimated that as of January 1987 there were 175,000 refugees in Mexico. The goals of the Commission include studying refugee needs and working with international organizations to formulate projects and seek permanent solutions to the refugee problem. Mexico has maintained that top priority be given to guarding the rights and integrity of refugees, and respecting the principle of non-intervention in other countries' internal matters. While the Government has no emigration policy, it acknowledges that the large flow of undocumented Mexicans to the United States requires negotiation between the two countries, and that the migrants be accorded appropriate human rights. There is also growing concern over the influx of returning undocumented Mexican immigrants from the United States as a consequence of the United States Immigration Reform and Control Act, which went into effect in May 1987. It is feared that the return movement will have significant repercussions for Mexico in terms of reduced remittances and higher unemployment.

<u>Spatial distribution</u>: The policy is to reduce migration to major metropolitan regions and other urban centres, and to decrease rural out-migration. Strategies include slowing metropolitan growth and promoting small and intermediate towns and rural development. In 1978, a regional demographic plan was adopted. It aims to adjust spatial distribution by retaining population in certain areas and channeling migration to new receiving areas, ensuring that no state grew by more than 4.5 per cent annually. One objective was to decrease the growth of the Federal District (by relocating public employees), Monterrey and the border cities in the region of Baja, California Norte. The National Urban and Housing Development Programme, 1984-1988, has as its objective the decentralization of functions, and territorial deconcentration by controlling the growth of large cities and developing medium-sized cities. The goal is to resettle 4 million people in 59 medium-sized cities by the year 2000.

<u>Status of women and population</u>: The Programme for Integrating Women in Development, one of seven programmes of the National Population Programme, 1984-1988, has several objectives, including enhancing the position of women in the family and in the labour market and encouraging women's participation in rural development. A National Commission for Women and Women's Commissions in federal and state agencies have been created to promote women's participation in development. Information on the minimum legal age at marriage for women varies: both 14 years and 18 years have been reported.

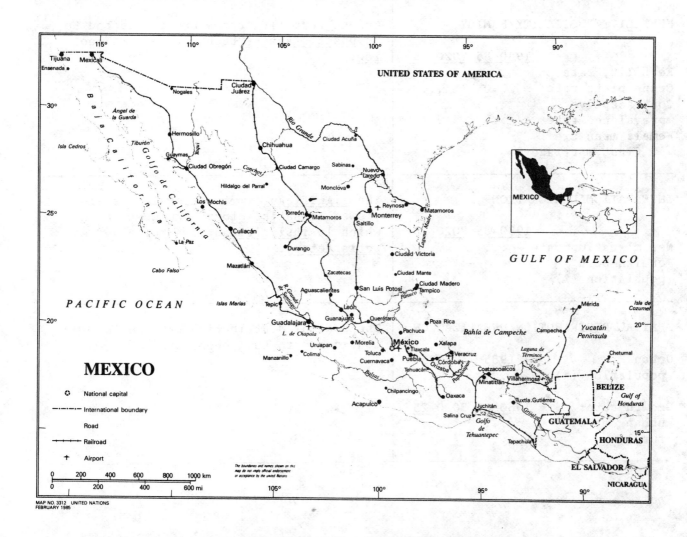

MONACO

DEMOGRAPHIC INDICATORS	CURRENT PERCEPTION
SIZE/AGE STRUCTURE/GROWTH	The Government perceives current growth rates as <u>unsatisfactory</u> and <u>too low</u>.

	1985	2025
Population:		
(thousands)	27	35
0-14 years (%)	...	...
60+ years (%)	29.0	...

Rate of:	1980-85	2020-25
growth	0.8	...
natural increase	0.0	...

MORTALITY/MORBIDITY	The Government considers levels of mortality to be <u>acceptable</u>.

	1980-85	2020-25
Life expectancy	...	...
Crude death rate	20.0	...
Infant mortality	...	...

FERTILITY/NUPTIALITY/FAMILY	Curent fertility rates are considered to be <u>unsatisfactory</u> because they are <u>too low</u>.

	1980-85	2020-25
Fertility rate	...	...
Crude birth rate	20.0	...
Contraceptive prevalence rate	...	...
Female mean age at first marriage	...	...

INTERNATIONAL MIGRATION	The <u>significant</u> immigration levels are viewed as <u>satisfactory</u>. Emigration, which is <u>insignificant</u>, is perceived as <u>satisfactory</u>.

	1980-85	2020-25
Net migration rate	...	...
Foreign-born population (%)	...	...

SPATIAL DISTRIBUTION/URBANIZATION	The spatial distribution pattern is considered to be <u>appropriate</u>.

Urban	1985	2025
population (%)	...	...

Growth rate:	1980-85	2020-25
urban	...	...
rural	...	...

GENERAL POLICY FRAMEWORK

Overall approach to population problems: Although there is no explicit population policy, the Government is concerned with the levels of immigration and low rates of fertility, and views intervention in both areas as appropriate.

Importance of population policy in achieving development objectives: The Government views the low rate of population growth as constraining development. Therefore, socio-economic adjustments have been implemented. Emphasis has been placed on a high capital/labour ratio, light industry and the service sector.

INSTITUTIONAL FRAMEWORK

Population data systems and development planning: The most recent population census was taken in 1982, and the next one has been scheduled for 1989. There is no information available on the status of vital registration data.

Integration of population within development planning: No information is readily available.

POLICIES AND MEASURES

Changes in population size and age structure: The Government is concerned about its aging population (about 25 per cent of the population is over the age of 65) and low growth rates. Consequently, higher rates of fertility are desired by the Government, which views intervention to raise growth rates as appropriate.

Mortality and morbidity: The country has no national health system. The right to health is recognized by the 1962 Constitution and free medical care is provided at the Princess Grace Hospital, the country's only public medical institution. France is relied upon for some types of highly specialized medical personnel. Efforts have been made to improve the quality of services provided, particularly making maternal and child health services more efficient and effective. To control pollution and its adverse consequences, economic development projects must take into consideration industrial pollution and occupational diseases. Environmental research deals primarily with pollution caused by the processing of waste. Research in this area is undertaken by the Centre Scientifique de Monaco.

MONACO

<u>Fertility and the family</u>: Government objectives are to increase fertility rates through a policy of social welfare support, family allowances and assistance to young married couples. The Government offers direct support for the effective use of modern methods of fertility regulation. Sterilization is permitted for contraceptive purposes.

<u>International migration</u>: Government policy favours curbing immigration flows in the future but maintaining the already established immigrant population. Various international agreements have been signed relating to controlling immigration levels based on the availability of employment, housing and other basic factors. The largest number of immigrants are made up of French nationals who comprise over one half of the total population. French nationals living in the principality are now liable to French taxation, while nationals of Monaco and foreign residents pay no income tax. No policy has been formulated regarding emigration.

<u>Spatial distribution/urbanization</u>: Urbanization is not viewed as a demographic problem, and Government policy concerning internal migration is one of non-intervention. The principality is completely urbanized. Concerted efforts at land reclamation in the past two decades have succeeded in expanding the principality's total area by 20 per cent, with some of the new acreage sold for private development. This is in keeping with the Government's urban master plan.

<u>Status of women and population</u>: Information on the status of women is not readily available.

EUROPE

ICELAND

ATLANTIC OCEAN

SWEDEN

FINLAND

NORWAY

UNION OF

SOVIET SOCIALIST REPUBLICS

UNITED KINGDOM

DENMARK

IRELAND

NETHERLANDS

BYELORUSSIAN SSR

GERMAN DEM. REP.

POLAND

FED. REP. OF GERMANY

BELGIUM

UKRAINIAN SSR

LUXEMBOURG

CZECHOSLOVAKIA

LIECHTENSTEIN

FRANCE

AUSTRIA

HUNGARY

SWITZERLAND

ROMANIA

BLACK SEA

SAN MARINO

YUGOSLAVIA

MONACO

BULGARIA

ITALY

ANDORRA

TURKEY

PORTUGAL

ALBANIA

SPAIN

GREECE

Gibraltar

MEDITERRANEAN

CYPRUS

MALTA

SEA

The boundaries shown on this map do not imply official
endorsement or acceptance by the United Nations.

0   200   400   600 mi

0   200   400   600 km

MAP NO. 2771.10   UNITED NATIONS
DECEMBER 1988

MONGOLIA

DEMOGRAPHIC INDICATORS	CURRENT PERCEPTION

SIZE/AGE STRUCTURE/GROWTH
 	
Population: <u>1985</u>   <u>2025</u>
  (thousands) 1 908 4 539
   0-14 years (%) 41.6 28.5
   60+ years (%)   5.2   9.0
 	
Rate of: <u>1980-85</u> <u>2020-25</u>
 growth   2.7   1.5
 natural increase 27.4   15.4
	The Government perceives current growth rates to be <u>too low</u> in relation to manpower demands.

MORTALITY/MORBIDITY <u>1980-85</u> <u>2020-25</u> Life expectancy 62.0 74.1 Crude death rate 8.5 5.1 Infant mortality 53.0 15.7	Present health conditions and mortality levels are viewed as <u>unacceptable</u> despite achievements in reducing morbidity and mortality. Special concern is expressed over maternal and child mortality.
FERTILITY/NUPTIALITY/FAMILY <u>1980-85</u> <u>2020-25</u> Fertility rate 5.1 2.5 Crude birth rate 35.9 20.6 Contraceptive prevalence rate ... ... Female mean age at first marriage	Fertility rates are considered to be <u>too low</u>.
INTERNATIONAL MIGRATION <u>1980-85</u> <u>2020-25</u> Net migration rate 0.0 0.0 Foreign-born population (%)	Immigration levels are considered to be <u>not significant</u> and <u>satisfactory</u>. Emigration is also considered to be <u>not significant</u> and <u>satisfactory</u>.
SPATIAL DISTRIBUTION/URBANIZATION Urban <u>1985</u> <u>2025</u> population (%) 50.8 69.6 Growth rate: <u>1980-85</u> <u>2020-25</u> urban 2.6 2.3 rural 2.9 -0.2	The pattern of spatial distribution is perceived as <u>partially appropriate</u>.

- 183 -

MONGOLIA

GENERAL POLICY FRAMEWORK

Overall approach to population problems: The basis of Mongolian
population policy is the provision of the right to work and participate in
social and productive life while improving one's material and spiritual
conditions. The Government seeks the modification of demographic
variables in combination with a policy of social and economic
restructuring. Specific emphasis is placed on increasing population size
by reducing mortality and improving the spatial distribution, with
attention to the rational use of labour resources.

Importance of population policy in achieving development objectives:
Population policy is considered an essential part of Mongolia's programme
for socio-economic development. A goal of development planning is to
transform Mongolia into an industrial-agrarian society rather than one
that is agrarian-industrial. Population policy is necessary to provide
enough labourers for development and utilization of the resource
potential. The Government has adopted policies to increase the size of
the labour force by way of natural increase and limited immigration in
order to achieve developmental objectives.

INSTITUTIONAL FRAMEWORK

Population data systems and development planning: Population censuses
have been conducted since 1918. The most recent census was taken in
1979. International assistance has been received for a population data
analysis project and a pilot population registration system. Since 1951,
the Central Statistical Bureau and the Ministry of Health have been
responsible for the implementation of the compulsory registration of
births and deaths. The Department of Civil Registration, created in 1977
within the Ministry of Justice is responsible for policies concerning data
collection and analysis and for collecting statistical data. The
Government considers its vital registration information reliable.
Development planning began in the early 1920s; however, the system of
five-year plans was instituted beginning with the period 1948-1952. The
current development plan is the eighth five-year plan, covering the period
1986-1990.

Integration of population within development planning: Although
population policies are considered an important part of development
planning, no institutions are reported that facilitate the integration of
population variables into planning.

POLICIES AND MEASURES

Changes in population size and age structure: The reduction of mortality is
seen as one of the primary ways to increase the rate of natural increase. To
that end, the Government has stressed mother and child health care programmes

and the expansion of general health care facilities to remote regions. The Government also plans to remove constraints to achieving desired birth spacing and completed family size in order to boost the growth rate. The Government feels that the country's young population (47 per cent of the population was below the age of 17 in 1982) has provided both an economic burden in terms of social expenditures and a rejuvenation of the active population.

Mortality and morbidity: Mongolia has achieved considerable success in lowering mortality and morbidity rates but still desires to reach the low levels observed in developed countries. The Government has instituted a mother and child health care project. A council was created in 1979 under the supervision of the Ministry of Health to organize maternal and child health research activities. In 1983 and 1984, the Government adopted a general plan for health resources to the year 2000. The incidence of infectious diseases has apparently been substantially reduced, due to improvements in health care. The Government plans to intensify efforts to combat occupational hazards. Measures are directed towards improving preventive medicine and expanding the number of medical examinations. The Government also plans to provide more and better trained medical personnel. The 1978 National Law on Health Services is the legal basis for the national network of health facilities which provide services free of charge. Special emphasis is placed on providing services in small and medium-sized towns and on instituting paramedic services on agricultural co-operatives and state farms. Overall objectives stress such preventive measures as environmental hygiene and sanitation. The eighth five-year plan notes that construction will begin on centralized water main and sewage systems in certain county centres. The Government has also targeted the improvement of food supplies as part of a drive to improve nutritional intake.

Fertility and the family: The Government's objectives have been to improve mother and child health care and to guarantee that women may easily combine labour force participation with motherhood. Government statements have been made in favour of higher fertility. A tax is levied on unmarried adults and childless parents. The labour code protects the rights of working mothers and ensures financial assistance. Other pro-natalist measures include fully paid maternity leave with post-maternity allowances for mothers with more than four children. Measures are planned to subsidize the cost of raising children for working mothers. The current development plan stresses the objective of extending the system of nurseries and kindergartens and increasing the hours of operation. The Government provides direct support for contraception. Abortion and sterilization are allowed only for health reasons.

International migration: Although immigration is considered insignificant, the Government has pursued a policy of low levels of temporary immigration on a contractual basis with countries of the Council for Mutual Economic Assistance (CMEA) to supplement labour resources. Emigration is limited to temporary residence of Mongolian students in countries of the Council for Mutual Economic Assistance.

Spatial distribution/urbanization: The Government adheres to a policy of adjusting the pattern of spatial distribution to coincide with the country's development objectives. People are encouraged to migrate from rural areas to second-order urban centres. Government policy also includes rural-to-rural migration, or the sedentarization of nomads in lower-order settlements. Rural restructuring covers two other goals: the growth of agricultural co-operatives and state farms in order to concentrate population in centres and provide a full range of public services and housing utilities, and the consolidating of co-operatives into more centralized state farms. Development measures include public infrastructure subsidies, the development of housing and social services, human resource investments, and rural development strategies.

<u>Status of women and population</u>: The Government ensures equal rights for men and women. One quarter of the 370 deputies to the Mongolian Parliament are women. The Code on Marriage and Family guarantees equal status within marriage and makes polygamy and marriage of minors illegal. The legal age at marriage for women is 18 years.

<u>Other issues</u>: The Government acknowledges that its population policy, geared towards redistributing and increasing the size of the population, has caused certain problems. The increasingly young population requires enormous expenditures. Rapid industrialization and urbanization have caused a labour deficit in agriculture. Agriculture is also plagued by unfavourable climatic conditions, necessitating additional expenditures. The eighth five-year plan aims to increase real incomes.

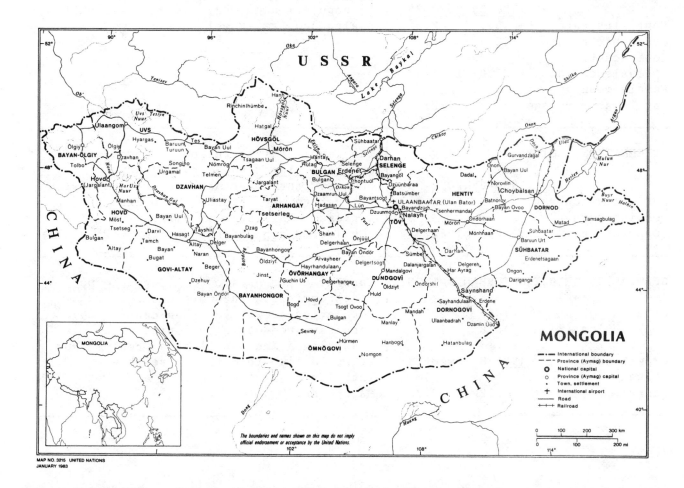

MONGOLIA

- · - · International boundary
- - - - Province (Aymag) boundary
- ⊚ National capital
- ○ Province (Aymag) capital
- · Town, settlement
- ✈ International airport
- —— Road
- +++ Railroad

The boundaries and names shown on this map do not imply official endorsement or acceptance by the United Nations.

MAP NO. 3215 UNITED NATIONS
JANUARY 1983

MOROCCO

DEMOGRAPHIC INDICATORS	CURRENT PERCEPTION

SIZE/AGE STRUCTURE/GROWTH
 	
Population: 1985   2025
 (thousands)   21 941   40 062
  0-14 years (%)   41.0   23.3
  60+ years (%)   5.7   12.2
 	
Rate of: 1980-85   2020-25
 growth   2.5   1.0
 natural increase   25.1   10.3
	The rate of population growth is considered to be <u>unsatisfactory</u> and <u>too high</u>, because it is regarded as a threat to the country's socio-economic equilibrium.

MORTALITY/MORBIDITY 1980-85 2020-25 Life expectancy 58.3 72.8 Crude death rate 11.3 6.4 Infant mortality 96.5 23.5	Levels and trends are considered to be <u>unacceptable</u>. Of particular concern are high rates of infant mortality, and associated diseases, including diarrhoea, malnutrition and polio.
FERTILITY/NUPTIALITY/FAMILY 1980-85 2020-25 Fertility rate 5.1 2.2 Crude birth rate 36.4 16.7 Contraceptive prevalence rate 26.0 (1983/4) Female mean age at first marriage 22.3 (1982)	Levels and trends are perceived as <u>unsatisfactory</u> and <u>too high</u> in relation to population growth, maternal and child health and family well-being.
INTERNATIONAL MIGRATION 1980-85 2020-25 Net migration rate -0.3 0.0 Foreign-born population (%) 0.3 (1982)	The level of immigration is perceived as <u>not significant</u> and <u>satisfactory</u>. However, the Government is concerned with the return migration of Moroccan workers. The level of emigration is considered <u>significant</u> and <u>too low</u>.
SPATIAL DISTRIBUTION/URBANIZATION Urban 1985 2025 population (%) 44.8 71.0 Growth rate: 1980-85 2020-25 urban 4.1 1.8 rural 1.2 -0.7	Current patterns are considered to be <u>inappropriate</u>. The Government views population growth in urban centres that were favoured during colonial rule (Casablanca and Rabat) as a problem, and it would like to deflect growth to interior areas (such as Fez and Marrakesh).

GENERAL POLICY FRAMEWORK

Overall approach to population problems: Although the Government has not yet formulated a comprehensive population policy, it accords great importance to population problems. There are official policies of intervention by the Government to lower population growth and fertility, to adjust the pattern of spatial distribution, and to reduce the infant mortality rate.

Importance of population policy in achieving development objectives: The Government considers the integration of population factors into development planning as essential in achieving an equilibrium between rates of population growth and economic growth. It is intended that a global population policy will eventually form an integral part of future development plans.

INSTITUTIONAL FRAMEWORK

Population data systems and development planning: National censuses were conducted in 1960, 1971, and 1982. The Division of Civil Registration of the Ministry of the Interior, charged with responsibility for vital statistics, is attempting to broaden national coverage. A vital registration system has been in effect for many years, but coverage is incomplete. The three-year development plan for 1986-1988, which was to have begun in 1986, has been postponed and will now commence in 1988, partly as a result of foreign debt problems.

Integration of population within development planning: The Planning Ministry is responsible for the integration of demographic variables into development planning. The Ministry of Planning's Directorate of Statistics, as well as its Centre for Demographic Research and Studies, analyses demographic data. The High Commission on Population is responsible for the formulation and co-ordination of population policies.

POLICIES AND MEASURES

Changes in population size and age structure: The Government wishes to reduce the rate of population growth. The growth rate is to be affected by policies to reduce fertility and infant mortality, to adjust the spatial distribution of the population, and to increase levels of emigration. No quantitative targets have been set regarding the rate of population growth. National approaches to issues of aging have stressed the need for intersectoral planning, research and training. The Ministry of Artisanat and Social Affairs has established the basic elements of the Government's policy for protecting the elderly and has promoted social projects for them. Social security is available for most employees; the self-employed are generally excluded.

<u>Mortality and morbidity</u>: Official policy is to reduce infant mortality, primarily through the provision of primary health care throughout the country. The policy also seeks to reduce general morbidity by combatting the most common diseases (e.g., typhoid, bilharzia, tuberculosis). Specific measures include nutrition and diarrhoeal-control programmes, an enlarged vaccination programme to increase the vaccination coverage of children to at least 80 per cent by the end of 1987, upgrading maternal and child health services, and efforts to expand the health infrastructure and to improve the provision of safe drinking water. Health policy is being reoriented, away from hospitals towards primary health care services. The official target for infant mortality was 65 per thousand live births in 1985, compared to 130 per thousand in 1981.

<u>Fertility and the family</u>: Official policy is to reduce fertility, primarily by means of expanded family planning services. Family planning has been included in the Government's development plans since 1968, and centres have been in operation since 1966. Family planning is to be practised solely on a voluntary basis. Child-spacing is emphasized. Fertility is to be affected also by measures to improve the status of women, child allowances, maternity and paternity benefits, and the protection of the aged. There is direct government support for access to modern contraceptive methods and information since 1966. Contraceptives have been distributed free of charge in government family planning centres in order to boost the rate of contraceptive use. Sterilization is limited to women over 28 years of age with at least four children. Abortion is illegal unless the woman's health is at risk. The Government had a goal of increasing the number of family planning acceptors among women aged 15-49 to 24 per cent by 1985.

<u>International migration</u>: Official policy is to maintain the level of immigration and increase the level of emigration in the future. At a meeting of Moroccan migrant organizations sponsored by the Government in 1986, the Amicale system, the network of migrant support groups under Government patronage which exists in countries with substantial numbers of Moroccan migrants, was reorganized. The Government has been very concerned by the passage of the <u>Loi Pasqua</u> in France in 1986, which permits the expulsion of any migrant convicted of an offense punishable by a prison sentence of at least six months, even if the migrant is legally resident in France.

<u>Spatial distribution/urbanization</u>: There are policies to modify the pattern of population distribution between urban zones, to modify the urban/rural balance, and to curb rural-to-urban migration. Specific measures include decentralization (including the creation of growth poles) in order to reduce regional disparities; the promotion of new provinces and small towns and intermediate cities, to redirect migrant flows away from the major urban areas; and rural development, including the construction of better housing and the provision of drinking water. A tax scheme is in effect to discourage land speculation. It is reported that the forthcoming development plan for the period 1988-1990 will give priority to rural development and food self-sufficiency by improving productivity through investment in infrastructure and land reclamation and by an improvement in rural living standards through the provision of electricity, safe drinking water and improved housing.

<u>Status of women and population</u>: The Government has been attempting to improve the status of women through projects of the Ministry of Youth and Sports by giving attention to rural women in illiteracy and income-generation programmes. The minimum legal age at marriage for women is 15 years.

<u>Other issues</u>: It was reported in 1987 that in order to ensure more effective and flexible control of development planning, the Government intends to introduce a new planning management structure. This will involve a ministerial-level monitoring committee and fulfillment control units operating at the project level. Potential projects will be evaluated in terms of their impact on regional economic factors before being implemented.

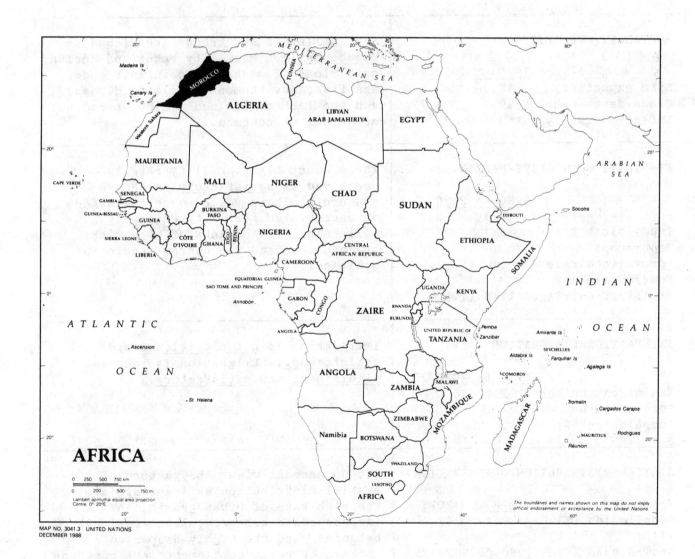

AFRICA

MAP NO. 3041.3 UNITED NATIONS
DECEMBER 1988

MOZAMBIQUE

DEMOGRAPHIC INDICATORS	CURRENT PERCEPTION

SIZE/AGE STRUCTURE/GROWTH
 	
Population: <u>1985</u>   <u>2025</u>
  (thousands) 13 961 37 154
    0–14 years (%) 43.2   34.1
    60+ years (%)   5.3   6.4
 	
Rate of: <u>1980–85</u> <u>2020–25</u>
 growth   2.8   1.7
 natural increase 25.4   16.8
	The present growth rate is considered to be <u>satisfactory</u>.

MORTALITY/MORBIDITY <u>1980–85</u> <u>2020–25</u> Life expectancy 45.3 61.3 Crude death rate 19.7 8.7 Infant mortality 153.5 71.6	Current levels and trends are viewed as <u>unacceptable</u>. Mortality rates and health conditions of mothers and infants under age five, environmental-related diseases, and the lack of trained medical personnel are areas of concern.
FERTILITY/NUPTIALITY/FAMILY <u>1980–85</u> <u>2020–25</u> Fertility rate 6.1 3.0 Crude birth rate 45.1 25.5 Contraceptive prevalence rate ... ... Female mean age at first marriage 17.6 (1980)	The present high fertility rate is perceived as <u>satisfactory</u>, although concern has been voiced over the effect of unregulated fertility on family well-being, the dangers of high-risk pregnancies, and the narrow spacing of pregnancies.
INTERNATIONAL MIGRATION <u>1980–85</u> <u>2020–25</u> Net migration rate 2.8 0.0 Foreign-born population (%)	Immigration is <u>not significant</u> and <u>satisfactory</u>. Emigration is seen as <u>significant</u> and <u>satisfactory</u>.
SPATIAL DISTRIBUTION/URBANIZATION Urban <u>1985</u> <u>2025</u> population (%) 19.4 52.6 Growth rate: <u>1980–85</u> <u>2020–25</u> urban 10.7 2.7 rural 1.3 0.6	The Government views the pattern of spatial distribution as <u>inappropriate</u>. The high rate of urban growth, the inappropriate urban/rural and regional balances, and the highly dispersed pattern of rural settlements are concerns.

GENERAL POLICY FRAMEWORK

Overall approach to population problems: There is no policy of direct governmental intervention to modify population growth or fertility, except in relation to family well-being. Major emphasis has been given to restructuring the economic and social sectors, reducing mortality and morbidity through primary health care in rural areas and adjusting the pattern of spatial distribution.

Importance of population policy in achieving development objectives: The Government considers that problems associated with demographic factors can be resolved by social and economic restructuring. While the Government has no comprehensive population policy, it is, progressively, taking demographic variables into consideration when formulating national development objectives. The Government reports that the integration of demographic variables in development planning has been hampered by the lack of adequate data.

INSTITUTIONAL FRAMEWORK

Population data systems and development planning: Five censuses were conducted in the colonial period and one following independence in 1980. The infrastructure created to conduct the post-independence 1980 census became the National Directorate of Statistics. The Ministry of Development and Economic Planning is responsible for development planning. The Economic and Social Directives resulting from the Fourth Party Congress in 1983 established indicative targets to be achieved by 1985. The current 10-year development plan is for the years 1980-1990. In January 1987 the Economic Rehabilitation Programme for the period 1987-1990 was launched, with the objective of arresting the decline of the country's economy.

Integration of population within development planning: Plans were initiated in 1986 to establish a population planning unit within the Ministry of Planning. The unit will eventually make possible the elaboration and evaluation of a population policy.

POLICIES AND MEASURES

Changes in population size and age structure: There is no official policy to modify the size and growth of population, although various indirect measures, such as social and economic restructuring, maternal and child health programmes, and adjusting the pattern of spatial distribution, may have an effect.

Mortality and morbidity: The Government aims at reducing the rate of general and infant mortality and the incidence of morbidity. Current policy is directed at eliminating regional disparities in health conditions and services, with priority given to preventive medicine, especially environmental sanitation, the organization of health programmes in schools and work places, and the establishment of rural health posts. The primary health care system includes programmes in maternal and child health and family planning and is the main policy approach in the Government's health efforts. This is accompanied by a system of socialized medicine. Some of the most important measures adopted include vaccination and immunization campaigns, sanitary and housing programmes, water programmes, personal hygiene instruction and increasing the number of health workers and facilities available. Recent efforts have focused on rehabilitating and upgrading existing infrastructure and improving services in those rural areas where security conditions permit such investments. The Government has set a goal of reducing the rate of infant mortality due to infectious and parasitic diseases to 50 per thousand by the year 2000.

Fertility and the family: There is a policy of intervention only to improve maternal and child health and overall family well-being. A family planning programme has been implemented to promote the spacing of births. The Government has attempted to educate women in family planning, through the maternal and child care programme and the Organization of Mozambican Women. It has recently begun structuring a programme to improve the quality of prenatal, natal and post-natal health care. There is also a policy of increasing the number of women covered by institutionalized deliveries. No quantitative targets have been established. Access to contraception is not restricted and receives direct government support. Abortion is permitted only when necessary to save the life of the mother. In 1980 the law was modified to permit sterilization of women above the age of 35 with spousal consent.

International migration: The Government has no official policy concerning immigration. Although it has not set an emigration target, the Government's policy is to reduce the level of emigration in the future. A policy to halt labour migration to South Africa was introduced in 1980, because it was considered impractical. In October 1986, South Africa ordered the repatriation of 30,000 Mozambican migrant workers. An additional 38,000 workers threatened with repatriation were granted a reprieve. It is estimated that as of mid 1987, 300,000 Mozambicans had fled into neighbouring Malawi, due to civil strife by rebel groups. Another 100,000 Mozambican refugees were estimated to be in South Africa, Swaziland, Zambia, and Zimbabwe in 1986. In 1987 the Government indicated that it intended to establish a programme for the repatriation of Mozambicans in Malawi.

Spatial distribution/urbanization: Official policy is to reduce migration to urban areas, primarily by concentrating development efforts in rural areas. Agricultural settlement schemes, including communal villages, have been created for that purpose. There has been an effort to build up basic services and infrastructure in rural communities. The policy is to direct development away from Maputo, the capital, and concentrate heavy industry in Beira, the second largest city and the second port. To make cities more self-sufficient in food production, a "cabinet of green zones" was created to support farmers in the greenbelt, including co-operatives. Regional centres have been created since independence to provide basic services in health, education and administration throughout the country, in an effort to promote a properly equilibrated national urban system. As a consequence of the drought and mounting security problems, it is estimated that over 1 million people have been displaced within the country. Large segments of the population have moved to more easily defensible coastal zones.

Status of women and population: In 1983 a study was undertaken by the National Commission on Women to improve the understanding of the status and role of women in Mozambique. The possibility of holding a national seminar on population and development and the training of women in organization and management was being discussed in 1985. Information on the minimum legal age at marriage for women is not readily available.

Other issues: The country in recent years has suffered severe economic deterioration as a result of a series of climatic disasters (severe drought alternating in some regions with flooding) and a mounting civil insurgency. Mainly as a result of insurgent activities, the emergency situation took a dramatic turn for the worse, with the number of the affected population more than doubling, to almost 4 million people. The total number of people in need of food assistance in early 1987 was estimated to be about 2 million.

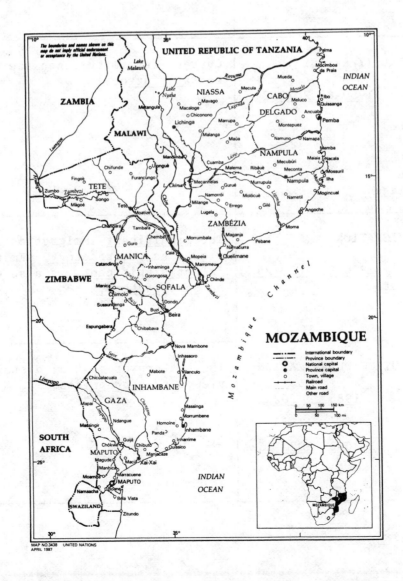

MAP NO.3438   UNITED NATIONS
APRIL 1987

NAURU

DEMOGRAPHIC INDICATORS	CURRENT PERCEPTION
SIZE/AGE STRUCTURE/GROWTH Population: <u>1985</u> <u>2025</u> (thousands) 8 11 0-14 years (%) ... ... 60+ years (%) ... ... Rate of: <u>1980-85</u> <u>2020-25</u> growth 0.9 ... natural increase	The Government perceives current growth rates as <u>unsatisfactory</u> and <u>too low</u>.
MORTALITY/MORBIDITY <u>1980-85</u> <u>2020-25</u> Life expectancy 55.0 ... Crude death rate ... ... Infant mortality	The Government considers present levels of mortality to be <u>acceptable</u>.

FERTILITY/NUPTIALITY/FAMILY
 	
           <u>1980-85</u> <u>2020-25</u>
Fertility rate   ...   ...
Crude birth rate   ...   ...
Contraceptive
  prevalence rate   ...   ...
Female mean age
  at first marriage   ...   ...
	Current fertility rates are considered to be <u>satisfactory</u>.

INTERNATIONAL MIGRATION <u>1980-85</u> <u>2020-25</u> Net migration rate ... ... Foreign-born population (%)	The <u>significant</u> immigration levels are viewed as <u>satisfactory</u>. Emigration, which is <u>not significant</u>, is also considered to be <u>satisfactory</u>.

SPATIAL DISTRIBUTION/URBANIZATION
 	
Urban   <u>1985</u> <u>2025</u>
  population (%)   ...   ...
 	
Growth rate: <u>1980-85</u> <u>2020-25</u>
  urban   ...   ...
  rural   ...   ...
	The pattern of spatial distribution is viewed as <u>appropriate</u>.

GENERAL POLICY FRAMEWORK

<u>Overall approach to population problems</u>: The Government has no explicit policy regarding its population, which lives in the world's least populous micro State. The Government believes in a general welfare strategy where all essential services, such as schooling, health and transportation, are provided at Government expense. Official policy emphasizes employment, dictating that any Naruan who needs employment will be guaranteed the minimum wage.

<u>Importance of population policy in achieving development objectives</u>: Government development objectives are strongly tied to the demographic situation since the entire economy is based on phosphate mining which, through its revenues, funds and supports all social services. Phosphate is the only resource the island has, and the supply is being rapidly depleted. The Government's response has been to make overseas investments in real estate, forming trust funds for the future welfare of its population. Secondary industries are also being established or considered as viable alternatives.

INSTITUTIONAL FRAMEWORK

<u>Population data systems and development planning</u>: The most recent population censuses were taken in 1977 and 1983. Vital registration of births and deaths is considered virtually complete. The Nauru Local Government Council is responsible for general planning and development.

<u>Integration of population within development planning</u>: There does not exist a single governmental agency responsible for the formulation and co-ordination of population policies. Demographic information is collected by the Chief Secretary's Office.

POLICIES AND MEASURES

<u>Changes in population size and age structure</u>: The Government desires increased growth rates and considers intervention to raise rates as appropriate. Improvements in health standards have slightly altered the age structure of the population, which still remains very young. There is no information readily available on the status of pension schemes.

<u>Mortality and morbidity</u>: All essential services provided by the Government are free of charge, including medical and dental care. The health system consists of two local hospitals on the island. Patients in need of treatment that cannot be provided in Nauru are flown to Australia for treatment at the Government's expense. Of particular concern are the large numbers of heart attacks and the high incidence of diabetes.

NAURU

<u>Fertility and the family</u>: Government policy concerning fertility and the family is based on a general welfare strategy, with measures supporting free social services, subsidized housing and child allowances. There also exists support for family planning services. Abortion is legal only if there is a risk to the woman's health.

<u>International migration</u>: Government policy aims at maintaining current levels of immigration. Contract labourers imported specifically for the phosphate industry come mainly from other island states in the Pacific and are hired to work for one-year renewable terms. The workers are not eligible for residency. Advancement in the phospate company is limited to Nauruans. Technicians and schoolteachers are recruited from Australia, New Zealand and the United Kingdom. Almost one half of the population is made up of immigrants, while citizenship is restricted to native Nauruans only.

<u>Spatial distribution/urbanization</u>: Since Nauru has no towns or urban centre, the Government perceives the pattern of spatial distribution and the level of urbanization as appropriate, with no policy to alter the situation. The Government, however, views housing as a problem in the near future since the only remaining phosphate lies below residential areas. The Government is considering the possibility of buying an island for living space to solve this problem since the island on which it is situated is not suitable for agriculture.

<u>Status of women and population</u>: There is no information readily available on the status of women.

<u>Other issues</u>: As Nauru approaches a total depletion of its phosphate reserves, the possibility of a physical removal from the island has been suggested. Government officials have discussed this possibility with neighbouring Pacific countries but have been rebuffed as a consequence of Nauru's insistence that it be granted legal sovereignty to any island to which its citizens might relocate. Since gaining independence in 1968, up to 30 per cent of all earnings from the phospate industry have been channelled into funds controlled by the Nauru Phosphate Royalties Trust. The funds had been designed to reinvest all earnings until 1995, the projected date for exhausting the phosphate reserves. It is hoped that by 1995 the funds will be able to provide an income equivalent to that generated by the phosphate industry.

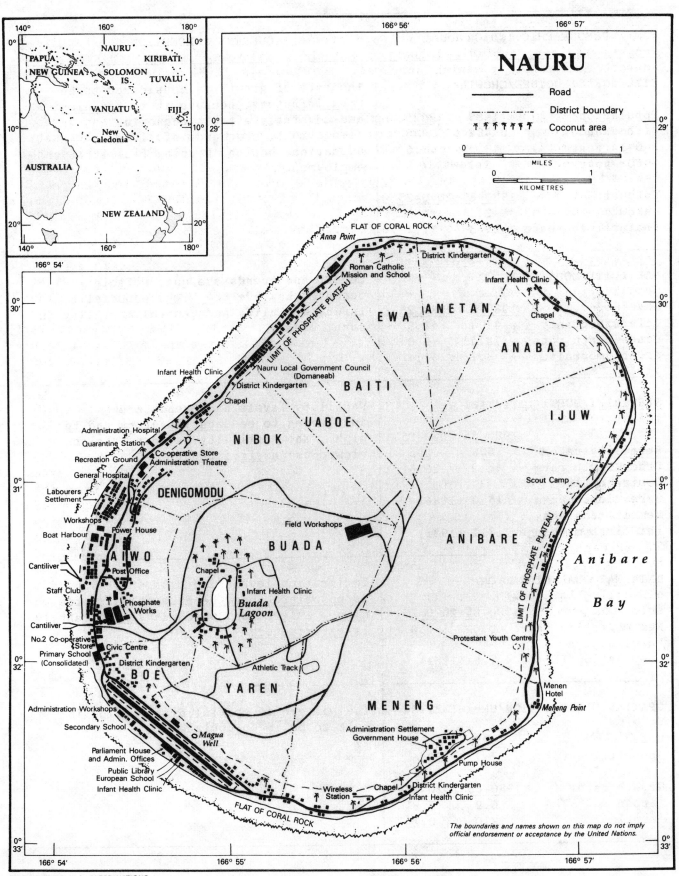

NAURU

Road
District boundary
Coconut area

MILES

KILOMETRES

NAURU
KIRIBATI
PAPUA
NEW GUINEA
SOLOMON
IS.
TUVALU
VANUATU
FIJI
New
Caledonia
AUSTRALIA
NEW ZEALAND

FLAT OF CORAL ROCK
Anna Point
District Kindergarten
Roman Catholic
Mission and School
Infant Health Clinic
Chapel

EWA ANETAN

ANABAR

Infant Health Clinic
Nauru Local Government Council
(Domaneab)
District Kindergarten
Chapel

BAITI

UABOE

IJUW

Administration Hospital
Quarantine Station
Recreation Ground
Co-operative Store
Administration Theatre
General Hospital
Labourers
Settlement
Workshops
Boat Harbour
Power House
Cantiliver
Post Office
Staff Club
Phosphate
Works
Cantiliver
No.2 Co-operative
Store
Civic Centre
Primary School
(Consolidated)
District Kindergarten
Administration Workshops
Secondary School
Parliament House
and Admin. Offices
Public Library
European School
Infant Health Clinic

NIBOK

DENIGOMODU

AIWO

BOE

YAREN

Field Workshops

BUADA

Chapel
Infant Health Clinic
Buada
Lagoon

Athletic Track

Magua
Well

ANIBARE

Anibare

Bay

Scout Camp

Protestant Youth Centre

Menen
Hotel
Meneng Point

MENENG

Administration Settlement
Government House
Pump House
Wireless
Station
Chapel
District Kindergarten
Infant Health Clinic

FLAT OF CORAL ROCK

LIMIT OF PHOSPHATE PLATEAU

The boundaries and names shown on this map do not imply
official endorsement or acceptance by the United Nations.

MAP NO. 845 Rev. 2 UNITED NATIONS
DECEMBER 1988

NEPAL

DEMOGRAPHIC INDICATORS	CURRENT PERCEPTION

SIZE/AGE STRUCTURE/GROWTH
 	
Population: 1985   2025
 (thousands) 16 482 33 946
  0–14 years (%) 43.3   28.6
  60+ years (%)   5.0   7.3
 	
Rate of: 1980–85 2020–25
 growth   2.3   1.2
 natural increase 23.3 11.7
	The rate of growth is considered to be <u>unsatisfactory</u>, because it is <u>too high</u> and adversely affects economic development, standards of living, education, health, housing facilities and employment.

MORTALITY/MORBIDITY 1980–85 2020–25 Life expectancy 45.9 61.8 Crude death rate 18.4 9.0 Infant mortality 138.7 61.4	Levels and trends are <u>unacceptable</u> because they are <u>too high</u>, especially infant mortality and general mortality in rural areas.
FERTILITY/NUPTIALITY/FAMILY 1980–85 2020–25 Fertility rate 6.3 2.5 Crude birth rate 41.7 20.6 Contraceptive prevalence rate 15.0 (1986) Female mean age at first marriage 17.1 (1981)	Fertility levels and trends are considered to be <u>unsatisfactory</u> and <u>too high</u>. The nuptiality pattern is also viewed as <u>unsatisfactory</u>.
INTERNATIONAL MIGRATION 1980–85 2020–25 Net migration rate 0.0 0.0 Foreign-born population (%) 1.6 (1981)	Immigration levels and trends are viewed as <u>unsatisfactory</u>, because they are <u>too high</u>. Emigration, which is <u>significant</u>, is <u>satisfactory</u>.
SPATIAL DISTRIBUTION/URBANIZATION Urban 1985 2025 population (%) 7.7 30.6 Growth rate: 1980–85 2020–25 urban 6.9 3.8 rural 2.0 0.1	The pattern of spatial distribution is felt to be <u>inappropriate</u>.

GENERAL POLICY FRAMEWORK

Overall approach to population problems: In order to maintain a balance between population growth and economic development, the Government seeks to reduce population growth through both direct and indirect intervention. The policy is to control population growth through basic development, reforms in the socio-cultural, economic and educational environment, and maternal and child health and family planning programmes. The Government seeks to reduce immigration and regulate migration from the Hills to the Terai, to achieve an optimal distribution of the population.

Importance of population policy in achieving development objectives: The Government realizes the negative effects of high population growth on national development and views population policy as an integral part of development policy, with priority given to questions of fertility, health, immigration and spatial distribution. It considers population control to be an essential way to raise the standard of living of the population, provide adequate education and health services, and to increase employment opportunities. The seventh five-year plan, in which the Government has given a strategic thrust to the population problem through quantified development objectives based on the interrelationship between population and development, builds upon the 1983 National Population Strategy.

INSTITUTIONAL FRAMEWORK

Population data systems and development planning: The most recent population census was taken in 1981. Major demographic sample surveys were conducted by the Central Bureau of Statistics with international assistance, in 1974-1975, 1976 and 1977-1978. The vital registration system is considered to be incomplete. As a part of the World Fertility Survey, the Nepal Fertility Survey was undertaken in 1976. The seventh five-year plan, 1985-1990, is currently in effect.

Integration of population within development planning: After several organizational changes, the National Population Commission was reconstituted in 1982 for the second time, with the specific aim of strengthening the Government's capacity to deal with population issues. Under the chairmanship of the Prime Minister, the Commission is responsible for formulating, implementing and evaluating population policies and integrating population into development plans and programmes.

POLICIES AND MEASURES

Changes in population size and age structure: The policy to lower population growth is to be achieved by reducing levels of fertility, mortality and immigration. The seventh five-year plan (1985-1990) places emphasis on policies to increase domestic production, expand family planning services to

NEPAL

satisfy the unmet demand, and integrate population programmes in all projects related to the environment, agriculture, forestry and rural development. A target has been established to lower the rate of population growth to 1.2 per cent a year by the year 2000. The 1983 National Population Strategy specifies a total population target of 21 million by the year 2000. Under the social security scheme, coverage is limited to permanent governmental employees and employees of autonomous corporate bodies, based on agreements between employers and the provident fund.

Mortality and morbidity: The seventh five-year plan emphasizes the reduction of mortality and morbidity through the expansion of health care facilities and the preventive and promotive aspects of health care. By the provision of basic health services, including environmental sanitation and nutritional supplies, the expansion of hospital facilities and malaria eradication programmes, the policies aim at reducing general and infant mortality and increasing life expectancy. Maternal and child health care services are given high priority in order to improve the health status of mothers and children and to reduce the incidence of illness and death. They focus on oral rehydration, nutrition, immunization, basic and natal care and birth-spacing. Structural reorganization of the health care sector was undertaken in order to resolve the rural/urban imbalance and to provide basic health care services to a maximum number of people. The Plan envisages the creation of 1,300-1,400 health posts at the local level.

Fertility and the family: The Government has adopted a multisectoral approach to reduce high fertility levels. Emphasis is given to family planning services, maternal and child health, basic education and the status of women. The family planning programme focuses on couples aged 20-30 years, by enhancing the use of temporary birth control methods through increased awareness and motivation. All family planning programmes include effective information, education and communication activities. Efforts are also being made to improve support services, including logistic, personnel, financial administration and programme management. Measures have been adopted to extend and strengthen family planning delivery services to all population segments, so as to meet the unmet demand. These include training more physicians in family planning methods, provision of family planning services in district and zonal hospitals, a contraceptive retail sales project and strengthening the concentration of family planning services in densely populated areas. Birth control pills and condoms are available free of charge at all health centres. Abortion is permitted only on medical grounds, and sterilization is legal for both men and women. The target is to reduce the total fertility rate to 4.0 by 1990 and to 2.5 by the year 2000.

International migration: The policy aims at controlling immigration. The measures include issuing citizenship certificates to distinguish nationals from non-nationals and prohibiting non-nationals from acquiring property in Nepal. A system of work permits for foreigners issued by the local panchayats is to be instituted. The policy on emigration aims at increasing the emigration of unskilled manual workers and agricultural workers and decreasing the emigration of professional and skilled workers. In 1983 the National Commission on Population created a task force to study internal and international migration. Policies and programmes will be based on the findings of the task force.

Spatial distribution/urbanization: The policies aim at reducing migration from the Hills to the Terai because of disparities in income levels between the two geographical regions. To adjust the distribution of population, a programme of allocative investment was undertaken, benefiting the least developed areas of the country. The Government envisages a long-term policy for the development of the Hill region, so as to provide adequate employment opportunities there. Measures are being taken to promote rural markets and growth centres. Appropriate programmes of land utilization in the Hills and Terai have been launched to optimize the use of natural and land resources. In addition, resettlement schemes have been implemented. A new dimension was added to local development with the 1982 Decentralization Act, which provides for the continuation of decentralization in formulating and implementing policies for socio-economic development at the local level.

Status of women and population: Efforts are under way to increase women's literacy rates and labour-force participation. The Government considers improving women's status to be an integral part of the development process and one of the most effective means for lowering population growth. Incentive schemes, initiated to improve women's education and employment opportunities, include boarding facilities in schools, scholarships, skill-oriented training, co-operatives and quota systems. The goal is to raise the social and economic status of women, to make them self-reliant and to gain their participation in development programmes. The minimum age at marriage for women is 18 years.

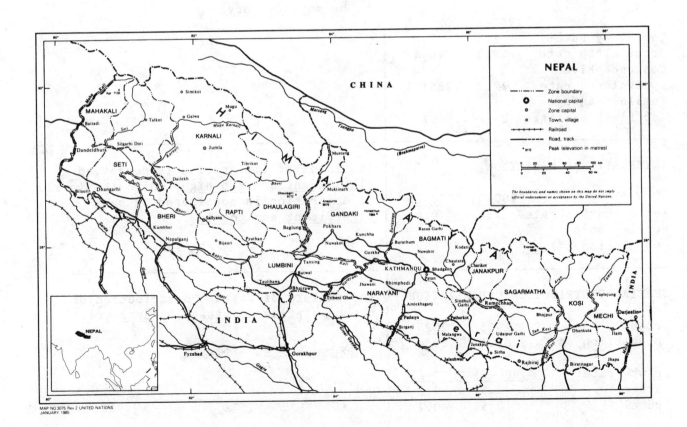

NETHERLANDS

DEMOGRAPHIC INDICATORS	CURRENT PERCEPTION
SIZE/AGE STRUCTURE/GROWTH	The Government considers the current growth rate of the population to be <u>satisfactory</u>.
Population: 1985 2025	
(thousands) 14 500 14 691	
0-14 years (%) 19.6 15.1	
60+ years (%) 16.5 30.1	
Rate of: 1980-85 2020-25	
growth 0.5 -0.2	
natural increase 3.8 -2.7	
MORTALITY/MORBIDITY	Present conditions of health and levels of mortality are viewed as <u>acceptable</u>.
1980-85 2020-25	
Life expectancy 76.0 78.2	
Crude death rate 8.7 13.0	
Infant mortality 8.3 5.2	
FERTILITY/NUPTIALITY/FAMILY	Present level of fertility is considered to be <u>satisfactory</u>.
1980-85 2020-25	
Fertility rate 1.6 1.9	
Crude birth rate 12.5 10.4	
Contraceptive	
prevalence rate 72.0 (1985)	
Female mean age	
at first marriage 23.2 (1980)	
INTERNATIONAL MIGRATION	The level of immigration is perceived as <u>significant</u> and <u>too high</u>, while the level of emigration is considered to be <u>significant</u> and <u>too low</u>.
1980-85 2020-25	
Net migration rate 1.0 0.4	
Foreign-born	
population (%)	
SPATIAL DISTRIBUTION/URBANIZATION	The pattern of spatial distribution of the population is viewed as <u>appropriate</u>.
Urban 1985 2025	
population (%) 88.4 89.6	
Growth rate: 1980-85 2020-25	
urban 0.5 -0.2	
rural 0.5 -0.7	

GENERAL POLICY FRAMEWORK

Overall approach to population problems: The Government has taken the following positions on population since 1979: population growth should cease, in the interest of national welfare; fertility should be 15-30 per cent below replacement level for the next few years since it will lead within the foreseeable future to a termination of population growth; immigration should be restricted so that it will have no appreciable impact on the population. The Government also believes that, in view of the high population density and the resulting pressure on the environment, it would be desirable for a stationary population to be achieved at a somewhat lower size than the present population.

Importance of population policy in achieving development objectives: The Government believes that population policy is an important instrument for the achievement of socio-economic goals. The prospect of reaching an end to population growth and of entering a period of temporary population decline is accompanied by challenges for social and economic policies.

INSTITUTIONAL FRAMEWORK

Population data systems and development planning: Census-taking is the responsibility of the Central Bureau of Statistics. The last population and housing census was conducted in 1971. The census scheduled for 1981 has been indefinitely postponed. However, the Netherlands has a complete population register that records births, deaths, and changes of residence as they occur. Special surveys on labour-force participation, housing requirements and so on are yielding data roughly comparable to those obtained through a census, and it is planned to include census-type data in the population registers. The Central Planning Bureau is responsible for economic forecasting and indicative planning and has a significant influence on general economic policy.

Integration of population within development planning: The Bureau for Population Affairs and the Interdepartmental Committee for Population Questions are responsible for the formulation and co-ordination of population policies. The Social and Cultural Planning Office is charged with the responsibility of taking into account population variables in planning. Population projections at the national level are prepared by the Central Bureau of Statistics. The Netherlands Interdisciplinary Demographic Institute, an independent Government-financed foundation, is responsible for providing information on population/development interrelationships.

POLICIES AND MEASURES

Changes in population size and age structure: The Government's position is that, in the interests of national welfare, population growth should cease and the population should ultimately become more or less stationary, at a level somewhat smaller than the current one. Although the Government pursues a policy of non-intervention, it feels that it is necessary to monitor demographic trends at regular intervals, since the transition from a population that is declining to one that is stationary creates new challenges for social and economic policy. The position resulted in a study on the consequences of continuing low fertility for future public expenditure. Special attention is being given to the continuing aging of the population. The Ministry of Welfare, Health and Cultural Affairs co-ordinates policies on the elderly and young people.

Mortality and morbidity: The Government is committed to improving the health of the population - in particular, through cancer control, open heart surgery and early detection programmes, especially those of developmental disturbances in children. The aging of the population has contributed to changes in the morbidity and mortality patterns, and greater efforts are now directed at adapting health and social security policies to the new trends. Health care is provided through a State insurance system, which covers some 70 per cent of the population, the remainder being covered by private insurance.

Fertility and the family: The Government firmly holds the position that policies should respect the basic right of all couples and individuals to decide freely and responsibly the number and spacing of their children. The Government's policy to influence fertility is only acceptable if broad layers of the population consider it to be ethically justified and only if one can depend on the voluntary co-operation of the population. The current level of fertility is regarded as favourable for the time being since it will lead within the foreseeable future to a termination of population growth. For the short term, a fertility rate within a margin of 15-30 per cent below replacement is accepted as a guideline. However, the Government has indicated that in the future, fertility must gradually rise to replacement level to ensure a stationary population. Diffusion of information on and access to all modern methods of contraception are permitted by law. All family planning services are privately run, but reimbursed by the Government. Contraceptives requiring medical supervision are free of charge to those covered by health insurance. The 1981 Abortion Law, legalizing abortion for physical, mental health and social reasons, replaced the 100-year-old law under which abortion was forbidden. Sterilization is available as a family planning method.

International migration: The Government has a policy of reducing the significant level of immigration in the future. It pursues a restrictive policy on the admission of aliens, in the interest of ensuring that resident aliens enjoy the best possible legal status, which forms part of governmental policy on minorities. Minority policy is aimed at achieving a society in which members of Dutch minority groups have an equal place and equal opportunities for developing, both as individuals and as members of a group. New measures were introduced in 1986 in the form of subsistence allowances to assist voluntary repatriation, particularly of unemployed males aged 55-65, residing in the country at least five years. In July 1986 the Government announced a doubling of the annual Dutch refugee resettlement quota to 500 places, effective January 1987. To restrict the flow of refugees, the Dutch Parliament approved measures in April 1987 requiring that refugees who passed through other Western countries or sought asylum there be refused entry to the Netherlands.

Spatial distribution/urbanization: The Government's overall policy regarding population distribution and internal migration were formulated in the Structural Outline Sketch for Urban Areas, 1985. The plan aims at the continuation of present internal migration trends, and towards developing the economic potential of the various regions. In addition, new residential, employment and recreation areas will be located as close as possible to the large- and medium-sized cities within the urban-regional framework.

Status of women and population: Equal rights and opportunities for women have been part of the Government's policy since 1974. The Government has stated that a purposeful emancipation policy should be pursued as an integral part of the general policy. The main objectives of the policy are to remove role restrictions, to help both sexes in sectors where they have fallen behind and to attach greater value to characteristics and activities which are traditionally ascribed to women. The National Advisory Committee on Emancipation acts as an advisory body to the Government. Equal pension rights are guaranteed under a new act which came into force in April 1985. The minimum age at marriage for women is 16 years.

NEW ZEALAND

DEMOGRAPHIC INDICATORS	CURRENT PERCEPTION

SIZE/AGE STRUCTURE/GROWTH
 	
Population: 1985   2025
 (thousands)   3 318   4 202
  0-14 years (%)   24.1   17.9
  60+ years (%)   14.6   23.1
 	
Rate of: 1980-85   2020-25
 growth   0.9   0.3
 natural increase   7.4   1.8
	The Government perceives current growth rates as <u>satisfactory</u>.

MORTALITY/MORBIDITY 1980-85 2020-25 Life expectancy 73.8 77.5 Crude death rate 8.4 10.2 Infant mortality 12.1 6.1	Present health conditions are considered to be <u>acceptable</u>.
FERTILITY/NUPTIALITY/FAMILY 1980-85 2020-25 Fertility rate 1.9 1.8 Crude birth rate 15.7 11.9 Contraceptive prevalence rate 41.0 (1976) Female mean age at first marriage 22.7 (1981)	Fertility rates and trends are regarded as <u>satisfactory</u>.
INTERNATIONAL MIGRATION 1980-85 2020-25 Net migration rate 1.8 1.2 Foreign-born population (%) 14.8 (1981)	Immigration levels are considered to be <u>satisfactory</u> and <u>not significant</u>. Emigration trends are viewed as <u>significant</u> because they are <u>too high</u>.
SPATIAL DISTRIBUTION/URBANIZATION Urban 1985 2025 population (%) 83.7 87.8 Growth rate: 1980-85 2020-25 urban 1.0 0.4 rural 0.4 -0.6	The Government considers the pattern of population distribution to be <u>partially appropriate</u>. Metropolitan growth is unsatisfactory because it is too high, and both urban and rural growth are unsatisfactory because they are too low.

GENERAL POLICY FRAMEWORK

Overall approach to population problems: The Government feels that it does not have any substantial population problems. No explicit population policy has been formulated; however, the Government acknowledges that indirect measures have influenced demographic trends. Indirect measures stem from policies affecting the family, health care, and immigration, the purpose of which is to promote the well-being of the population.

Importance of population policy in achieving development objectives: The official view is that population issues do not adversely affect national development objectives in New Zealand; consequently, the Government has not attempted to influence demographic factors in order to achieve socio-economic objectives and has not developed any population policy.

INSTITUTIONAL FRAMEWORK

Population data systems and development planning: The first population census was conducted in 1858; the most recent, in 1986. Modern censuses of the Maori population began in 1926. The New Zealand Statistics Act of 1975 mandates a quinquennial census. Vital registration of the European population began in 1848, with published data commencing in 1860. Maori vital registration was introduced in 1913, but was not considered complete until the 1950s. A centralized development planning structure does not exist.

Integration of population within development planning: No single governmental agency co-ordinates or formulates population policy. Furthermore, governmental apparatus does not include machinery for integrating population into sectoral and central planning. The New Zealand Planning Council, created in 1977, is responsible for reporting to the Government on socio-economic and cultural development. The Population Monitoring Group was established in 1982, within the Council, to identify population issues and to report on the impact of development on population. The Department of Statistics conducts research into the social, economic and demographic factors which influence migration and is also responsible for population projections.

POLICIES AND MEASURES

Changes in population size and age structure: The Government has no explicit policy for affecting population growth. However, because of a declining birth rate, the Government has given more attention to the changing age structure of the population. Measures for the aged include increased geriatric medical care. Regional governments have provided rental accommodations for the aged.

Mortality and morbidity: Although New Zealand is a low mortality country, the Government believes that health for all is an investment and thus devotes special attention to improving health conditions, particularly those of women and children. Health policy has three goals: improve the health of all, provide health services at a minimum cost in all areas, reform health services to include community involvement. Measures aim to increase access to primary medical services by subsidizing visits to general practitioners and providing free prescriptions. Mortality and morbidity policy centres on preventive medicine aimed at specific diseases and high-risk groups. Major issues are heart disease, cancer, teen-age pregnancies, alcohol and drug abuse, tobacco smoking, and accidents. The Government has expressed special concern over the morbidity and mortality rates of infants and the Maori population.

Fertility and the family: The policy is to improve maternal and child health and family well-being. Fertility decisions are considered an individual matter, to be determined by couples, and there is no attempt to influence fertility patterns. The Government provides child welfare allowances and family benefits, adjusted for inflation and dependent upon family income. In 1984, a supplement was added for low-income and large families because of a wage freeze. Subsidies are provided for day-care if parents cannot afford it. The taxation system allows for rebates according to family circumstances. A 1981 law provides for the institution of a family court system. Maternity benefits are provided for unmarried women and the New Zealand Working Women's Charter includes provisions for paid parental leave. The Government provides financial support for family planning to improve maternal and child health. Contraceptive advice is available to those over the age of 16. Parental or medical permission is required for women under 16 years of age. Sterilization is allowed for contraceptive purposes. Abortion is not available for contraceptive purposes. In 1985 the Ministry of Education introduced a programme of sex education in selected intermediate schools, on a trial basis.

International migration: The policy on immigration is to maintain the present level so as to achieve essentially non-demographic goals, such as admitting workers with skills that are deemed necessary. New Zealand has historically been a country of immigration but has recently enacted restrictions to control the flows. New Zealand allows for the reunification of families and the settlement of refugees. In the economic sector, immigration serves as a supply of needed, trained personnel for new industries and labour-deficient industries. The number of permanent immigrants admitted is a function of the capacity to provide them with adequate employment, housing, and community services. Attempts to control illegal immigration include requiring work permits and imposing employer sanctions for illegal hiring. Although emigration is perceived as significant and detrimental to the country's development, the Government wants to maintain current levels.

Spatial distribution/urbanization: The goals for internal migration are to maintain in-migration to metropolitan areas and decrease out-migration from other urban areas and rural regions. The concentration of population in the urban areas of North Island is of particular concern. A growth centre strategy targets industrial development for 11 locations outside of three major metropolitan areas. Measures include public infrastructure subsidies, housing and social services, human resource investments and job training. To reduce out-migration from non-metropolitan regions, tax concessions are offered to industrial relocatees. The Government has encouraged relocation by decentralizing its offices to regions outside of Wellington, the capital city.

Status of women and population: The Government has indicated its commitment to improving the status of women by means of national programmes and legislation. The 1972 Equal Pay Act and the 1977 Human Rights Commission Act promote the economic and social advancement of women. Discrimination against women because of sex or marital status is prohibited. The Positive Action Programme of the Department of Labour is responsible for broadening occupational horizons for women to include non-traditional jobs. A Minister of Women's Affairs was appointed in 1985 to ensure the achievment of genuine equality. The minimum legal age at marriage for women is 16 years, but parental permission is required for men and women under the age of 20.

Other issues: Socio-economic differentials exist between the European, Maori, and Polynesian populations. Policies advocate integrating ethnic groups, while maintaining ethnic cultures.

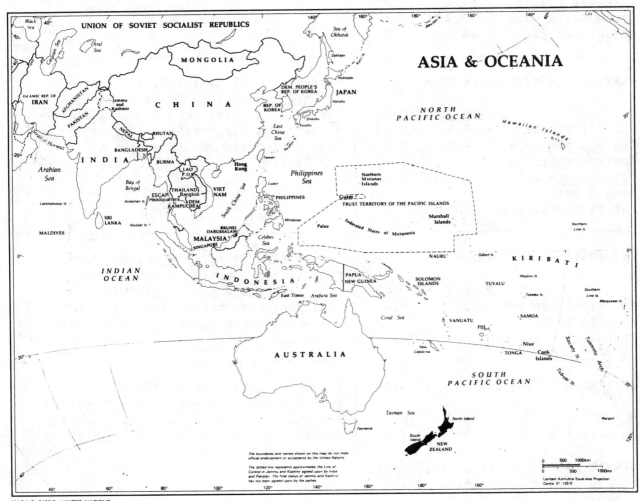

NICARAGUA

DEMOGRAPHIC INDICATORS			CURRENT PERCEPTION
SIZE/AGE STRUCTURE/GROWTH			The Government views the current rate of population growth as <u>satisfactory</u>, partly because of Nicaragua's small population size.
Population:	1985	2025	
(thousands)	3 272	9 219	
0-14 years (%)	46.7	31.1	
60+ years (%)	4.1	7.8	
Rate of:	1980-85	2020-25	
growth	3.3	1.8	
natural increase	34.5	17.8	
MORTALITY/MORBIDITY			Current levels and trends are considered to be <u>unacceptable</u>.
	1980-85	2020-25	
Life expectancy	59.8	72.6	
Crude death rate	9.7	5.1	
Infant mortality	76.4	26.9	
FERTILITY/NUPTIALITY/FAMILY			Current fertility levels are viewed as <u>satisfactory</u>, since it is felt that Nicaragua's relatively low population density and large expanses of undeveloped land could accommodate a larger population.
	1980-85	2020-25	
Fertility rate	5.9	2.7	
Crude birth rate	44.2	22.9	
Contraceptive prevalence rate	27.0 (1981)		
Female mean age at first marriage	20.2 (1971)		
INTERNATIONAL MIGRATION			Immigration is <u>not significant</u> and <u>satisfactory</u>, while emigration is <u>significant</u> and <u>too high</u>. During the civil war and post-war period about 200,000 Nicaraguans have sought refuge in other countries.
	1980-85	2020-25	
Net migration rate	-1.3	0.0	
Foreign-born population (%)	1.2 (1971)		
SPATIAL DISTRIBUTION/URBANIZATION			The distribution is viewed as <u>inappropriate</u>. The growth rate of the Managua metropolitan area is too high, whereas the growth rate in rural areas is considered too low.
Urban	1985	2025	
population (%)	56.6	77.9	
Growth rate:	1980-85	2020-25	
urban	4.5	2.3	
rural	1.9	0.0	

GENERAL POLICY FRAMEWORK

Overall approach to population problems: No explicit policy to modify population growth has been reported, mainly because the Government considers the country to be sparsely populated. The major population concern is the high level of morbidity and mortality. In addition, adjustments in the pattern of spatial distribution, reducing urban migration and encouraging rural migration, are desired. Nicaragua has adopted an open-door policy regarding political refugees and seeks repatriation of Nicaraguans living abroad.

Importance of population policy in achieving development objectives: The Government has not adopted a specific population policy it considers the current rate of population growth to be satisfactory and population policies and family planning programmes to be of low priority. One of the Government's chief priorities has been reducing the country's high levels of morbidity and mortality. The collection and analysis of demograpahic data is another area of concern.

INSTITUTIONAL FRAMEWORK

Population data systems and development planning: The National Statistical System (SEN) co-ordinates all national demographic activities. The National Institute of Statistics and Censuses (INEC) collects national statistics, analyses demographic data, prepares population data and conducts censuses. Three censuses have been conducted since 1950; the most recent was in 1971. A census scheduled for 1984 was not held because of violence in the region; instead, a household survey was conducted in 1986. The Ministry of Planning (MIPLAN) is responsible for formulating economic and social development plans at the regional and national levels. A 1987 economic plan has been prepared.

Integration of population within development planning: Population factors are integrated within development planning by the Ministry of Planning and Budget. The National Institute of Statistics and Censuses provides information regarding the interrelationships between population and development. There are no formal institutional arrangements for integrating population policies into development plans. With international assistance, the Ministry of Planning and Budget analysed the interrelationships between population trends and socio-economic variables. The results were used in preparing short- and medium-term national and sectoral policies and programmes.

POLICIES AND MEASURES

Changes in population size and age structure: The Government has not reported any policies with the aim of modifying population growth or natural increase. It is felt that population growth is essential for the country's economic revitalization, that some regions are sparsely populated, and that there are recurring labour shortages in the agricultural sector. The Government recently acknowledged some problems associated with population growth, such as additional housing and employment opportunities. Beginning in 1984 social security coverage is gradually being broadened to include the rural population.

Mortality and morbidity: A chief priority of the Government has been reducing the country's high levels of morbidity and mortality. Policy has focused on the integration of the national health care system. By unifying the previously scattered health care units into one body, and simultaneously expanding the number of health care centres in underserved areas, the Government reports that more than 80 per cent of the population has access to some type of health care. Mass-based health campaigns such as vaccination and environmental sanitation programmes have contributed to a reduction in the incidence of communicable diseases and have aided malaria control. In an attempt to reduce the high incidence of gastroenteritis and diarrhoeal diseases, the Ministry of Health has begun distribution of free rehydration salts throughout Nicaragua's newly constructed oral rehydrator centres.

Fertility and the family: The Government has neither formulated an explicit policy to modify fertility nor identified any desirable future level of fertility. This non-intervention policy is related to the view that Nicaragua has relatively low population density and much undeveloped land which could accommodate future population growth. However, family planning services are available within maternal and child health programmes of the Ministry of Health and by the Social Security Institute, as well as from private organizations receiving government support. Under the child care programme priority is given to children in rural areas, to promote health and nutrition and to facilitate the integration of mothers in production and service employment. One hundred and seventy-seven centres have been constructed throughout the country, providing a variety of services such as cafeterias, social assistance, advisory services and re-education. There is no official policy on sterilization. Abortion is illegal except to save the mother's life.

International migration: The Government has adopted an open-door policy with respect to political refugees and qualified migrant workers. As of mid 1987, it was estimated that there were about 20,000 Salvadorean refugees in Nicaragua. As means of encouraging repatriation, in January 1984 the Government announced an amnesty decree permitting Nicaraguans to return, although few have availed themselves of the offer. The displacement of Miskitos from their ancestral villages in 1981 led to the flight of over 20,000 to neighbouring Honduras. The Office of the United Nations High Commissioner for Refugees estimates that as of mid 1987 it was assisting nearly 11,000 Nicaraguan Ladino refugees in Honduras. Another 18,000 Nicaraguans were in Costa Rica in mid 1986.

Spatial distribution/urbanization: National policies are aimed at reducing migration to metropolitan areas and increasing migration to rural areas and other less populated urban centres. The problems posed by an inappropriate pattern of population dispersion have been aggravated by an acute shortage of electrical power, drinking water, health and education facilities and services in general. Policy measures include developing growth poles to redistribute population growth; agrarian reform and infrastructure programmes to reduce out-migration from rural areas; exploitation of natural resources in the isolated Atlantic coast; and integration of the Indian and black populations into the larger social and economic community. The revision of the land reform law in January 1986 has accelerated the process of granting title to landless peasants. The Minister of Agriculture has estimated that 20,000 farmers benefited from the new policy in 1986. The conflict along the northern border has adversely affected the pattern of spatial distribution and has displaced up to 200,000 people within the country, according to Government estimates.

Status of women and population: The Government has taken an active role in regard to family welfare and women's issues, instituting special maternal/child health programmes. The Government seeks to improve the status of women and guarantee the active and absolute participation of women in the economic, political, social and cultural milieu. The Government has passed legislation clarifying responsibilities of both spouses in regard to sharing household work and child-rearing. The minimum legal age at marriage for women is 14 years. Equal pay for equal work is guaranteed by the new Constitution, which came into force in January 1987.

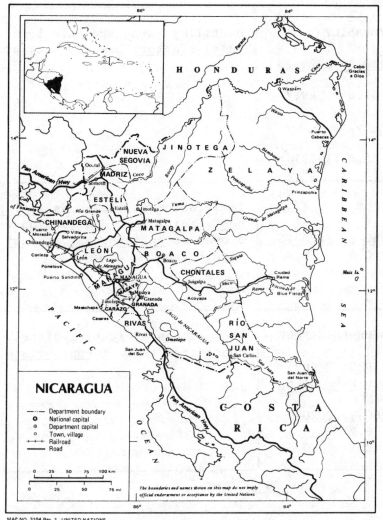

MAP NO. 3104 Rev. 2 UNITED NATIONS
FEBRUARY 1984

- 214 -

NIGER

DEMOGRAPHIC INDICATORS	CURRENT PERCEPTION
SIZE/AGE STRUCTURE/GROWTH	Population growth is considered to be unsatisfactory because it is too high.

Population:	1985	2025
(thousands)	6 115	18 940
0-14 years (%)	46.7	38.0
60+ years (%)	4.9	4.8

Rate of:	1980-85	2020-25
growth	2.8	2.0
natural increase	28.1	20.3

MORTALITY/MORBIDITY

Levels and trends of mortality and morbidity are regarded as unacceptable.

	1980-85	2020-25
Life expectancy	42.5	58.5
Crude death rate	22.9	9.4
Infant mortality	145.7	70.9

FERTILITY/NUPTIALITY/FAMILY

Fertility rates are perceived as unsatisfactory because they are too high.

	1980-85	2020-25
Fertility rate	7.1	3.6
Crude birth rate	51.0	29.7
Contraceptive prevalence rate	...	...
Female mean age at first marriage	15.8 (1959)	

INTERNATIONAL MIGRATION

Immigration is viewed as satisfactory and not significant. Emigration is also viewed as satisfactory and not significant.

	1980-85	2020-25
Net migration rate	0.0	0.0
Foreign-born population (%)	...	...

SPATIAL DISTRIBUTION/URBANIZATION

The pattern of spatial distribution is considered to be inappropriate.

Urban	1985	2025
population (%)	16.2	46.6

Growth rate:	1980-85	2020-25
urban	6.9	3.8
rural	2.1	0.6

GENERAL POLICY FRAMEWORK

Overall approach to population problems: The Government has not yet developed a long-term policy but has instituted a network of measures devoted to improving living and health conditions, particularly in rural areas. Improvement in health care, education, and food supply is a Government priority. The Government attaches particular importance to temporal and spatial population trends. International assistance is sought, to improve population data collection and analysis, in order to increase knowledge of demographic trends and processes.

Importance of population policy in achieving development objectives: The Government has stated that population cannot be viewed in isolation from socio-economic development and recently increased its attention to high rates of population growth, reduction of the drain on resources, and the attainment of food self-sufficiency. The Government emphasizes agricultural and rural development. In 1985 the President of Niger announced that the Government intended to formulate a population policy.

INSTITUTIONAL FRAMEWORK

Population data systems and development planning: The first general census was conducted in 1977; another had been provisionally planned for May 1988. Before 1977, demographic data were available only from a 1960 demographic survey and a 1963-1964 survey of nomads. Civil registration has existed since 1956; however, the Government has a civil registration and statistics project to improve reporting of vital statistics. The Ministry of the Interior, Department of Civil Registration and Population has established a special unit to process vital statistics. The Three-Year Programme (1976-1978) was followed by the first five-year National Development Plan (1979-1983). The Government followed up with an interim plan for 1984-1985 as a transitional measure for the next five-year development plan. A structural adjustment programme has been formulated for the period 1986-1988. In April 1987, a round table of aid donors achieved consensus on the main trends of the economic and social development plan for the period 1987-1991.

Integration of population within development planning: The Government is in the process of creating a population unit within the Ministry of Planning to formulate population policies and integrate population variables into the planning process. The Survey and Demographic Section of the Statistical and Information Office is responsible for data collection and census enumeration. The Section includes the Permanent Survey Division, the Central Census Division, the Demographic Research Division, and the Cartographic Division.

NIGER

POLICIES AND MEASURES

<u>Changes in population size and age structure</u>: The Government has recently issued statements indicating deep concern over the growing size of the population in relation to severe food shortages and economic growth. Measures are directed towards reducing mortality and morbidity, improving living conditions and reducing fertility. Although the Government considers its population to be young, measures to protect the aged constitute a particular concern. Social security provides old-age benefits for employed persons, while a special system exists for public employees.

<u>Mortality and morbidity</u>: The Government aims rapidly to reduce mortality and morbidity rates. Policy objectives are to expand health care coverage, train medical personnel, produce and distribute medicines and medical equipment, and maintain an adequate food supply. The 1979-1983 National Development Plan specified intentions to improve the hospital system and build more dispensaries. Improving the water supply and providing safe drinking water in urban and rural locations are also goals of the Plan. The health system emphasizes the integration of curative and preventive medicine, immunization, and health education (particularly in regard to nutrition). In addition to measures directed towards improving health and sanitary conditions in rural areas, in 1979 a Government order required nurses and midwives to spend one year in a rural area after the completion of their studies. Concern over the health of the active population, infants, children, and women in the child-bearing years led to the creation in 1984 of the National Centre for Family Health. In a break with its previous position, the Government in 1985 endorsed family planning education (including contraception and birth-spacing) as a means of improving maternal and child health and family well-being.

<u>Fertility and the family</u>: The Government has changed its policy and now intervenes to lower the rate of fertility. The Government has modified its policy towards family planning since 1983. Direct support for family planning with the stated objective of improving family health and well-being is now available. The Government views the promotion of later marriage, birth-spacing, breast-feeding and nutritional education as a means towards improving maternal health. Employed women and social insurance beneficiaries receive pre-natal allowances, lump-sum birth grants, and benefits for children between the ages of 1 and 14 years (benefits extend beyond age 14 if the child is a student or an apprentice). Abortion is available only for narrow medical reasons.

<u>International migration</u>: Neither immigration nor emigration is considered an active policy concern. However, in 1982 the Government placed legal restrictions on jobs which foreigners may hold. Since 1985 more than 5,000 migrant workers have returned to Niger from the Libyan Arab Jamahiriya, as a consequence of that country's campaign to reduce its foreign labour supply in the wake of falling oil revenues.

<u>Spatial distribution/urbanization</u>: The major focus of policy affecting the pattern of spatial distribution is rural development. The Government estimates that, despite the rural exodus, 90 per cent of the working population lives in rural areas. The Government desires the maintenance of

rural-to-urban migration but would like to control the growth of the capital, Niamey, by creating a second pole of development. Irrigation and food supply projects are part of the overall programme to improve rural conditions. Additional measures include public infrastructure subsidies, direct state investment, housing and social services, human resource investment, and job training. Concern is also expressed over the sedentarization of nomads who comprise approximately one-fifth of the total population of Niger.

Status of women and population: The Government advocates the education of women and their integration into various aspects of development. The Women's Association endeavours to mobilize women and acquaint them with their basic rights. Its objective is to lessen the burden on rural women by providing them with agricultural equipment. The legal age at marriage for women is 16 years.

Other issues: The draft five-year development plan, 1987-1991, aims to reduce disparities in living conditions by improved health coverage and facilities and information programmes to inform the population of the significance of population problems. A draft plan of action has been issued which calls for liberalizing family planning, preparing a family code, supporting an integrated programme of sex education, strengthening data collection and appointing a group to implement the plan.

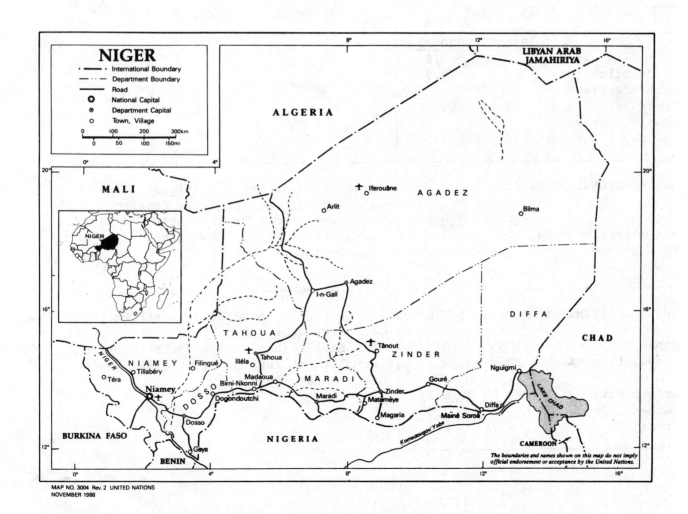

NIGERIA

- 218 -

DEMOGRAPHIC INDICATORS	CURRENT PERCEPTION
SIZE/AGE STRUCTURE/GROWTH	The Government considers the growth rate to be _too high_.
Population: 1985 2025 (thousands) 95 198 338 105 0-14 years (%) 48.3 38.8 60+ years (%) 4.0 4.6	
Rate of: 1980-85 2020-25 growth 3.3 2.3 natural increase 33.3 22.7	
MORTALITY/MORBIDITY	Levels and trends are _unacceptable_. Concerns are infant, child and maternal mortality, malaria, gastro-intestinal, respiratory and preventable diseases, lack of piped water, sanitation, and health workers and facilities.
1980-85 2020-25 Life expectancy 48.5 64.5 Crude death rate 17.1 6.8 Infant mortality 114.2 48.5	
FERTILITY/NUPTIALITY/FAMILY	The Government perceives fertility as being _too high_.
1980-85 2020-25 Fertility rate 7.1 3.6 Crude birth rate 50.4 29.5 Contraceptive prevalence rate 5.0 (1981/2) Female mean age at first marriage 18.7 (1981/2)	
INTERNATIONAL MIGRATION	Immigration is _not significant_ and _satisfactory_, although the Government has been concerned over the influx of illegal immigrants. Emigration is _not significant_ and _satisfactory_.
1980-85 2020-25 Net migration rate 0.0 0.0 Foreign-born population (%)	
SPATIAL DISTRIBUTION/URBANIZATION	The pattern of population distribution is perceived as _inappropriate_. It is felt that rapid urbanization contributes to unemployment and the deterioration of urban amenities.
Urban 1985 2025 population (%) 23.0 53.0	
Growth rate: 1980-85 2020-25 urban 5.8 3.8 rural 2.7 0.7	

GENERAL POLICY FRAMEWORK

Overall approach to population problems: In a major policy shift from its
previous policy of non-intervention, the Government since 1985 has a
policy directed towards lowering population growth and fertility, while
continuing the policy of reducing morbidity/mortality and controlling the
pace of urbanization.

Importance of population policy in achieving development objectives: The
Government's growing awareness of the importance of population policy is
expressed in the 1988 national population policy, which spoke of the
urgent need to formulate a national policy on population and development,
in order to ensure Nigeria's unity, progress and self-reliance. The draft
policy was approved by the Council of Ministers in August 1986 and the
Armed Forces Ruling Council in March 1988.

INSTITUTIONAL FRAMEWORK

Population data systems and development planning: Censuses have been
conducted since 1866; the latest available census was in 1963.   The
results of the 1973 census were not released.   In July 1987 the Government
reported that a census would be held in 1991.   Registration of births and
deaths is incomplete.   The most recent published development plan is the
Fourth Development Plan (1981-1985).   The launching of the Fifth Five-Year
Development Plan, 1986-1990, which was to have begun in January 1986, was
tentatively postponed until late 1987 because of the national economic
emergency declared by the new Government in 1985.

Integration of population within development planning: The national
population policy issued in 1985 and approved by the Armed Forces Ruling
Council in 1988 calls for the creation of a Centre for Population and
Development Activities. The Centre would provide the institutional basis
to ensure adequate co-ordination and integration between population and
development programmes. An interministerial co-ordinating committee has
been established to advise the Centre. The Ministry of Health has
responsibility for the formulation of population policy.

POLICIES AND MEASURES

Changes in population size and age structure: In a dramatic shift from a
policy of non-intervention, the new population policy approved in 1988
acknowledges the dangers of rapid population growth and emphasizes
child-spacing, delayed marriages, and a limited number of pregnancies per
woman in order to brake the rate of growth. The major strategies include
family planning, maternal and child health, greater male responsibilities in
family life, enhancement of women's status, population education and
information, intensified rural and urban development, and improved data
collection for planning. The goal is to reduce the rate of population growth

NIGERIA

from 3.3 per cent to 2.5 per cent by 1995, and to 2.0 per cent by the year 2000. Under the social security scheme, coverage is limited to employees of firms with at least 10 employees.

Mortality and morbidity: The Government aims at the provision of basic health for the entire population by the year 2000. This is to be accomplished through the Primary Health Care System which currently represents the main policy approach. To reduce mortality rates, the system will be strengthened. In general, policies call for the extension of preventive and curative health services. Specific measures adopted include the training of front-line workers and health assistants, water supply and sanitation projects, family health projects, programmes of nutrition, oral rehydration and the provision of clean water. In addition, several immunization programmes have been undertaken, and the share of budget expenditures devoted to primary health care has increased. A target has been set to cut the infant mortality rate from about 90 per thousand, to 50 by 1995, and to 30 by the year 2000.

Fertility and the family: Based on the 1988 population policy, the Government hopes to lower fertility by a number of measures. They include boosting the availability of family planning methods to all those of reproductive age through both the public and private sector, a vigourous population education campaign, to limit maternity benefits to three children, and to raise the minimum age at marriage for women. Among the targets specified are the following: to reduce the proportion of women marrying before age 18 by 50 per cent by 1995 and 80 per cent by the year 2000; to reduce the likely completed family size from six to four by the year 2000; to achieve a birth-spacing interval of at least two years for 50 per cent of the country's mothers by 1995 and for 80 per cent by the year 2000. Contraceptives are widely available and access to them is provided through direct governmental support; they have not been emphasized by the Government though, to the same extent as other measures (e.g., education, counselling, information services) and in practice, contraceptives are not widely used. Abortion is permitted in the southern states if there is a risk to the mother's physical or mental health. In the northern states it is only permitted if the mother's life is at risk.

International migration: Despite its policy to maintain immigration, the Government has resorted to strong measures to curb undocumented immigration. In January 1983, deportation was instituted, forcing the departure of as many as 3 million undocumented immigrants, including more than 1 million Ghanaians. After having closed its borders in 1984 to control immigration, the Government reopened them in April 1985 to repatriate an estimated 700,000 undocumented immigrants, including about 300,000 Ghanaians. The acts were the result of the official recognition that Nigeria's faltering oil revenues would not provide the high level of prosperity believed possible in the 1970s. The border was once again reopened in Feburary 1986. Official policy allows for the emigration, for employment purposes, of unskilled labourers. Such emigration, however, has been minimal in recent years.

Spatial distribution/urbanization: The Government has developed an explicit
policy to curb rural-to-urban migration.   Features of the policy include a
programme of integrated urban and rural development; self-sufficiency in food
production, ensuring a balance in the distribution of productive facilities
and social amenities between urban and rural areas; and strengthening the
primary health care system in rural areas.   Another important measure is the
planning and designing of a new capital, Abuja, in the interior and near the
country's geographic centre which is intended to lessen population pressure in
congested coastal areas, particularly Lagos.   Abuja was originally planned to
have a population of 250,000 by 1987 and 1.5 million by the year 2000.   In the
mid 1980s, the city's population was estimated to be about 15,000.   Two
government ministeries have so far been transferred to Abuja and it is
expected that by 1990, the target date for the official transfer of the
capital from Lagos, 75 per cent of the government ministries will have moved.

Status of women and population: The 1988 population policy recognizes the
need to improve the status of women.   A variety of women's groups and women's
co-operatives are acting in the political and development areas.   The draft
included a proposal to raise the minimum legal age at marriage for women from
15 to 18 years.   There are plans to introduce programmes to guarantee equal
opportunities for women in education, employment, housing and business, and to
provide day-care centres.

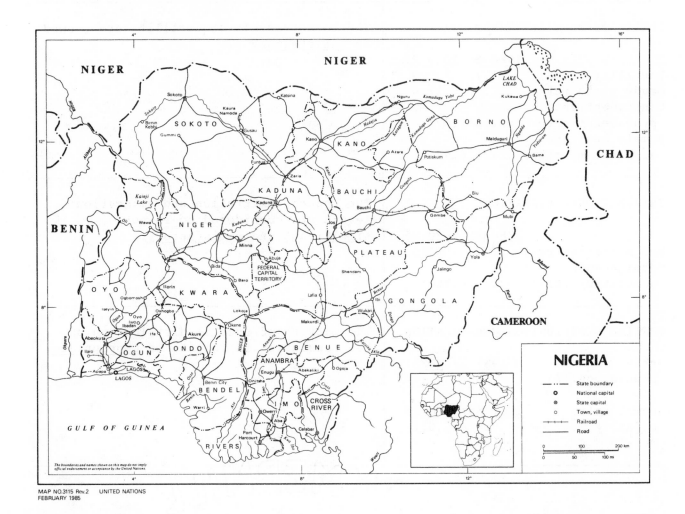

MAP NO.3115 Rev.2   UNITED NATIONS
FEBRUARY 1985

NORWAY

DEMOGRAPHIC INDICATORS	CURRENT PERCEPTION
SIZE/AGE STRUCTURE/GROWTH	The growth rate of the population is regarded as <u>satisfactory</u>.
Population: <u>1985</u> <u>2025</u>	
(thousands) 4 142 4 261	
0-14 years (%) 20.1 16.9	
60+ years (%) 21.1 27.1	
Rate of: <u>1980-85</u> <u>2020-25</u>	
growth 0.3 0.0	
natural increase 1.8 -0.8	
MORTALITY/MORBIDITY	The present conditions of health and levels of mortality are considered to be <u>acceptable</u>.
<u>1980-85</u> <u>2020-25</u>	
Life expectancy 76.0 78.1	
Crude death rate 10.7 12.2	
Infant mortality 8.0 5.0	
FERTILITY/NUPTIALITY/FAMILY	The recent levels of fertility are viewed as <u>satisfactory</u>.
<u>1980-85</u> <u>2020-25</u>	
Fertility rate 1.7 2.0	
Crude birth rate 12.5 11.4	
Contraceptive	
prevalence rate 71.0 (1977)	
Female mean age	
at first marriage 24.0 (1980)	
INTERNATIONAL MIGRATION	The recent immigration and emigration levels are considered to be <u>not significant</u> and <u>satisfactory</u>.
<u>1980-85</u> <u>2020-25</u>	
Net migration rate 1.0 0.9	
Foreign-born	
population (%) 2.0 (1980)	
SPATIAL DISTRIBUTION/URBANIZATION	The pattern of spatial distribution of the population is felt to be <u>appropriate</u>.
Urban <u>1985</u> <u>2025</u>	
population (%) 72.8 79.9	
Growth rate: <u>1980-85</u> <u>2020-25</u>	
urban 0.9 0.1	
rural -1.3 -0.2	

GENERAL POLICY FRAMEWORK

<u>Overall approach to population problems</u>: There is no explicit policy to modify population growth. The Government aims at providing for the health of the population, maintaining the level of immigration and improving the status of women. As a result of the Government's awareness of the considerable changes in the age structure of population that will take place in the coming decades and the impact that that will have on social development, a population committee was established in 1981 to study in depth the issue of population and development.

<u>Importance of population policy in achieving development objectives</u>: The Government believes that the ultimate goal of population policies is to improve the health and welfare of individuals. Another essential element in population policy is the promotion of the status of women, which has the positive effect of strengthening the role of the family as a basic unit in society.

INSTITUTIONAL FRAMEWORK

<u>Population data systems and development planning</u>: Norway has a long history of census-taking dating as far back as 1769. National censuses and major surveys have been conducted by the Central Bureau of Statistics since 1890. The latest population and housing census was taken in November 1980. Vital registration is complete, and administrative responsibilities lie with the Central Bureau of Statistics. A medium-term plan is usually presented every fourth year, before the general elections. There is a general socio-economic plan for the period 1986-1989.

<u>Integration of population within development planning</u>: There is no single governmental agency responsible for the formulation or co-ordination of population policies. However, population variables are taken into consideration by planning units in various ministries such as those dealing with labour markets, schools, family policies and health services. The Central Bureau of Statistics prepares population projections for the whole country. In 1981 the Government appointed a Committee to elucidate possible consequences of future demographic developments.

POLICIES AND MEASURES

<u>Changes in population size and age structure</u>: There is no policy of intervention designed to change population size. However, the establishment of the Population Committee was intended, among other things, to discuss whether it would be desirable or even possible for the Government actively to influence population and development. The report of the Committee, submitted in 1984, attached little importance to the growth rate. The Committee had

given most emphasis to the problems of adapting personnel and other resources within the many welfare sectors to the changing needs brought about by demographic processes. Increasing attention is given to the elderly and concomittant problems such as the burden placed on the national insurance scheme by the increasing expenditures on pensions. At the central governmental level, care of the elderly is the responsibility of the Ministry of Social Affairs. There are three co-ordinating and/or research agencies responsible for the development of overall social policies for the elderly; the National Council for Care of the Aged, the Norwegian Gerontological Institute, and the Committee on Preparation for Retirement.

Mortality and morbidity: The policy aims at achieving a proper balance between primary health care and institutional and specialist health services. The 1982 Act on Municipal Health Services, which came into effect in January 1984, is intended to strengthen primary health care in the local community. The Act provides the legal basis for unifying the different elements of primary health care. The general socio-economic plan for the period 1986-1989 gives priority to health services to meet the needs of the growing number of elderly and to expand local services for the aged, the disabled and the mentally ill to increase the possibility of their remaining in the local community and in their homes. Another stated priority of the plan is a greater emphasis on prevention to curb the increase in diseases related to lifestyles and the human environment. Great importance is also attached to the prevention of accidents at work. A National Board of Pollution Control was established in 1981 to promote health considerations in industrial and other economic development schemes. Health services are three-tiered, consisting of municipal, country and regional health services.

Fertility and the family: There is no policy of intervention to affect the level of fertility. Regardless of population policy aims, the Population Committee stressed the necessity of a radical improvement in the living conditions of families with children. According to the Committee, changes in living conditions in general and especially in the social role of female family members, had accentuated the needs for public support to families in the reproductive phases of their life cycle. Measures proposed are extended leaves for nurses and taking care of children, construction of kindergartens to cover the total requirements of all preschool children, and increased money allowances and transfers to families with children. Diffusion of information on, and access to, all modern methods of contraception are permitted by law. While first trimester abortion is legal, second trimester abortion is subject to a medical committee's decision. Sterilization is permitted on request for those over 25 years of age.

International migration: The policy aims at maintaining a constant level of immigration in the future. No quantitative targets have been set. Immigration policy is based on the following principles: restricted and controlled immigration; integration based on equality and equal rights; freedom for immigrants to choose jobs and their degree of association with Norway; the right of family reunification. Norway has undertaken an international commitment to receive more refugees. As a step towards improving the co-ordination of refugee services, it was announced in August 1986 that all governmental services and departments dealing with refugees and asylum seekers would be regrouped under a single Directorate for Aliens as from January 1988. In addition, all laws and regulations dealing with foreigners were under revision in 1986. Norway's humanitarian tradition towards asylum seekers is now being placed under strains as the number of asylum seekers rapidly increases. The number of those requesting asylum jumped from 300 in 1984 to about 8,000 by the end of 1987. The Government has not expressed a policy concerning emigration.

Spatial distribution/urbanization: The spatial distribution policy aims at maintaining the present pattern. The Government believes that the greatest threat to stability in population distribution is the loss of competitive ability, which puts jobs in local industries at risk. Changes that will have to be made in the industrial sector will necessitate some increase in mobility. The Government wishes to conduct a policy that can secure the degree of growth necessary to bring about the creation of new jobs and to make it possible to change jobs for those who desire to do so.

Status of women and population: The 1978 Equal Status Act aims at promoting equal status between the sexes, particularly at improving the position of women. The Family Affairs and Equal Status Department in the Ministry of Consumer Affairs and Government Administration directs and co-ordinates the work on equal status in the central administration. The Cabinet has declared its intention to extend paid maternity leave from 18 weeks to 26 weeks by 1990. The minimum legal age at marriage for women is 18 years.

EUROPE

The boundaries shown on this map do not imply official endorsement or acceptance by the United Nations.

MAP NO. 2771.12 UNITED NATIONS
DECEMBER 1988

SELECTED REFERENCES

Except for the indicators mentioned below, the source of the demographic estimates and projections is World Population Prospects: Estimates and Projections as Assessed in 1984 (United Nations publication, Sales No. E.86.XIII.3). Additional information on demographic estimates and projections may also be found in the companion publications Global Estimates and Projections of Population by Sex and Age (United Nations publication, ST/ESA/SER.R/70) and The Prospects of World Urbanization, Revised as of 1984-1985 (United Nations publication, Sales No. E.87.XIII.3). For several countries, recent political upheavals have had considerable impact on their demographic phenomena. Therefore, the demographic estimates and projections cited for such countries should be used with caution.

It should also be noted that the estimates of international migration are the most problematic of the demographic estimates due to the shortage of appropriate data. Even more uncertain are the projected rates of international migration, shown in this publication for the period 2020-25. As international migration is influenced greatly by social, economic and political conditions in countries of origin and destination, projecting future trends in international migration is a highly risky undertaking. In the United Nations projections, it is assumed that the volume of net migration will progressively move to zero as time passes except for those countries for which the evidence strongly suggests a continuation of current migration levels for a considerable time into the future (for example, Australia, Canada, Mexico and the United States).

Replies from Governments to a United Nations questionnaire entitled "Fifth Population Inquiry Among Governments: monitoring of Government perceptions and policies on demographic trends and levels in relation to development", where received, constitute important sources for the individual country narratives. (Annex II lists those countries that have responded to the five questionnaires.)

Figures on the contraceptive prevalence rate are from Recent Levels and Trends of Contraceptive Use as Assessed in 1987 (United Nations publication, forthcoming). The reader is advised to consult the country-specific notes given below for deviations from the standard age group of 15-49 years of age for the contraceptive prevalence rate. Information on national pension schemes has for the most part been taken from Social Security Programs Throughout the World-1985; Research report No. 60 (Washington, D.C., United States Department of Health and Human Services, Social Security Administration, 1986). The female mean ages at first marriage are from World Population Trends and Policies: 1987 Monitoring Report (United Nations publication, Sales No. E.88.XIII.3). The source for the minimum legal age of marriage for women is First Marriage: Patterns and Determinants (United Nations publication, ST/ESA/SER.R/76).

GABON

Daily Nation (1985), "Gabon rewards mothers for having children" (11 May) (Gaborone).

République gabonaise, Ministère de la santé publique et de la population (1985), "Evaluation de la stratégie de la santé pour tous d'ici l'an 2000 du Gabon".

United Nations, Population Division (1985), "The Mexico City Conference: the debate on the review and appraisal of the World Population Plan of Action".

United Nations Population Fund (1986), 1985 Report by the Executive Director of the United Nations Fund for Population Activities.

GAMBIA*

Gambia, Central Statistics Division (1976), Population census, 1973, vol. III, General report.

_____, Ministry for Economic Planning and Industrial Development (1983), Five-year plan for economic and social development, 1981/1982-1985/1986.

United Nations, Population Division (1985), "The Mexico City Conference: the debate on the review and appraisal of the World Population Plan of Action".

United Nations/United Nations Population Fund (1986), "Population policy compendium: Gambia".

GERMAN DEMOCRATIC REPUBLIC

German Democratic Republic, Academy of Sciences, Institute for Sociology and Social Policy (1985), "Demographic processes and population policies in the German Democratic Republic, 1970-1984".

International Labour Office (1986), Social and Labour Bulletin, vol. 3/4, pp. 408-409.

United Nations, Population Division (1985), "The Mexico City Conference: the debate on the review and appraisal of the World Population Plan of Action".

---

* Contraceptive prevalence rate is for women aged 15-44.

GERMANY, FEDERAL REPUBLIC OF*

Commission of the European Communities (1986), Report on Social Developments (Brussels).

Germany, Federal Republic of (1984), Statistisches Jahrbuch, 1984 (Wiesbaden).

United Nations, Population Division (1985), "The Mexico City Conference: the debate on the review and appraisal of the World Population Plan of Action".

United Nations High Commissioner for Refugees (1986), Refugees (October), pp. 32-33.

World Health Organization (1986), Evaluation of the Strategy for Health for All by the Year 2000: Seventh Report on the World Health Situation, vol. 5 (Copenhagen).

GHANA

Ghana, Central Bureau of Statistics (1975), 1970 Population Census of Ghana, vol. III.

United Nations, Population Division (1985), "The Mexico City Conference: the debate on the review and appraisal of the World Population Plan of Action".

United Nations/United Nations Population Fund (1981), "Population policy compendium: Ghana".

World Health Organization (1986), Evaluation of the Strategy for Health for All by the Year 2000: Seventh Report on the World Health Situation, vol. 2 (Brazzaville).

GREECE

Greece, National Statistical Service of Greece (1986), Statistical Yearbook of Greece, 1985.

International Labour Office (1986), Women at Work, No. 1, p.22.

Organisation for Economic Co-operation and Development, Conference of National Experts on the Future of Migration (1986), "Future problems and prospects of migration in the Southern European OECD countries: Greece".

---

* Contraceptive prevalence rate is for women aged 15-44 reporting a method "usually" used. Foreign-born population: data are reported by nationality rather than by place of birth.

United Nations, Population Division (1985), "The Mexico City Conference: the debate on the review and appraisal of the World Population Plan of Action".

World Health Organization (1986), Evaluation of the Strategy for Health for All by the Year 2000: Seventh Report on the World Health Situation, vol. 5 (Copenhagen).

GRENADA

Caribbean Community Secretariat (1985), 1980-1981 Population Census of the Commonwealth Caribbean: Grenada, vol. 1.

Population Reference Bureau (1984), Grenada: Yesterday, Today and Tomorrow, p.16.

United Nations Development Programme, Country and Intercountry Programmes and Projects (1986), "Second country programme for Grenada" (DP/CP/GRN/2), 28 October.

World Health Organization (1986), Evaluation of the Strategy for Health for All by the Year 2000: Seventh Report on the World Health Situation, vol. 3 (Washington, D.C.).

GUATEMALA*

República de Guatemala, Instituto nacional de estadística (1985), Censos nacionales de 1981; IX censo de poblacion, tome I, Cifras definitivas.

Pan American Health Organization (1986), Health Conditions in the Americas, 1981-1984.

United Nations High Commissioner for Refugees (1986), Refugees. No. 1 (July), p. 22.

United Nations, Population Division (1985), "The Mexico City Conference: the debate on the review and appraisal of the World Population Plan of Action".

United Nations/United Nations Population Fund (1985), "Population policy compendium: Guatemala".

---

* Contraceptive prevalence rate is for women aged 15-44.

GUINEA*

Africa Research Bulletin (1986) (31 August), pp. 8331-8332.

International Labour Office (1985), Social and Labour Bulletin, vols. 3-4, p. 560.

United Nations High Commissioner for Refugees (1984), Refugees (September), pp. 9-10.

United Nations, Population Division (1985), "The Mexico City Conference: the debate on the review and appraisal of the World Population Plan of Action".

United Nations/United Nations Population Fund, "Population policy compendium: Guinea".

GUINEA-BISSAU

United Nations (1984), Demographic Yearbook, 1983 (United Nations publication, Sales No. E/F.84.XIII.1).

United Nations Population Fund (1987), "Assistance to the Government of Guinea-Bissau" (DP/FPA/CP/11), 2 March.

_____ (1986), "Population perspectives: statements by world leaders", 2nd ed.

World Health Organization (1986), Evaluation of the Strategy for Health for All by the Year 2000: Seventh Report on the World Health Situation, vol. 2 (Brazzaville).

GUYANA

Caribbean Community Secretariat (1985), 1980-1981 Population Census of the Commonwealth Caribbean: Guyana, vol. I.

Economist Intelligence Unit (1986), Country Profile: Guyana, Barbados, Windward & Leeward Islands, 1986-87 (London, Economist Publications).

International Labour Office (1984), Women at Work, No. 4, p. 26.

Pan American Health Organization (1986), Health Conditions in the Americas, 1981-1984.

United Nations Children's Fund (1987), Country programme recommendation: Guyana (E/ICEF/1987/P/L.17), 5 February.

---

* Contraceptive prevalence rate is for women aged 15-44.

HAITI

Haiti, Institut de statistique et d'informatique (1984), Résultats anticipés du recensement général, 1982, échantillon 2.

Pan American Health Organization (1986), Health Conditions in the Americas, 1981-1984.

United Nations High Commissioner for Refugees (1987), Refugees, No. 39 (March), pp.15-22.

United Nations, Population Division (1985), "The Mexico City Conference: the debate on the review and appraisal of the World Population Plan of Action".

United Nations/United Nations Population Fund (1980), "Population policy compendium: Haiti".

HONDURAS*

Pan American Health Organization (1986), Health Conditions in the Americas, 1981-1984.

United Nations, Population Division (1985), "The Mexico City Conference: the debate on the review and appraisal of the World Population Plan of Action".

United Nations/United Nations Population Fund (1985), "Population policy compendium: Honduras".

United Nations High Commissioner for Refugees (1985), Refugees, No.20 (August), pp.27-28.

HUNGARY**

United Nations, Population Division (1985), "The Mexico City Conference: the debate on the review and appraisal of the World Population Plan of Action".

_____ (1987), Case Studies in Population Policy: Hungary (ST/ESA/SER.R/87).

United Nations, Economic Commission for Europe, Second Informal Working Group on Economic and Social Implications of Changing Age Distribution in Selected ECE Countries, (1985), "Economic and social implications of aging in Hungary" (ESAA/WP/7).

World Health Organization (1986), Evaluation of the Strategy for Health for All by the Year 2000: Seventh Report on the World Health Situation, vol. 5 (Copenhagen).

---

* Contraceptive prevalence rate is for women aged 15-44 years.
** Contraceptive prevalence rate is for women aged 15-39 years.

ICELAND

Banks, Arthur, ed. (1987), Political Handbook of the the World (Binghampton, CSA Publications).

Council of Europe (1987), Recent Demographic Developments in the Member States of the Council of Europe, 1986.

Economist Intelligence Unit (1985), Quarterly Economic Review of Denmark, Iceland: 1985 Annual Supplement (London, Economist Publications).

World Health Organization (1986), Evaluation of the Strategy for Health for All by the Year 2000: Seventh Report on the World Health Situation, vol. 5 (Copenhagen).

INDIA

India, Registrar General and Census Commissioner (1983), Census of India, 1981. Series 1, part II.

_____, Ministry of Health and Family Welfare (1986), "Revised strategy for the national family welfare programme, a summary".

United Nations, Population Division (1985), "The Mexico City Conference: the debate on the review and appraisal of the World Population Plan of Action".

United Nations/United Nations Population Fund (1982), "Population policy compendium: India".

World Health Organization (1986), Evaluation of the Strategy for Health for All by the Year 2000: Seventh Report on the World Health Situation, vol. 4 (New Delhi).

INDONESIA*

Indonesia (1984), Department of Information. Repelita IV, 1986/86-1989-90.

United Nations, Population Division (1985), "The Mexico City Conference: the debate on the review and appraisal of the World Population Plan of Action".

United Nations/United Nations Population Fund (1979), "Population policy compendium: Indonesia".

World Health Organization. (1986), Evaluation of the Strategy for Health for All by the Year 2000: Seventh Report on the World Health Situation, vol. 4 (New Delhi).

---

* Contraceptive prevalence rate is for women aged 10-49 years.
Foreign-born population: 1980 census data, as cited in Government reply to United Nations Demographic Yearbook questionnaire.

IRAN*

United Nations, Economic and Social Commission for Asia and the Pacific (1987), Population Headliners. "Iran conducts first household survey" (July), p. 1.

United Nations High Commissioner for Refugees (1987), Refugees (February), p. 10.

United Nations, Population Division (1985), "The Mexico City Conference: the debate on the review and appraisal of the World Population Plan of Action".

United Nations (1984), Demographic Yearbook, 1983 (United Nations publication, Sales No. E/F.83.XIII.1).

World Health Organization (1987), Evaluation of the Strategy for Health for All by the Year 2000: Seventh Report on the World Health Situation, vol. 6 (Alexandria).

IRAQ

International Labour Office (1986), Women at Work, No. 1, p. 33.

United Nations Population Division (1985), "The Mexico City Conference: the debate on the review and appraisal of the World Population Plan of Action".

United Nations/United Nations Population Fund (1980), "Population policy compendium: Iraq".

United Nations Population Fund (1985), "Population perspectives: statements by world leaders", 2nd ed.

World Health Organization. (1987), Evaluation of the Strategy for Health for All by the Year 2000: Seventh Report on the World Health Situation, vol. 6 (Alexandria).

IRELAND

Commission of the European Communities (1986), Report on Social Developments, 1985.

International Labour Office (1986), Women at Work, No. 1, p. 19.

---

* Contraceptive prevalence rate is for women aged 15-44.

United Nations, Population Division (1985), "The Mexico City Conference: the debate on the review and appraisal of the World Population Plan of Action".

United Nations, Economic Commission for Europe, Joint ECE/INSTRAW Meeting on Statistics and Indicators on the Role of Women and Situation of Women (1984), "Statistics on women in the labour force and related topics: what do we need to know?" (CES/AC.60/7).

World Health Organization (1986), _Evaluation of the Strategy for Health for All by the Year 2000: Seventh Report on the World Health Situation_, vol. 5 (Copenhagen).

ISRAEL

International Planned Parenthood Federation (1986), _People_, vol. 13, No. 4, pp. 27-28.

Population Reference Bureau (1984), _Population Bulletin_, "Israel's population: the challenge of pluralism", vol. 39, No. 2 (April).

United Nations, Population Division (1985), "The Mexico City Conference: the debate on the review and appraisal of the World Population Plan of Action".

World Health Organization (1986), _Evaluation of the Strategy for Health for All by the Year 2000: Seventh Report on the World Health Situation_, vol. 5 (Copenhagen).

ITALY*

Council of Europe (1987), "Recent demographic developments in the Member States of the Council of Europe".

International Labour Office (1986), _Women at Work_, No. 2.

_____(1987), _Social and Labour Bulletin_, No. 2. p. 14.

United Nations, Population Division (1985), "The Mexico City Conference: the debate on the review and appraisal of the World Population Plan of Action".

World Health Organization (1986), _Evaluation of the Strategy for Health for All by the Year 2000: Seventh Report on the World Health Situation_, vol. 5 (Copenhagen).

---

* Contraceptive prevalence rate is for women aged 18-44 years.

JAMAICA

Jamaica, Statistical Institute (1983), Population Census, 1982, vol. 1.

_____, Planning Institute of Jamaica (1984), Economic and Social Survey, 1983.

United Nations, Population Division (1985), "The Mexico City Conference: the debate on the review and appraisal of the World Population Plan of Action".

United Nations/United Nations Population Fund (1980), "Population policy compendium: Jamaica".

World Health Organization (1986), Evaluation of the Strategy for Health for All by the Year 2000: Seventh Report on the World Health Situation, vol. 3 (Washington, D.C.).

JAPAN

Asian Population and Development Association (1985), Demographic Transition in Japan and Rural Development. Population and development series No. 1.

Nihon University, Population Research Institute (1985), Population of Japan: Population Policy. Reprint series, No. 14.

United Nations, Population Division (1985), "The Mexico City Conference: the debate on the review and appraisal of the World Population Plan of Action".

World Health Organization (1986), Evaluation of the Strategy for Health for All by the Year 2000: Seventh Report on the World Health Situation, vol. 7 (Manila).

JORDAN

Jordan, National Planning Council (1981), Five-year Plan for Economic and Social Development, 1981-1985.

United Nations (1985), Bulletin on Aging, vol. X, No. 4. p. 15.

_____, Population Division (1985), "The Mexico City Conference: the debate on the review and appraisal of the World Population Plan of Action".

United Nations Population Fund (1985), "Report on second mission on needs assessment for population assistance: Jordan", Report No. 83.

World Health Organization (1987), Evaluation of the Strategy for Health for All by the Year 2000: Seventh Report on the World Health Situation, vol. 6 (Alexandria).

KENYA

Africa Parliamentary Conference on Population and Development (1986), Status of Population Policy and Family Planning Programmes in Kenya.

Institute for Resource Development (1986), "Demographic data for development. Population policy brief, Kenya".

United Nations, Population Division (1985), "The Mexico City Conference: the debate on the review and appraisal of the World Population Plan of Action".

United Nations/United Nations Population Fund (1985), "Population policy compendium: Kenya".

World Health Organization (1986), Evaluation of the Strategy for Health for All by the Year 2000: Seventh Report on the World Health Situation, vol. 2 (Brazzaville).

KIRIBATI

Banks, Arthur, ed.(1987), Political Handbook of the the World (Binghampton, CSA Publications).

Kiribati (1983), National Development Plan, 1983-1986.

South Pacific Commission (1987), Monthly News of Activities, No. 102 (December).

United Nations, Economic and Social Commission for Asia and the Pacific, Third Asian and Pacific Population Conference, (1982), "Country statement: Kiribati".

United Nations, Economic and Social Commisssion for Asia and the Pacific/ South Pacific Commission, ESCAP/SPC Conference Seminar on Population Problems of Small Island Countries of the ESCAP/SPC Region, (1982), "Country statement: Kiribati". Noumea, New Caledonia, 15-19 February.

KUWAIT*

Economist Intelligence Unit (1985), Quarterly Economic Review of Kuwait: 1985 Annual Supplement (London, Economist Publications).

Kuwait, Ministry of Planning, Central Statistical Office (1987). Research studies on population: 1985 census analysis, No. 1, "Major demographic features of the population of Kuwait".

---

* Foreign-born population: data are reported by nationality rather than by place of birth.

United Nations, Population Division (1985), "The Mexico City Conference: the debate on the review and appraisal of the World Population Plan of Action".

_____ (1987), Case Studies in Population Policy: Kuwait (ST/ESA/SER.R/82).

World Health Organization (1987), Evaluation of the Strategy for Health for All by the Year 2000: Seventh Report on the World Health Situation, vol. 6 (Alexandria).

LAO PEOPLE'S DEMOCRATIC REPUBLIC

Lao People's Democratic Republic (1983), "Report on the economic and social situation, development strategy and assistance requirements", vol. 1. Prepared for the Asian-Pacific Round Table Meeting Concerning the Implementation of the Substantial New Programme of Action for the Least Developed Countries (AP/RTM//83/LAO).

United Nations/United Nations Population Fund (1983), "Population policy compendium: Lao People's Democratic Republic".

United Nations Children's Fund, Programme Committee (1987), "Country programme recommendation: Lao People's Democratic Republic" (E/ICEF/1987/P/L.22).

United Nations High Commissioner for Refugees (1987), Refugees (April), pp. 11-13.

LEBANON

United Nations Development Programme, Governing Council (1984), "Consideration and approval of country programmes: second country programme for Lebanon" (DP/CP/LEB/2).

United Nations Fund for Population Activities (1985), "Population perspectives: statements by world leaders", 2nd ed.

United Nations (1987), "Special programmes of economic assistance: Assistance for the reconstruction and development of Lebanon" (A/42/553).

_____ (1984), "Special economic and disaster relief assistance: Special programmes of economic assistance. Assistance for the reconstruction and development of Lebanon" (A/39/390).

World Health Organization (1987), Evaluation of the Strategy for Health for All by the Year 2000: Seventh Report on the World Health Situation, vol. 6 (Alexandria).

United Nations High Commissioner for Refugees (1984), Refugees (May), pp. 9-11.

United Nations, Population Division (1985), "The Mexico City Conference: the debate on the review and appraisal of the World Population Plan of Action".

LESOTHO

United Nations Children's Fund, Programme Committee (1987), "Country programme recommendation: Lesotho" (E/ICEF/1987/P/L.4).

United Nations High Commissioner for Refugees (1986), Fact Sheet (November).

United Nations, Population Division (1985), "The Mexico City Conference: the debate on the review and appraisal of the World Population Plan of Action".

World Health Organization (1986), Evaluation of the Strategy for Health for All by the Year 2000: Seventh Report on the World Health Situation, vol. 2 (Brazzaville).

LIBERIA

Liberia, Ministry of Planning and Economic Affairs (1977), 1974 Population and Housing Census of Liberia; Population Characteristics of Major Areas, vol. PC-1.

United Nations Development Programme, Country and Intercountry Programmes and Projects (1986), "Fourth country programme for Liberia. Note by the Administrator" (DP/CP/LIR/NOTE/4).

United Nations Population Fund (1986), Report of second mission on needs assessment for population assistance: Liberia", Report No. 87.

United Nations, Population Division (1985), "The Mexico City Conference: the debate on the review and appraisal of the World Population Plan of Action".

World Health Organization (1986), Evaluation of the Strategy for Health for All by the Year 2000: Seventh Report on the World Health Situation, vol. 2 (Brazzaville).

LIBYAN ARAB JAMAHIRIYA*

Economist Intelligence Unit (1986), Country Profile: Libya, 1986-87 (London, Economist Publications).

Kezeiri, S. (1986), "Growth and change in Libya's settlement system", Ekistics, vol. 317 (March/April).

Libyan Arab Jamahiriya, Secretariat of Planning, Census and Statistics Department (1975), 1973 Population Census; Final All-country Results.

---

* Foreign-born population: Data are reported by nationality rather than by place of birth.

Population Reference Bureau (1984), Population Today. "Spotlight"
     (July/August).

Qadhafi, Muammar Al (1980), "A letter to the World Conference of the United
     Nations Decade for Women".

World Health Organization (1987), Evaluation of the Strategy for Health for
     All by the Year 2000: Seventh Report on the World Health Situation,
     vol. 6 (Alexandria).

LIECHTENSTEIN

Banks, Arthur, ed. (1987), Political Handbook of the the World (Binghampton,
     CSA Publications).

Keesing's Contemporary Archives, Record of World Events (1986), February
     (London, Longman).

New Encyclopaedia Britannica (1987), vol. 7, 15th ed.

LUXEMBOURG*

Commission of European Communities (1986), Report on Social Developments
     (Brussels).

Council of Europe (1987), "Recent demographic developments in the member
     States of the Council of Europe".

Luxembourg, Ministère de l'économie (1984), Recensement général de la
     population du 31 mars 1981, Résultats par subdivision territoriale,
     vol. 6.

_____, Service central de la statistique et des études économiques (1986),
     "Bulletin du STATEC", No. 3.

Organisation de coopération et de développement économiques, Conference
     d'experts nationaux sur l'avenir des migrations (1986), "Politiques et
     pratiques nationales en matière d'admission dans les pays membres de
     l'OCDE: Luxembourg".

World Health Organization (1986), Evaluation of the Strategy for Health for
     All by the Year 2000: Seventh Report on the World Health Situation,
     vol. 5 (Copenhagen).

---

* Foreign-born population: Data are reported by nationality rather than
by place of birth.

MADAGASCAR

Africa Research Bulletin (1986), "Five year plan: further details",
    pp. 8,405-8,406.

United Nations, Population Division (1985), "The Mexico City Conference: the
    debate on the review and appraisal of the World Population Plan of
    Action".

United Nations/United Nations Population Fund (1981), "Population policy
    compendium: Madagascar".

United Nations Population Fund (1987), "Assistance to the Government of
    Madagascar: support for a comprehensive population programme",
    (DP/FPA/CP/28).

World Health Organization (1986), Evaluation of the Strategy for Health for
    All by the Year 2000: Seventh Report on the World Health Situation,
    vol. 2 (Brazzaville).

MALAWI

United Nations Development Programme, Country and Intercountry Programmes and
    Projects: (1986), "Fourth country programme for Malawi", 20 October
    (DP/CP/MLW/4).

United Nations (1984), Demographic Yearbook, 1983 (United Nations publication,
    Sales No. E/F.84.XIII.1).

_____, Population Division (1985), "The Mexico City Conference: the
    debate on the review and appraisal of the World Population Plan of
    Action".

United Nations/United Nations Population Fund (1983), "Population policy
    compendium: Malawi".

United Nations High Commissioner for Refugees (1987). Refugees (May), p. 7.

World Health Organization (1986), Evaluation of the Strategy for Health for
    All by the Year 2000: Seventh Report on the World Health Situation,
    vol. 2 (Brazzaville).

MALAYSIA

Malaysia (1983), Population and Housing Census of Malaysia, 1980. General
    Report of the Population Census, vol. 2.

_____ (1986), Fifth Malaysia Plan, 1986-1990.

United Nations, Population Division (1985), "The Mexico City Conference: the debate on the review and appraisal of the World Population Plan of Action".

_____ (1987), Case studies in population policy: Malaysia (ST/ESA/SER.R/80).

United Nations/United Nations Population Fund (1980), "Population policy compendium: Malaysia".

MALDIVES

Banks, Arthur ed. (1987), Political Handbook of the World (Binghampton, CSA Publications).

Maldives (1985), National Development Plan, 1985-1987, vol. 1.

United Nations, Population Division (1985), "The Mexico City Conference: the debate on the review and appraisal of the World Population Plan of Action".

United Nations, Economic and Social Commission for Asia and the Pacific (1987), "Asian-Pacific population programme news", vol. 12, No. 1.

United Nations Children's Fund (1987), "Country programme recommendation: Maldives" (E/ICEF/1987/P/L.23).

MALI

Mali, Ministère du plan, Direction nationale de la statistique et de l'informatique (1983), "Rapport final du seminaire national sur les politiques de population", 22-26 mars.

United Nations (1984), Demographic Yearbook, 1983 (United Nations publication, Sales No. E/F.84.XIII.1).

_____, Population Division (1985), "The Mexico City Conference: the debate on the review and appraisal of the World Population Plan of Action".

United Nations/United Nations Population Fund (1984), "Population policy compendium: Mali".

United Nations, Economic Commission for Africa (1984), "Second African Population Conference: country statements" (ST/ECE/POP/1).

MALTA

Council of Europe (1987), "Recent demographic developments in the member States of the Council of Europe" (Strasbourg).

Malta review (1986), "Census: the Maltese example", No. 8/86. pp. 12-13.

_____ (1987), "The Government's social policy", No. 5/87. p. 13.

United Nations (1986), "Report of the Interregional Seminar to Promote the Implementation of the International Plan of Action on Aging", Kiev, Ukrainian Soviet Socialist Republic, 9-20 September 1985.

MAURITANIA*

Mauritanie, Ministère de l'économie et de la comptabilité nationale, Direction de la statistique, Recensement général de la population, 1977, vol. I, Résultats prioritaires.

_____ (1985), "Recensement général de la population et de l'habitat, 1987".

United Nations Population Fund, Proposed Projects and Programmes (1987), "Assistance to the Government of Mauritania" (DP/FPA/CP/23).

Vie de la Nation (1983), "Les orientations du 4ème plan de developpement économique et social", 4 juillet.

MAURITIUS*

Mauritius, Central Statistical Office (1985), 1983 Housing and Population Census of Mauritius, vol. III.

United Nations, Population Division (1985), "The Mexico City Conference: the debate on the review and appraisal of the World Population Plan of Action".

United Nations/United Nations Population Fund (1982), "Population policy compendium: Mauritius".

United Nations, Economic Commission for Africa (1984), "Second African Population Conference: country statements" (ST/ECE/POP/1).

---

* Foreign-born population: Data are reported by nationality rather than by place of birth.

MEXICO*

Pan American Health Organization (1986). "Health conditions in the Americas, 1981-1984", vol. II.

United Nations, Population Division (1987), "Case studies in population policy: Mexico" (ST/ESA/SER.R/89).

_____, _____ (1985), "The Mexico City Conference: the debate on the review and appraisal of the World Population Plan of Action".

United Nations/United Nations Population Fund (1979), "Population policy compendium: Mexico".

United Nations High Commissioner for Refugees (1986). Refugees (October), pp. 2-22.

MONACO

World Health Organization (1986), Evaluation of the Strategy for Health for All by the Year 2000: Seventh Report on the World Health Situation, vol. 5 (Copenhagen).

MONGOLIA

Mongolia (1980), National report presented to the United Nations Conference on the Decade for Women.

United Nations/United Nations Population Fund (1979), "Population policy compendium: Mongolia".

United Nations, Economic and Social Commission for Asia and the Pacific (1984), Asian-Pacific Population Programme News, vol.13, No. 2. pp. 35-37.

World Health Organization (1986), Evaluation of the Strategy for Health for All by the Year 2000: Seventh Report on the World Health Situation, vol. 4 (New Delhi).

---

* Foreign-born population: 1980 census data as cited in Government reply to a United Nations Demographic Yearbook questionnaire.

MOROCCO*

Economist Intelligence Unit (1986), Country Profile: Morocco 1986-87.
(London, Economist Publications).

Maroc, Ministère du Plan, Direction de la statistique (1983), Population
légale du Maroc, 1982.

_____, _____ (1986), "Seminaire national sur l'integration des variables
demographiques dans la planification du développement économique et
social". Rapport final.

United Nations (1986), "Report of the Interregional Seminar to Promote the
Implementation of the International Plan of Action on Aging", Kiev,
Ukrainian Soviet Socialist Republic, 9-20 September 1985.

_____, Population Division (1985), "The Mexico City Conference: the debate
on the review and appraisal of the World Population Plan of Action".

MOZAMBIQUE

United Nations, Population Division (1985), "The Mexico City Conference: the
debate on the review and appraisal of the World Population Plan of
Action".

United Nations/United Nations Population Fund (1982), "Population policy
compendium: Mozambique".

United Nations High Commissioner for Refugees (1987), Refugees (May),
pp. 42-43.

United Nations Development Programme, Country and Intercountry Programmes and
Projects (1987), "Third country programme for Mozambique" (DP/CP/MOZ/3).

NAURU

Banks, Arthur, ed. (1987), Political Handbook of the World (Binghampton,
CSA Publications).

Economist Intelligence Unit (1986), Country Profile: Pacific Islands, 1986-87.
(London, Economist Publications).

Pacific Publications (1985), 1984 Pacific Islands Yearbook, pp. 269-273.

---

* Foreign-born population: Data are reported by nationality rather than
by place of birth.

NEPAL*

Nepal, National Planning Commission (1985), The Seventh Plan, 1985-1990, A Summary.

_____, National Commission on Population Secretariat (1983), Unofficial translation of the decisions of the National Commission on Population meeting of 7 January, 1983.

United Nations (1985), Demographic Yearbook, 1983 (United Nations publication, Sales No. EF.84.XIII.1).

_____, Population Division (1985), "The Mexico City Conference: the debate on the review and appraisal of the World Population Plan of Action".

United Nations/United Nations Population Fund (1979), "Population policy compendium: Nepal".

NETHERLANDS**

Netherlands (1983), Statement of the Netherlands delegation to the United Nations Economic Commission for Europe meeting on population, 6-12 October.

United Nations, Population Division (1985), "The Mexico City Conference: the debate on the review and appraisal of the World Population Plan of Action".

United Nations, Economic Commission for Europe, Second Informal Working Group on Economic and Social Implications of Changing Age Distribution in Selected ECE Countries (1985), "The consequences of demographic trends for public expenditures in the Netherlands, 1981-2030" (ESAA/WP/5).

United Nations, Economic Commission for Europe/Conference of European Statisticians, Joint ECE/INSTRAW Meeting on Statistics and Indicators on the Role and Situation of Women (1985), "Statistical information on the role and position of women in the Netherlands" (CES/AC.60/9).

---

* Contraceptive prevalence rate is for currently married non-pregnant women.

** Contraceptive prevalence rate is for women aged 21-37 years.

NEW ZEALAND*

New Zealand, Planning Council (1986), "The New Zealand population: change, composition and policy implications". Population Monitoring Group report No. 4.

_____ (1985), "The New Zealand population: trends and their policy implications", Population monitoring group report no. 3.

United Nations (1985), Demographic Yearbook, 1983 (United Nations publication, Sales No. EF.84.XIII.1).

_____, Population Division (1985), "The Mexico City Conference: the debate on the review and appraisal of the World Population Plan of Action".

United Nations, Economic and Social Commission for Asia and the Pacific (1985), Country monograph series No. 12: "The population of New Zealand", vol. 2 (ST/ESCAP/378).

NICARAGUA

Nicaragua, Banco y Ministerio de Economia, Industria y Comercio (1974), Censos nacionales, 1971, vol. 1, Poblacion.

United Nations, Population Division (1985), "The Mexico City Conference: the debate on the review and appraisal of the World Population Plan of Action".

United Nations/United Nations Population Fund (1979), "Population policy compendium, Nicaragua".

United Nations High Commissioner for Refugees (1985), Refugees (August), pp. 30-31.

World Health Organization (1986), Evaluation of the Strategy for Health for All by the Year 2000: Seventh Report on the World Health Situation, vol. 3 (Washington D.C.).

NIGER

Economist Intelligence Unit (1985), Quarterly Economic Review of Togo, Niger, Benin, Burkina Faso: 1985 Annual Supplement (London, Economist Publications).

Futures Group (1986), Report of the RAPID II Population Policy Workshop held in conjunction with the All-Africa Parliamentary Conference on Population and Development, Harare, Zimbabwe, 12-16 May 1986.

---

* Contraceptive prevalence rate is for women aged 15 years and over who considered that they were at risk of pregnancy.

United Nations, Economic Commission for Africa (1986), "Rapport de mission à Niamey", 17-29 octobre 1985.

_____, Population Division (1985), "The Mexico City Conference: the debate on the review and appraisal of the World Population Plan of Action".

United Nations Population Fund (1987), "Assistance to the Government of Niger: support for a comprehensive population programme" (DP/FPA/CP/17).

NIGERIA

Futures Group (1986), Report of the RAPID II Population Policy Workshop held in conjunction with the All-Africa Parliamentary Conference on Population and Development, Harare, Zimbabwe, 12-16 May 1986.

International Planned Parenthood Federation (1987), People, vol. 14, No. 1. pp. 27-30.

United Nations, Population Division (1985), "The Mexico City Conference: the debate on the review and appraisal of the World Population Plan of Action".

United Nations/United Nations Population Fund (1981), "Population policy compendium: Nigeria".

United Nations Population Fund (1987), "Assistance to the Government of Nigeria: support for a comprehensive population programme" (DP/FPA/CP/19).

NORWAY*

Organisation for Economic Co-Operation and Development, Conference of National Experts on the Future of Migration (1986), "National policies and practices of entry control in OECD countries: Norway".

Population Research Institute (1986), Yearbook of Population Research in Finland, 1985, "The Norwegian report on population", pp. 11-30.

United Nations, Population Divison (1985), "The Mexico City Conference: the debate on the review and appraisal of the World Population Plan of Action".

World Health Organization (1986), Evaluation of the Strategy for Health for All by the Year 2000: Seventh Report on the World Health Situation, vol. 5 (Copenhagen).

---

* Contraceptive prevalence rate is for women aged 18-44 years.
Foreign-born population: 1980 census data as cited in Government reply to United Nations Demographic Yearbook questionnaire.

كيفية الحصول على منشورات الأمم المتحدة

يمكن الحصول على منشورات الأمم المتحدة من المكتبات ودور التوزيع في جميع أنحاء العالم . استعلم عنها من المكتبة التي تتعامل معها أو اكتب إلى : الأمم المتحدة ، قسم البيع في نيويورك أو في جنيف .

如何购取联合国出版物

联合国出版物在全世界各地的书店和经售处均有发售。请向书店询问或写信到纽约或日内瓦的联合国销售组。

HOW TO OBTAIN UNITED NATIONS PUBLICATIONS

United Nations publications may be obtained from bookstores and distributors throughout the world. Consult your bookstore or write to: United Nations, Sales Section, New York or Geneva.

COMMENT SE PROCURER LES PUBLICATIONS DES NATIONS UNIES

Les publications des Nations Unies sont en vente dans les librairies et les agences dépositaires du monde entier. Informez-vous auprès de votre libraire ou adressez-vous à : Nations Unies, Section des ventes, New York ou Genève.

КАК ПОЛУЧИТЬ ИЗДАНИЯ ОРГАНИЗАЦИИ ОБЪЕДИНЕННЫХ НАЦИЙ

Издания Организации Объединенных Наций можно купить в книжных магазинах и агентствах во всех районах мира. Наводите справки об изданиях в вашем книжном магазине или пишите по адресу: Организация Объединенных Наций, Секция по продаже изданий, Нью-Йорк или Женева.

COMO CONSEGUIR PUBLICACIONES DE LAS NACIONES UNIDAS

Las publicaciones de las Naciones Unidas están en venta en librerías y casas distribuidoras en todas partes del mundo. Consulte a su librero o diríjase a: Naciones Unidas, Sección de Ventas, Nueva York o Ginebra.

Litho in United Nations, New York
00141—January 1989—5,175
ISBN 92-1-151175-5

02800

United Nations publication
Sales No. E.89.XIII.3
ST/ESA/SER.A/102/Add.1

COUNTRY	First Inquiry	Second Inquiry	Third Inquiry	Fourth Inquiry	Fifth Inquiry
Mali	–	–	–	+	+
Malta	..	–	–	–	+
Mauritania	–	–	–	+	+
Mauritius	..	–	+	–	+
Mexico	–	+	+	+	+
Monaco	–	–	–	–	–
Mongolia	–	–	–	–	–
Morocco	+	–	+	+	+
Mozambique	..	..	–	–	+
Nauru	–	–	–	–	–
Nepal	–	+	+	+	+
Netherlands	+	+	+	+	+
New Zealand	+	+	+	+	+
Nicaragua	–	–	+	–	+
Niger	–	–	+	+	–
Nigeria	–	–	+	+	–
Norway	+	+	+	–	+

Note: A plus (+) means reply received.
A minus (–) means reply not received.
Two dots (..) mean not applicable because country neither a United Nations Member State nor an observer at the time of the Inquiry.

Annex II

List of countries replying to the First, Second, Third, Fourth and Fifth Inquiries

---

COUNTRY	First Inquiry	Second Inquiry	Third Inquiry	Fourth Inquiry	Fifth Inquiry
Gabon	–	+	+	+	+
Gambia	..	–	–	–	+
German Democratic Republic	..	..	+	+	+
Germany, Federal Republic of	+	+	+	+	+
Ghana	+	–	+	–	–
Greece	+	+	+	+	+
Grenada	..	..	..	..	..
Guatemala	+	+	+	+	+
Guinea	–	–	–	–	–
Guinea-Bissau	..	..	–	+	+
Guyana	..	–	+	+	–
Haiti	–	–	+	–	+
Honduras	–	–	+	+	+
Hungary	+	+	+	+	+
Iceland	–	+	+	–	–
India	+	+	+	+	+
Indonesia	–	–	+	–	+
Iran (Islamic Republic of)	+	+	+	+	+
Iraq	–	+	+	+	+
Ireland	+	–	+	+	–
Israel	–	+	–	–	–
Italy	+	+	+	–	+
Jamaica	+	–	+	–	+
Japan	+	+	+	+	+
Jordan	+	+	+	+	+
Kenya	..	+	+	+	–
Kiribati	..	..	..	..	+
Kuwait	+	+	–	–	+
Lao People's Democratic Republic	–	+	–	–	–
Lebanon	+	+	–	–	–
Lesotho	..	+	+	–	+
Liberia	+	+	+	–	+
Libyan Arab Jamahiriya	–	+	+	–	+
Liechtenstein	–	–	–	–	–
Luxembourg	–	–	+	+	+
Madagascar	–	+	+	+	+
Malawi	..	+	–	–	–
Malaysia	+	–	+	+	+
Maldives	..	–	–	+	+

- 251 -

Net migration rate: the difference between gross immigration and gross emigration per 1,000 of the mid-year population.

Net reproduction rate: a refined measure of the reproduction of population expressed as an average number of daughters that a cohort of newly born girl babies will bear during their lifetime, assuming fixed schedules of age-specific fertility and mortality rates. In other words, it is the measure of the extent to which a cohort of newly born girls will replace themselves under given schedules of age-specific fertility and mortality rates.

Rate of growth: the exponential average annual rate of population growth, expressed as a percentage.

Sex ratio: the number of men per 100 women.

Survival ratio: the probability of surviving from one age to an older one; it is often computed for five-year age groups and a five-year time period.

Total fertility rate: the sum of the age-specific fertility rates over all ages of the child-bearing period; if five-year age groups are used, the sum of the rates is multiplied by 5. This measure gives the approximate magnitude of "completed family size", that is, the total number of children an average woman will bear in her lifetime, assuming no mortality.

Urban population: population living in areas defined as urban by national authorities.

Annex I

GLOSSARY

<u>Contraceptive prevalence rate</u>: percentage currently using contraception; usually based on married or sexually active couples with women in the reproductive age.

<u>Crude birth rate</u>: the number of births in a year per 1,000 mid-year population.

<u>Crude death rate</u>: the number of deaths in a year per 1,000 mid-year population.

<u>Dependency ratio or age dependency ratio</u>: the ratio of the combined child population under 15 years of age and adult population 65 years and over to the population of intermediate age per 100.

<u>Foreign-born population</u>: persons born outside the country or area in which they were enumerated at the time of the census.

<u>General fertility rate</u>: the annual number of births divided by the mid-year population of women aged 15 to 49 years multiplied by 1,000.

<u>Gross reproduction rate</u>: a measure of the reproduction of a population expressed as an average number of daughters to be born to a cohort of women during their reproductive age, assuming no mortality and a fixed schedule of age-specific fertility rates. More specifically, it is the sum of age-specific fertility rates for the period multiplied by the proportion of the total births of girl babies.

<u>Infant mortality rate</u>: the probability of dying between birth and age 1 multiplied by 1,000; commonly calculated as the number of deaths of infants under one year of age in any given calendar year divided by the number of births in that year and multiplied by 1,000.

<u>Life expectancy at birth</u>: a life-table function to indicate the expected average number of years to be lived by a newly born baby, assuming a fixed schedule of age-specific mortality rates.

<u>Mean age at first marriage (females)</u>: the average age at which women marry for the first time.

<u>Median age</u>: the age which divides the population into two groups of equal size, one of which is younger and the other of which is older.

<u>Natural rate of increase</u>: the difference between the crude birth rate and the crude death rate, expressed per 1,000 mid-year population.

<u>Net migration</u>: the difference between gross immigration and gross emigration.

ANNEXES